For God's
Glory
and the
Church's
Consolation

For God's Glory and the Church's Consolation

400 YEARS OF THE SYNOD OF DORDT

Ronald L. Cammenga, Editor

REFORMED FREE PUBLISHING ASSOCIATION
Jenison, Michigan

©2019 Reformed Free Publishing Association
All rights reserved
Printed in the United States of America

No part of this publication may be reproduced, stored in a retrieval system, or transmitted in any form or by any means—electronic, mechanical, photocopying, recording, or otherwise—without the prior written permission of the publisher. The only exception is brief quotations in printed reviews.

Scripture cited is taken from the King James (Authorized) Version

Reformed Free Publishing Association
1894 Georgetown Center Drive
Jenison, Michigan 49428
616-457-5970
rfpa.org
mail@rfpa.org

The painting used in the cover design is *View of Dordrecht*, ca. 1660, by Salomon van Ruysdael.
Cover design by Erika Kiel
Interior design by Katherine Lloyd / theDESKonline.com

ISBN: 978-1-944555-57-3 (hardcover)
ISBN: 978-1-944555-58-0 (ebook)
LCCN: 2019948883

Contents

Editor's Preface vii

Chapter 1
Controversy Regarding Sovereign Grace: The Synod of Dordt and Its Relevance for Today
Douglas J. Kuiper 1

Chapter 2
The Canons as the Original Five Points of Calvinism
Angus Stewart 23

Chapter 3
Warring a Good Warfare with the Canons
Brian Huizinga 55

Chapter 4
Dordt's Unfeigned Call of the Gospel
Mark Shand 71

Chapter 5
The Doctrine of the Covenant in the Canons of Dordt
Douglas J. Kuiper 99

Chapter 6
The Polity of Dordt: *Om Goede Orde in de Gemeente Christi te Onderhouden* (To Maintain Good Order in the Church of Christ)
William A. Langerak 127

Chapter 7
ILLUSTRATING AND RECOMMENDING THE GRACE
OF ELECTION: DORDT'S DOCTRINE OF REPROBATION
Ronald L. Cammenga 161

Chapter 8
ASSURANCE: SOVEREIGN GRACE'S SPEECH TO THE HEART
Barrett Gritters 201

Appendix 1
THE SESSIONS OF THE SYNOD OF DORDT, 1618–1619
Douglas J. Kuiper 223

Appendix 2
BALTHASAR LYDIUS' PRAYER AT THE CONVENING OF
THE SYNOD OF DORDT
Translated and edited by
Prof. Douglas J. Kuiper and Dr. H. David Schuringa 295

Editor's Preface

The Synod of Dordt, 1618–19, is, for good reason, often referred to as "the great synod." *Great* is certainly the right adjective to describe the Synod of Dordt. It was great because of the central issue with which the synod dealt. That issue was the heresy of Arminianism that had infected the Dutch Reformed churches. So critical was the error that the embrace of it meant a fundamental denial of the gospel of grace. Clearly, great things were at stake, so far as the church was concerned. No greater issue can be imagined than the issue that confronted the Synod of Dordt. Is man saved because of his own works and will, or because of the efficacious grace of God? Who ought to receive the glory for salvation? Does glory belong to God alone, or does man, at least in part, receive a portion of the glory? Clearly, there is no greater issue.

The Synod of Dordt was also great because of the representation at the synod. The Dutch Reformed churches understood that the error that was troubling their churches was not unique to them. They were keenly aware that this error was not uniquely Dutch but was an error that was no respecter of persons. It was an error that threatened the Reformed faith everywhere. Seeing that and understanding the truth of the oneness and catholicity of the church, the Dutch invited representatives of the Reformed faith from around the world—and they came, they contributed, and they joined hands with the Dutch in condemning the heresy that threatened the universal church of Christ. Great was the Synod of Dordt in its scope.

And great has the Synod of Dordt proved to be in the history of the Reformed church that followed Dordt. Great has the synod been in its enduring legacy. For generations—fifteen or sixteen generations—the Synod of Dordt has served with its clear articulation of the truth and its uncompromising rejection of error. In the church and on the mission field, the Canons of Dordt have served as the confessional standard for instruction in the doctrines of grace—the five points of Calvinism.

But the Synod of Dordt was much more than the Canons of Dordt and the Arminian heresy. It dealt with the matter of a proper view and observance of the New Testament Sabbath, establishing principles that serve the church today. It dealt with Bible translation, authorizing a new Dutch translation of the Bible, the *Statenvertaling*. It dealt with church polity and formulated the Church Order that is still in use in Reformed churches around the world. It dealt with church-state issues, and although more would need to be done following Dordt, it showed the way by insisting that the church must be free to govern its own affairs. Dordt was polemical and showed how properly the church ought to deal with error and errorists. And in so many other ways, the work done by the Synod of Dordt endures to the present. Throughout the centuries following Dordt, like the aging fig tree of Psalm 92:14, its fruit would only ripen and become the sweeter. Great was the Synod of Dordt!

The chapters in this book began as speeches at a conference sponsored by the Protestant Reformed Theological Seminary (PRTS). The theme of the conference was *Dordt 400: Safeguarding the Reformed Tradition*. Among the speakers were faculty members of PRTS, ministers in the Protestant Reformed Churches of America (PRCA), and ministers from churches with whom the PRCA have official ecumenical relationships. The conference was hosted by the Trinity Protestant Reformed Church in Hudsonville, Michigan. Trinity's evangelism committee did a great deal of work in planning, advertising, and arranging the conference, for which the seminary was deeply appreciative. The conference was spread over three days and was very well attended. There were many out-of-state visitors, as well as numerous foreign guests. Special arrangements were made, making possible the presence of as many friends of the PRCA from abroad as were able to attend. In their honor, a pre-conference banquet was held, which provided an opportunity for our guests to become acquainted with each other. Just as delegates to the Synod of Dordt came from abroad, so did many come from abroad to commemorate with us the anniversary of the Synod of Dordt. Great was our celebration.

Although before the conference the seminary faculty had already made plans with the Reformed Free Publishing Association to publish the speeches given at the conference, many who attended the conference expressed the hope that the speeches would be made into a book. What we believed going into the conference, many who attended the conference confirmed—that the material presented is of enduring value. In addition, a book reaches a wider audience than a three-day conference. And that too is our hope.

With deepest appreciation and thanksgiving to the Lord for what he wrought at the Synod of Dordt, and with the prayer that Dordt's unique contribution may impact future generations, we are glad to present this book. May the Lord use it to endear to us and to our children the Reformed tradition that was preserved and developed through the Synod of Dordt. May the zeal for the truth and the boldness in rejecting heresy also be our zeal and boldness. And may it be the zeal and boldness of our children and our children's children, as well as all who embrace the doctrines of grace that were defended by the great synod.

—Ronald L. Cammenga, editor
Wyoming, Michigan
May 2019

Chapter 1

CONTROVERSY REGARDING SOVEREIGN GRACE: THE SYNOD OF DORDT AND ITS RELEVANCE FOR TODAY

Douglas J. Kuiper

Introduction

November 13, 2018, marked the four hundredth anniversary of the opening of the Synod of Dordt. Four centuries later, how ought we to evaluate this synod?

Throughout the centuries some have expressed their praises of the synod in superlatives. One church historian has said that it was "the greatest synod of Reformed churches ever held."[1] Another has expressed the judgment that it was "one of the two or three decisive events in the history of the Netherlands."[2] Yet another has referred to the Synod of Dordt as the "most holy Synod."[3] Expressing the

---

1 B. K. Kuiper, *The Church in History* (Grand Rapids, MI: Eerdmans, 1964), 268.
2 Peter Y. DeJong, ed., "The Rise of the Reformed Churches in the Netherlands," in *Crisis in the Reformed Churches: Essays in Commemoration of the Great Synod of Dort, 1618–1619* (Grand Rapids, MI: Reformed Fellowship, Inc., 1968), 1.
3 As quoted by David Engelsma, "The Significance of Dordt for Today," in *Always Reforming: Continuation of the Sixteenth-Century Reformation*, ed. David J. Engelsma (Jenison, MI: Reformed Free Publishing Association, 2009), 36. Additionally, Gerard Brandt relates what Wolfgang Mayer, minister in Basil,

same idea in other words, the church historian J. Wylie says, "Than the Synod of Dort there is perhaps no more remarkable Assembly in the annals of the Protestant Church."[4] Should we evaluate the synod similarly?

At the same time the criticisms of the Synod of Dordt have also been sharp. One would expect nothing less from Remonstrant sympathizers.[5] However, even some who are more orthodox have criticized the synod. John Hales and Walter Balcanquhall wrote letters to Dudley Carleton (the political ambassador from Britain to the United Provinces of the Netherlands) regarding the proceedings of the synod.[6] Informed only by these letters, the English-speaking people have long understood "that the Synod was relentlessly partisan and severe in its doctrine; that the Dutch provincial delegates were extreme, biased, and ignorant parties who had complete control over the debates and the decisions; that the Canons themselves were drawn up in private and foisted upon the

---

Switzerland, did whenever anyone in his presence made mention of the Synod of Dordt: "He frequently stiled them the holy Synod, and every time he gave them that title, he pulled off his velvet cap with great respect, saying, among other things…'Hearken to a word of prophecy, O holy Synod! the older you grow, the more you flourish.'" See Brandt, *The History of the Reformation and Other Ecclesiastical Transactions in and about the Low-Countries* (London: T. Wood, for John Nicks, 1722), 3:230.

4 J. A. Wylie, *The History of Protestantism*, 3 vols. (London: Cassell Petter and Galpin, 1899), 3:152.

5 Gerard Brandt was sympathetic to the Remonstrant cause. In his third volume, he portrays the synod as biased against and spiteful to the Remonstrants. Nevertheless, the historical data that he provides regarding the meetings of the synod is generally reliable and can be confirmed from other sources.

6 Walter Balcanquhall was a delegate to the Synod of Dordt from Great Britain, the only delegate representing the Scottish churches. John Hales was Dudley Carleton's chaplain. Hales was not a delegate but could only observe the synod at its open sessions. Both men kept Carleton informed of the proceedings of the synod. Hales's letters are preserved in the *Golden Remains of the Ever Memorable Mr. John Hales of Eton College* (London: Printed for Tim Garthwait, 1659).

foreign delegates."[7] Even Dutch Reformed men who lived within a century of the synod expressed their reservations.[8] Four hundred years later, should we also judge the synod severely?

A third response to the synod is a nuanced approach. Those who take this approach would commemorate the synod and its work by recognizing its historical significance but would express some degree of embarrassment at Dordt's theology and would explain its theology as irrelevant for today. Should this be our approach?

Whichever approach we take is determined by our answer to a fundamental question: are the truths that Dordt defended in the Canons of Dordt essential components of the gospel? The totality of the depravity of humans, the irresistible character of God's grace in the hearts and lives of his elect, the death of Christ on the cross to atone for those whom the Father had given him, and the decree of election and reprobation that governed the death of Christ and what it accomplished—are these the heart of the gospel? Or are they peripheral to the gospel? Or are they neither of these; are they entirely unrelated to the gospel?

If the truths that Dordt defended are entirely unrelated to the gospel, or peripheral matters, or matters of indifference, we may be ambivalent or critical in our evaluation of the synod. If the Canons of Dordt are only one way of expressing the gospel, but the Remonstrant expression is another equally valid way, once again, our response may be ambivalent or critical. However, if these doctrines make up the heart of the gospel—and they do—and if the controversy really concerned sovereign grace—and it did—then we may be neither ambivalent nor critical. Rather, we ought to praise and thank God for what he accomplished at the great synod.

---

7   Anthony Milton, "The Hales and Balcanquahall Letters," in *Revisiting the Synod of Dordt (1618–1619)*, ed. Aza Goudriaan and Fred van Lieburg (Leiden: Brill, 2011), 137.
8   Willem J. op 't Hof, "Ambivalent Assessments of the Synod of Dordt by Dutch Contra-Remonstrants," in Goudriaan, *Revisiting the Synod of Dordt*, 367–96.

It is our firm conviction that the Synod of Dordt defended the true gospel and opposed an erroneous, indeed heretical, form of the gospel. To say nothing of the other points of doctrine in the Canons, this is clear from the issue treated in the second head of the Canons, the death of the Son of God. By his death on the cross Christ completely and efficaciously atoned for the sins of all the elect. This concerns the heart of the gospel!

The Synod of Dordt is worth remembering. Its four hundredth anniversary is an appropriate time for Reformed churches throughout the world to renew their appreciation for the synod. What *men* did at the synod is not what needs emphasizing. But what *God* did through sinful men is praiseworthy. In fact, what God was pleased to accomplish through weak and sinful men is nothing short of amazing.

No single chapter can exhaust the subject of the relevance or significance of the synod for today.[9] This chapter will highlight three ways in which the Synod of Dordt is relevant for today.

1. The Synod of Dordt spelled out clearly the boundaries of the Reformed faith.

For several reasons, the fathers at Dordt understood the need to spell out clearly the boundaries of the Reformed faith. One reason for this is that the Remonstrants taught the wrong view regarding five foundational doctrines pertaining to sovereign grace. Another is that Remonstrant theology was an erroneous theological *system*. Yet these errors were found within Reformed churches, rather than outside Reformed churches. Furthermore, the Remonstrants claimed to be faithful to scripture in their teachings. Promoting their theological system within Reformed churches, they were trying to push the boundaries of Reformed orthodoxy to allow their views.

---

9 For other presentations of the significance of Dordt, see Engelsma, *Always Reforming*, 36–41; and DeJong, *Crisis in the Reformed Churches*.

That the Remonstrants were attempting to extend the boundaries of the Reformed faith had become clear to many delegates at the Synod of Dordt. As evidence of this, note three points. First, for over a decade the Remonstrants had been calling for the national government to convene a national synod in order to revise the Reformed confessions (the Belgic Confession and Heidelberg Catechism).[10] Soon after the Belgic Confession was written, some ministers in Reformed churches expressed reservations about some of its teachings. The number of those critical of the Belgic Confession grew in the decades preceding the Synod of Dordt. Rather than leaving the Reformed churches in the Netherlands, thereby acknowledging that their views did not harmonize with the Reformed confessions, these ministers desired to revise the confessions in order to eliminate certain teachings that were objectionable to them. The Remonstrants were trying to extend the boundaries of the Reformed faith.

Second, several months before the synod convened, Festus Hommius, who would be chosen as one of the synod's clerks, wrote a book in which he demonstrated that the Remonstrants opposed Reformed theology.[11] The Remonstrants, Hommius argued, did not merely disagree on the five points of doctrine that would later be embodied in the Canons of Dordt. Rather, Hommius showed, they differed from the teachings of the Belgic Confession on numerous

---

10 See "Historical Foreword Addressed to the Reformed Churches of Christ," in Homer C. Hoeksema, *The Voice of Our Fathers: An Exposition of the Canons of Dordrecht*, rev. ed. (Jenison, MI: Reformed Free Publishing Association, 2013), 567–64. See also Arminius' tenth point in his "Declaration of Sentiments," delivered to the national government on October 30, 1608. This can be found in *The Writings of James Arminius, Translated from the Latin in Three Volumes*, vol. 1, trans. James Nichols and W. R. Bagnall (Grand Rapids, MI: Baker, 1956), 193–275.

11 Festus Hommius, *Specimen Controversiarum Belgicarum Seu Confessio Ecclesiarum Reformatarum in Belgio*, 1618. As the title indicates, the book is written in Latin. As of January 31, 2019, a PDF version of the book, in Latin, was available at www.prdl.org.

points. In fact, they were Socinians theologically. Socinians maintained a wrong view of soteriology, which followed from their denial of the Trinity and the deity of Christ. This view was essentially the view embraced by the Remonstrants, argued Hommius.[12]

Third, that the delegates at the synod realized that the Remonstrants were attempting to extend the boundaries of the Reformed faith is evident from their decision to require the Remonstrants to provide synod in writing with all their objections to any point of doctrine in the Belgic Confession and the Heidelberg Catechism. The synod required this of them first on December 10, 1618.[13] That synod expected them to do this promptly is evident from its repeated reminders, which came in quick succession, on December 12, 17, and 20. When on December 21 the Remonstrants finally brought some observations regarding the Belgic Confession, the synod rebuked them for not providing their objections to the Heidelberg Catechism. The Remonstrants submitted these finally on December 27. On February 4, 1619, the synod appointed committees to respond to these objections.

In three ways the Synod of Dordt responded to this need to spell out the boundaries of the Reformed faith. First, the synod did review the two Reformed confessions of the Dutch churches, though its motive in doing so was not to appease the Remonstrants. On April

---

12 Aza Goudriaan, "The Synod of Dordt on Arminian Anthropology," in Goudriaan, *Revisiting the Synod of Dordt*, 81–83.

13 All references to specific decisions of the synod on specific dates at specific sessions can be verified by consulting the Latin critical edition and the Dutch translations of the Acts of the Synod of Dordt. For the Latin critical edition, see Donald Sinnema, Christian Moser, and Herman J. Selderhuis, eds., *Acta et Documenta Synodi Nationalis Dordrechtanae (1618–1619): Vol. 1, Acta of the Synod of Dordt* (Göttingen: Vanderhoeck & Ruprecht, 2015), 3–189. For the Dutch translation, see *Acta of Handelingen der Nationale Synode te Dordrecht*, J. H. Donner and S. A. Van Den Hoorn, eds. (Utrecht: Den Hertog's Uitgeverij en Boekhandel, n.d.). The English-speaking reader can confer with my summary of the sessions of the Synod of Dordt, found elsewhere in this volume.

30, 1619, at sessions 145 and 146, the delegates declared that they had reviewed the Belgic Confession and found nothing in it that conflicted with scripture. They declared the same of the Heidelberg Catechism at the 148th session on May 1. Second, at the 155th session (May 13), synod appointed four men to compare the Latin, Dutch, and French translations of the Belgic Confession in order to produce a standard authorized translation. It completed this work at the 173rd session on May 24. Third, at its 164th session (May 17), synod adopted the Formula of Subscription, requiring officebearers to declare:

> We…heartily believe and are persuaded that all the articles and points of doctrine contained in the Confession and Catechism of the Reformed Churches, together with the explanation of some points of the aforesaid doctrine made by the National Synod of Dordrecht, 1618–'19, do fully agree with the Word of God.
>
> We promise therefore diligently to teach and faithfully to defend the aforesaid doctrine, without either directly or indirectly contradicting the same, by our public preaching or writing. We declare, moreover, that we not only reject all errors that militate against this doctrine, and particularly those which were condemned by the above-mentioned synod, but that we are disposed to refute and contradict these, and to exert ourselves in keeping the church free from such errors.[14]

Thus the Synod of Dordt spelled out clearly that the doctrines contained in the Belgic Confession, Heidelberg Catechism, and Canons of Dordt were and are the boundaries of the Reformed

---

14 Formula of Subscription, in *The Confessions and the Church Order of the Protestant Reformed Churches* (Grandville, MI: Protestant Reformed Churches in America, 2005), 326. The Formula as used in the PRCA is essentially that which the Synod of Dordt adopted, with one minor change to include the word "elders and deacons." See "Introduction to the Formula of Subscription" in *Confessions and Church Order*, 324.

faith. The synod viewed the boundaries as fixed and unbending. The teachings of the Remonstrants were outside these boundaries; they contradicted the doctrines set forth in the Reformed confessions.

Reformed churches today must recognize the boundaries that the Reformed churches have previously set, and that Dordt declared to be fixed and unbending. They must love these doctrines and the confessions that contain them and be faithful to them. The way to guard against novelty and heresy is *not* to throw away the confessions and claim to derive our doctrines from scripture alone. Rather, the way in which to safeguard them is to know and love the doctrines embodied in the confessions.

It is urgent that Reformed churches and officebearers take this calling seriously. Those in Reformed churches who begin to teach heretical views generally do not immediately acknowledge that their views do not conform to the Reformed confessional standards, at least not at first. Rather, they claim either that the confessions allow room for their views or that their views are the only proper interpretations of the confessions.

Reformed churches and officebearers ought to also be alarmed at the idea that one's signature on the Formula of Subscription is an expression of agreement *insofar as* the doctrines taught in the confessions accord with scripture. "Insofar as" suggests that one does have reservations regarding some of the doctrines taught in the confessions, and that one considers them not to accord with scripture. The Formula of Subscription requires us to say that these doctrines "do fully agree with the Word of God."

2. The Synod of Dordt defended and reinforced the foundation of the Reformed faith.

The foundation of the Reformed faith is the five points of sovereign grace that Dordt spelled out and defended. To call these the foundation is to acknowledge that the sovereign grace of God toward sinners, manifested from eternity by electing them to salvation and manifested in time by sending Christ to the death of the cross, as well as by regenerating and sanctifying them, is the bedrock of all biblical and Reformed orthodoxy. To go wrong in regard to these five doctrines will inevitably lead to error regarding many other doctrines as well.

Specific attacks on these foundational doctrines made Dordt's defense and reinforcement of these doctrines both necessary and urgent. Allusion was made earlier to the fact that some pastors in Reformed churches had reservations with regard to some of the doctrines embodied in the Belgic Confession and Heidelberg Catechism. We will limit ourselves in this chapter to the reservations regarding—really, attacks on—the doctrine of election and the doctrine of man.

Before the Canons were written, the Reformed churches had already stated their doctrine of election in confessional form. They had done so in article 16 of the Belgic Confession, entitled "Eternal Election:"

> We believe that, all the posterity of Adam being thus fallen into perdition and ruin by the sin of our first parents, God then did manifest himself such as he is; that is to say, merciful and just: merciful, since he delivers and preserves from this perdition all whom he in his eternal and unchangeable counsel, of mere goodness, hath elected in Christ Jesus our Lord, without any respect to their works; just, in leaving others in the fall and perdition wherein they have involved themselves.[15]

Briefly, this article expresses as Reformed creedal teaching that God's decree of predestination is double—election *and* reprobation.

---

15 *Confessions and Church Order*, 41–42.

It confesses that God's decree is *personal and specific*—God did not merely choose a category of people, but elected particular persons. And it clearly maintains that election is *unconditional*—"without any respect to their works."

To this doctrine the Remonstrants objected. Their view, in sum, was that God had decreed to save and bring to heaven all who would believe and obey, and to condemn to everlasting punishment all who would not believe and obey.[16] However, from eternity God did not determine who would believe and obey. Rather, he foresaw who would and who would not believe and obey. Although in words they would not deny that faith and obedience were God's gifts to mankind, the Remonstrants insisted that natural man has the ability to believe and obey, and can choose to do so. Accordingly, God's decree of election is essentially his determination that everyone who would believe, obey, and persevere in faith and obedience to the end, in his own power, would be brought to heaven.

Even before Jacob Arminius publicly taught this, other ministers in Reformed churches were teaching these ideas in seed form. In 1586 the National Synod of The Hague treated the case of Herman Herberts, minister at Gouda, who had reservations with several articles in the Confession and Catechism. He was willing to subscribe to the sixteenth article of the Belgic Confession only as long as it was clear that the article did not teach God to be the author or cause of sin.[17] Of course, the article does not teach that God is the author of sin; but the accusation that it did would be regularly repeated by the Remonstrants.

---

16 The essential aspects of the Remonstrant view can be gleaned from the rejection of errors section of the first head of the Canons. As an aside, even though the Remonstrants were wrong, they were not as far down the road theologically as many liberals today. Many liberals today deny that hell exists as a place of everlasting torment, and they teach that in some way Christ's death does save all. The Remonstrants did not teach that; they acknowledged that some were everlastingly punished in hell.

17 Brandt, *History of the Reformation*, 1:405.

In 1591 the Provincial Synod of Zeeland treated the case of Rev. Gisbert Samuels, who had declared to the Classis of Tholen that he did not, and would not, believe the doctrine expressed in article 16. The classis condemned him, as did the provincial synod. However, the synod was willing to restore him to office if he signed the Belgic Confession, including the sixteenth article. This Samuels did, and he served again in pastoral ministry, although controversy dogged him at every step thereafter.[18]

When the Synod of Zeeland treated the case of Samuels, Jacob Arminius had served almost three years as a pastor. He had been ordained in the Reformed Church of Amsterdam in 1588 and had signed the Belgic Confession and Heidelberg Catechism in connection with his ordination. Soon after his ordination, his consistory assigned him to refute the teachings of Dick Coornheert, who had been opposing the Reformed doctrine of predestination as early as 1578. As Arminius studied Coornheert's writings, he became convinced of Coornheert's position and found himself unable to refute Coornheert's teachings.[19] From that point on, Arminius became known as the leader of the opposition to the doctrine of predestination embodied in the Belgic Confession. None of Arminius' works were published during his lifetime. However, his views of

---

18 Fred van Lieburg, "Gisbertus Samuels, A Reformed Minister Sentenced by the Synod of Zeeland in 1591 for his Opinions on Predestination," in Goudriaan, *Revisiting the Synod of Dordt*, 1–22.
19 Exactly when Arminius first realized that he did not agree with the Reformed doctrine of predestination is not clear. Some scholars suggest that Arminius never agreed with it and signed the Belgic Confession with some silent reservations. W. Robert Godfrey's recent reevaluation of this scholarship is convincing. Although it is not possible to say exactly when Arminius changed his mind, evidence can be brought forward to demonstrate that he did do so. See W. Robert Godfrey, *Saving the Reformation: The Pastoral Theology of the Canons of Dort* (Orlando: Reformation Trust, 2019), 191–95. See also A. W. Harrison, *The Beginnings of Arminianism to the Synod of Dort* (London: University of London Press, 1926), 25.

predestination embodied in his "Declaration of Sentiments," his "Twenty-Five Public Disputations," and his analysis of Romans 7 and 9 were well known.[20]

Arminius popularized the opposition to the doctrine of predestination contained in article 16 of the Belgic Confession. However, he was certainly not the first to oppose that doctrine. The same can be said of his opposition to the doctrine of humanity as taught in articles 14 and 15 of the Belgic Confession. These articles teach that Adam's fall into sin corrupted his entire human nature and left him unable to do anything that is truly good. They teach also that this depravity of Adam has been passed from generation to generation, so that the entire human race is infected with it. Consequently, article 14 says, even the will of every human is enslaved to evil and unable to choose what is good.

In his summary of the Remonstrant opposition to the Belgic Confession, Festus Hommius alleged that the Remonstrant doctrine of fallen humanity differed from that of the Reformed in three key areas. First, they denied that the will of fallen humans is a slave to sin and taught instead that the human will is able to will good as well as evil. Second, they asserted that God's grace works with the human will. The point is not that God's grace *renews* one's will, as the Reformed taught. Rather, the Remonstrants taught that the will of fallen humans cooperates with God's grace, and that God cannot do for humans what humans do not desire or permit God to do. Third, Hommius noted that Simon Episcopius taught that fallen, unregenerated humans can understand the spiritual truths embodied in the Bible apart from the gracious illumination of the Holy Spirit.[21]

---

20 These documents can be found in any complete collection of Arminius's writings, such as the *Writings of James Arminius*, trans. Nichols and Bagnall.
21 Aza Goudriaan, "The Synod of Dordt on Arminian Anthropology," in Goudriaan, *Revisiting the Synod of Dordt*, 82.

The Remonstrant view of the powers of the will of fallen humans reflected their view of God's justice. God's justice, they taught, leads God to require of humans only that which we are able to do. God would not require of us what we could not do. This is a different view of God's justice than is taught in Lord's Day 4 of the Heidelberg Catechism.

The Reformed understanding of divine election and of human depravity, as well as the Reformed understanding of the irresistible grace of God renewing and transforming the will, is part of the foundation of the Reformed faith. The Remonstrants were attacking this foundation. "If the foundations be destroyed, what can the righteous do?" (Psalm 11:3).

Dordt's response, then, was significant. It drafted and approved the Canons of Dordt, and particularly the first, third, and fourth heads, which responded to these Remonstrant errors. Thus Dordt defended the foundation of the Reformed faith, without compromise. The doctrines embodied in the Canons are the gospel. The gospel includes much more than is found in the five doctrines of sovereign grace. But the true gospel cannot dismiss these five doctrines; it cannot exist apart from these five doctrines.

That Dordt's response was the decisive response of the Reformed churches is evident from three considerations. First, the Reformed churches adopted the Canons of Dordt as a confessional statement. In connection with this, as already noted, the synod required officebearers to sign the Formula of Subscription as a statement that one fully agreed with the Reformed teaching. Every decision of an ecclesiastical assembly is settled and binding on the churches that are part of that assembly. However, not every decision of an assembly is raised to confessional status. This decision was.

Second, the synod adopted this response to the Remonstrants with the approval of the international delegates from Reformed churches in many different parts of the world. Before the Dutch delegates spoke their sentiments regarding the proposed Canons, each international delegation gave its judgment. The foreign delegations were unanimous in their advice that the Dutch delegates adopt the Canons.[22] They did not merely concur with the decision of the Dutch delegates to adopt the Canons; their advice was essentially a recommendation to the Dutch delegations to adopt the Canons.

Third, the decisiveness of Dordt's response is evident from the format of the Canons. This Reformed confession not only stated the true presentation of the doctrines of sovereign grace, but also explicitly rejected the erroneous presentation of the Remonstrants. One cannot claim that the Canons are vague on some points relating to the five doctrines of grace and that subscribing to them gives freedom for varying opinions regarding the doctrines they treat. The Canons are not vague. They are clear both regarding what they teach positively and regarding what they reject.

Today Arminianism holds sway in evangelical circles and in many Reformed churches. In them the Canons of Dordt are forgotten, and the doctrines of the Canons viewed as narrow and overly strict. However, the Reformed faith has not changed, and the gospel of sovereign grace has not changed. Those who profess to be Reformed, who go to churches that share the name Reformed, must know, confess, defend, and promote these doctrines. They are the foundation of the Reformed faith. To destroy the foundation is to destroy not only the Reformed system of theology, but to destroy the gospel itself.

---

22 Individual members of some delegations, such as those from Great Britain and Bremen, had some reservations regarding some statements in the Canons, particularly in the second head. However, at the synod each delegation voted as a block, and each had one vote. Each delegation voted to adopt the Canons.

3. The Synod of Dordt's defense of the Reformed confessional faith was a concrete instance of God's providential governing of all history with a view to preserving the truth.

A survey of history will demonstrate that God governed the affairs of history so that this synod happened at exactly the right moment. The course of history was such that it seemed that this synod might not be held; or, worse, that it might be held and conclude with a decisive victory for the Remonstrants. But God directed the affairs of history so that the synod was held and was a decisive victory for Reformed orthodoxy.

First, take note of the political history of the time. Philip II became lord of the Netherlands in 1555 and king of Spain in 1556. Spain and the Netherlands were at opposite ends of the religious spectrum. By the time Philip became lord of the Netherlands, many Reformed believers lived there, alongside Roman Catholics and Anabaptists. By contrast, Spain was committed to Roman Catholicism. Trying to destroy the Reformed faith in the Netherlands, Philip sent an army against the provinces. The Dutch defended themselves; the year 1568 marks the beginning of the Eighty Years War between Spain and the Netherlands. During these eighty years the Dutch national government was preoccupied with foreign affairs. However, during this eighty-year time, one truce was declared, the Twelve Years Truce, which was agreed on in 1609, with war scheduled to resume in 1621. During the years of this truce, the synod met.

Turning to the domestic aspect of the political situation, one cannot overestimate the role of Johan van Oldenbarnevelt, the "Land's Advocate" for the States of Holland from 1586 to 1618. In this position he had helped unite the Dutch provinces and had helped negotiate the truce with Spain. The position was not that of a prime minister, but Oldenbarnevelt soon exercised the authority of a prime minister. Oldenbarnevelt was opposed to calling a national synod as long as he was in power. And he was sympathetic to the Remonstrants.

Second, the economic situation must be considered. The Dutch Golden Age had begun. Dutch merchant ships were sailing to the East and West Indies and establishing Dutch colonies in both Indies as well as at other points along the shipping route. These ships were bringing goods from foreign countries into the Netherlands. The Dutch economy was booming, and the Netherlands was wealthy. The Dutch national government was able to afford the considerable expense of the Synod of Dordt. At the outset, the government budgeted 100,000 guilders; but, as one scholar suggests, "In practice this amount was exceeded by far."[23]

Because of the wealth of the Netherlands, Spain could not afford to lose the Eighty Years War—a factor in its decision to resume the war after the truce was over. Spain depended heavily on the Dutch economy. And the Netherlands had everything to gain by defeating Spain: the Dutch could afford to prolong the war and desired to be free from religious persecution.

In this intriguing economic and political climate, a theological and church-political controversy was brewing. The theological controversy had begun earlier, even before Jacob Arminius was theological professor at Leiden University, though it intensified during his time there. He was appointed in 1603. Within a year, he and fellow professor Franciscus Gomarus were sparring over the doctrine of predestination. Arminius died in 1609, but his followers continued his opposition to the Reformed creedal understanding of election and reprobation.

Arminius knew his theology was different from that which was spelled out in the Reformed confessions; for this reason, he desired

---

[23] Fred van Lieburg, *The Synod of Dordrecht 1618–1619*, trans. Dick Swier (Dordrecht: Stichting Historisch Platform Dordrecht, 2017), 19. To put the sum of 100,000 guilders into context, bear in mind that a laborer made 300 guilders a year and a pastor made 500 guilders a year; see http://www.vanosnabrugge.org/docs/dutchmoney.htm, accessed May 10, 2019.

a revision of the confessions. At the same time, he knew the best way—humanly speaking—to accomplish this. The Church Order adopted by the National Synod of 's Gravenhage in 1586 provided not only for annual meetings of provincial synods, but also for a national synod to be held ordinarily every third year. Arminius wanted this provision for a national synod dropped. If there were no national synod, and if Arminius' views were upheld in a province, his views would hold in that province; there would be no higher court of appeal. Also, Arminius desired the state government to send as many, or more, delegates to each provincial synod as did the churches. When Arminius lived, the state government was sympathetic to him; opposition to Arminius came primarily from those in the churches. But he died, and a national synod would not be held for another decade. When it *was* finally held, it adopted a Church Order that provided for the very opposite of that for which Arminius had hoped.

All these loose ends come together. It was possible for the synod to be held during the years 1609–1621 only because of the Twelve Years Truce with Spain. However, Oldenbarnevelt opposed the idea of a synod and defended the Remonstrants, effectively preventing the synod from being held. Had it been held during Oldenbarnevelt's tenure, when the national government and some notable provincial governments were sympathetic toward the Remonstrants, the Remonstrants might have been completely exonerated. At the worst, looking at the matter from their viewpoint, they would not have been decisively condemned.

Under the sovereign hand of God, the tide turned quickly. The national government became sympathetic toward the Contra-Remonstrant cause. The national government saw that it was *politically* expedient to call a national synod, because the theological issue was threatening the unity of the United Provinces, and because King James I of England was pressuring the United Provinces to do so.

The national government managed to convene the synod within about one year of calling it—a major feat, considering the fact that international delegates had to be invited and other arrangements be made for what would be the longest and largest synod in Dutch history.

The tide turned when Prince Maurice sided with the Contra-Remonstrants in early 1617. Maurice was the *stadtholder* of the United Provinces. This position had evolved from that of a medieval duke or earl and meant that Maurice was the head of the United Provinces and the one charged with ensuring peace and order. It was a different position than Oldenbarnevelt's, but the nation's wellbeing required both to work together harmoniously. However, they took different sides in the theological issue, which led them to oppose each other politically. Oldenbarnevelt—by now over seventy years old—began losing support from all the provinces except Holland and Utrecht, while Maurice grew in favor. In this political and theological divide, civil violence was common and riots were threatened, and provincial governments lined up on each side.

In this context, in 1617 the national government approved the calling of a national synod. The Province of Holland, sympathetic to Oldenbarnevelt, refused to support this decision and formed civil militias in each town to keep the peace. The other provinces perceived this as a *de facto* declaration of independence from the United Provinces, and Maurice was sent with his army to force Holland's subjection. Some local militias readily laid down their arms when they saw his army coming. Maurice was able to remove local magistrates who favored the Remonstrants, replacing them with Contra-Remonstrant supporters. Maurice's actions sealed the support of all the provinces for the national synod.

The intrigue continued even after the synod had been called. Maurice was instrumental in having Oldenbarnevelt arrested for treason and deposed from political office in August 1618.

Oldenbarnevelt was beheaded the following May, shortly before the synod adjourned.

Two years earlier, it appeared that the national synod would not be held, or, if it were, that it would favor the Remonstrants. The tables had turned. God's providential hand, never idle, was busy directing history to serve his great purpose of preserving the truth. God governed every detail of the history of the United Provinces with a view to this synod. He even directed the lives of everyone who would be a delegate, preparing them for their service. How he did so with respect to certain men makes for interesting stories, but they are beyond the scope of this chapter.

It is striking how long it took the churches to respond to the error of Arminianism. Arminius himself had died in 1609, almost a decade earlier. The churches had been dealing with opposition to the Belgic Confession's teachings for at least three decades. The synod was not held until 1618. The historical factors in this delay have been explained. But what was God's purpose? He who governs history could have governed all events so that the matter was dealt with sooner. Why did he not? While we do not know the mind of God entirely, two answers can be given.

One is that God, in his wisdom, permitted the churches to respond to the Remonstrant error only after that error had matured and developed into an entire theological system, and after its pernicious and destructive character had become evident. Had the church officially and creedally opposed the Remonstrant view of predestination twenty years earlier, other aspects of Remonstrant teaching would have later developed to which the churches would need to respond further. However, when the Synod of Dordt convened, the entire system of Remonstrant teaching could be condemned. That those who taught Remonstrant teachings sincerely meant them and deliberately opposed the confessions had to become apparent to the churches. All this meant that the error had to develop into its mature form.

A benefit of this is that the church today can, on the basis of the Canons of Dordt, condemn Arminianism in every stripe and form. Arminian thinking has developed beyond what the Remonstrants of Dordt's day taught. However, even if the form has changed, the essence of Arminian thinking has not changed. Dordt's condemnation of a mature presentation of Remonstrant teaching allows the churches today to use the Canons of Dordt to oppose present-day forms of Arminianism. The Canons are not outdated; they are relevant.

A second answer is practical and is a lesson that God has taught his church time and again throughout history: he does not deliver us until we see how great our need is and cry out to him for deliverance. Israel in Egypt waited four hundred years but only cried to God for deliverance after her affliction had become great. During the time of the judges in the Old Testament, the church was oppressed by heathen nations for many years, sometimes decades, before she cried to God. When God performs a great deliverance for his church, he often waits for her to understand her great need for it. Understanding this need, and her own inability to deliver herself, the church is the more thankful to God for his deliverance.

So it was with the Synod of Dordt. The heresy would not quietly go away; the churches had to address it. But for their deliverance they had to rely on God and praise him for his victories. The orthodox would be (and were) alarmed by the enemy and would earnestly beseech God to deliver them. This lesson we do well to take to heart as we wait for the appointed hour of God's great deliverance of his church. This last deliverance will come about not by the agency of a national government, nor by an ecclesiastical assembly. It will come about by the return of Jesus Christ. But it will come about after iniquity has developed to the full and in the way of the church's cry to God for deliverance.

Even a right eschatology depends on a right understanding of the gospel of sovereign grace. Until he comes again, the church of Christ on earth will be continually troubled by heresies and ungodliness. Realizing our great need, we cry often and urgently for him to deliver us. We cry in the confidence that one day, at last, when it seems that the cause of the truth and his church is all but lost, God will turn the course of history to manifest his great purpose: the deliverance of his church from all trouble, sin, heresy, and persecution.

We know he will, for he died effectually to save the elect, and his goal in the salvation of the elect is the praise of God by the church in every age, and in the age to come. The ninth article of the second head of the Canons speaks of this purpose of God in bringing his church to glory:

> This purpose, proceeding from everlasting love toward the elect, has from the beginning of the world to this day been powerfully accomplished, and will henceforward still continue to be accomplished, notwithstanding all the ineffectual opposition of the gates of hell, so that the elect in due time may be gathered together into one, and that there never may be wanting a church composed of believers, the foundation of which is laid in the blood of Christ, which may steadfastly love and faithfully serve him as their savior, who as a bridegroom for his bride, laid down his life for them upon the cross, and which may celebrate his praises here and through all eternity.[24]

Many historical events in the history of the church demonstrate that the opposition of the gates of hell will be, in the end, ineffectual. One such event is the Synod of Dordt.

---

24 *Confessions and Church Order*, 164.

Chapter 2

THE CANONS AS THE ORIGINAL FIVE POINTS OF CALVINISM

Angus Stewart

Introduction

The year of our Lord 2019 marks the four hundredth anniversary of the conclusion of the great Synod of Dordrecht or Dordt in the Netherlands. This synod did sterling work by God's grace in various areas, including commissioning a Dutch Bible translation (the *Statenvertaling* or the state's translation, published in 1637), approving six fine articles on the Lord's day, and developing the Church Order of Dordt, which is still of great benefit in many Reformed churches around the world.[1]

The main achievement of the synod, however, is the Canons of Dordt, which set forth the truth of the absolute sovereignty of God in salvation over against the heresies of Arminianism. This was the principal reason for calling the synod in the first place. This was the explanation for the invitation of the foreign delegates from Great Britain and France and various parts of Switzerland and Germany. This is what took most of the synod's time.[2]

---

1   For more on the last subject, see William A. Langerak, "The Polity of Dordt: *Om Goede Orde in de Gemeente Christi te Onderhouden* (To Maintain Good Order in the Church of Christ)," in chapter 6 of this book.
2   From November 13, 1618, to May 29, 1619, the Synod of Dordt met in 180

When they were produced, the Canons of Dordt were the most developed creed on Jehovah's particular grace in Jesus Christ in the history of the church. Four hundred years later, they are still the greatest confessional statement specifically dealing with the sovereignty of God over various aspects of man's salvation.[3] They may well remain such until the Lord's return.

In this fourth centenary year, we rightly celebrate Jehovah's blessed work at the Synod of Dordt and especially its chief fruit, the Canons of Dordt, which is one of our three forms of unity, along with the Belgic Confession (1561) and the Heidelberg Catechism (1563).

At this massive Dordtian milestone, our heavenly Father is calling us to a closer study of, a stronger faith in, and a deeper love for his utterly gracious salvation in Christ. This not only applies to those of us who have the Canons of Dordt as one of our church's official creeds, but it also holds good for all who are the true, spiritual children of the Reformation. American Presbyterian B. B. Warfield points out that the Canons were

> published authoritatively in 1619 as the finding of the Synod [of Dordt] with the aid of a large body of foreign assessors, representative practically of the whole Reformed world. The Canons...therefore...[possess] the moral authority of

---

sessions, exactly two-thirds of which were occupied with the Arminian error. In sessions 21–57 (December 5–January 14), procedural issues were discussed and the Remonstrants were interviewed; while the matter itself was debated and the Canons were drafted in sessions 58–140 (January 14–April 25).

3   In refuting the heresies of Amyrauldianism, a more subtle error than Arminianism, the Geneva Theses (1649) and the Formula Consensus Helvetica (1675) are more explicit and antithetical than the Canons on some points, but neither of these Swiss confessions present a lengthy, full-orbed treatment of the doctrines of grace. For both of these creeds, see James T. Dennison Jr., *Reformed Confessions of the 16th and 17th Centuries in English Translation*, 4 vols. (Grand Rapids, MI: Reformation Heritage Books, 2008–2014), 4:413–22, 516–30.

the decrees of practically an Ecumenical Council throughout the whole body of Reformed Churches...for the points of doctrine with which they deal they provide a singularly well-considered, prudent, and restrained Reformed formulary.[4]

Likewise, this is the considered opinion regarding Dordt of the great Scottish Presbyterian theologian George Smeaton:

> This great Synod, equal in importance to any of the Ecumenical Councils, is the glory of the Reformed Church. Since the first four General Councils, none have ever assembled with a more momentous charge or commission. It gave forth in its decrees a full and all-sided outline of the doctrines of special grace; and nobly was its work discharged. The decrees of the Synod were not only made the fundamental articles of the Dutch Church, but continue as part of the literature of these questions, to have a significance for all time. And it may be questioned whether anything more valuable as an ecclesiastical testimony for the doctrines of sovereign, special, efficacious grace was ever prepared on this important theme since the days of the apostles... Nowhere has the renewing work of the Holy Spirit been more correctly and fully exhibited than in the Canons of the Synod of Dort.[5]

In short, the triune God is calling all who believe the Bible to dig more deeply into the truth taught in this great Christian creed, which summarizes precious doctrines of holy scripture.

---

[4] B. B. Warfield, "Predestination in the Reformed Confessions," in *The Works of B. B. Warfield*, 10 vols. (1932; repr., Grand Rapids, MI: Baker, 2000), 9:144–45.

[5] George Smeaton, *The Doctrine of the Holy Spirit* (1858; repr., Edinburgh: The Banner of Truth Trust, 1974), 358–59.

The Five Points of Calvinism Moniker

The Canons of Dordt are the original five points of Calvinism. There are some who are familiar with the five points of Calvinism but who have never heard of the Canons of Dordt from which they are derived. The five *points* of Calvinism summarize the five *heads* of the Canons of Dordt (1618–19), which are a response to, and a refutation of, the Five *Articles* of the Remonstrants or Arminians at Gouda in the Dutch province of South Holland in 1610.[6]

Even the number of the five points of Calvinism needs some clarification in comparison with the Canons of Dordt. The third and the fourth heads of the Canons are combined, so that this confession consists of head one, head two, heads three and four, and head five. Why? In the "Remonstrance of 1610," the Arminians' third article on man's sinfulness was not, in itself, false, though it was ambiguous, deliberately avoiding the key issue. Their fourth article, which denied that God's grace is irresistible, revealed that the Remonstrants did not believe that man's depravity is total, for he could evidently choose not to resist Jehovah's mercy. Just as it is the combination of the Arminians' third and fourth articles that exposes the error in the former, so the Canons set forth the truth regarding these issues together in heads three and four.

Moreover, the word *Calvinism* in this moniker requires explanation. John Calvin died in 1564, whereas the Canons were completed fifty-five years later in 1619. Obviously, the original five points of Calvinism were not written by the long-dead, Genevan reformer. The five points of Calvinism were not even culled from his writings. They were drawn from the inexhaustible treasury of sacred scripture.

Thus the five points of Calvinism, based on the Canons of Dordt, summarize the truth of God's word, which is in accordance

---

6   The "Remonstrance of 1610" is included as an appendix in De Jong, *Crisis in the Reformed Churches,* 207–209.

with the genius of John Calvin's biblical theology. So what is known as the five points of Calvinism is really an abbreviation of the five heads (with two of them combined) on the absolute sovereignty of God in salvation set forth by the Synod of Dordt from the holy scriptures in the form of ninety-three articles, of which fifty-four are positive and thirty-nine are negative (the rejection of errors). But since this is too much of a mouthful, the five points of Calvinism moniker is understandably the prevailing terminology and will be for the foreseeable future.

THE ACRONYM *TULIP*

What then about the acronym TULIP used for the five points of Calvinism? *T* is for total depravity, *U* for unconditional election, *L* for limited atonement, *I* for irresistible grace, and *P* for the perseverance of the saints. This is a handy memory aid that has been, and is, helpful for many.

The acronym TULIP is appropriate because Dordt is in the Netherlands, where the tulip is the unofficial national flower. This TULIP is a beautiful flower of God's grace, for the root meaning of grace is beauty.[7] This lovely flower of divine grace grew, blossomed, and unfolded in Dutch Reformed soil and has been transplanted all around the world. The spouse of Jesus Christ admires and cherishes this precious flower.[8]

The order of the five petals of the TULIP differs from that of the five heads of the Canons. TULIP begins with *T* for total depravity, which is the third topic in the Canons. Thus the TULIP acronym, when transposed to the Canons themselves, is actually ordered as ULTIP: unconditional election, limited atonement, total depravity, irresistible grace, and the perseverance of the saints.

---

7 Cf. Herman Hoeksema, *Reformed Dogmatics*, 2 vols., 2nd ed. (Grandville, MI: Reformed Free Publishing Association, 2004–2005), 1:154–60.
8 Compare the language of Canons 5.15.

How does TULIP compare with the titles of the Canons of Dordt's five heads of doctrine, which occur in the order of ULTIP? What the five points of Calvinism calls unconditional election is entitled "Of Divine Predestination" in the Canons themselves. *Unconditional* election focuses on our main battleground with the Arminians. Arminianism is all about conditions.[9] The Canons of Dordt repeatedly condemn conditionalism, both conditions in general and, especially, in election. So the *U* of ULTIP, *unconditional* election, hits the nail right on its head. However, as unconditional *election*, it can be misleading, because head one of the Canons deals with predestination, understood theologically as referring to both election and reprobation, which the Canons rightly identify as components in one, single, divine "decree."[10]

There are some who call themselves Calvinists who claim to believe all the five points of Calvinism, but they hold only to unconditional election and not unconditional reprobation. However, the true, biblical Calvinism of the Canons of Dordt, and of John Calvin himself, insists on both election and reprobation.[11]

The *U* of TULIP, unconditional *election*, would be more faithful to scripture and the Canons, and a lot sharper, if it were changed to unconditional *predestination*, with predestination being understood in theological parlance as including both election and reprobation.[12]

The next letter in ULTIP is *L* for limited atonement. The title of the corresponding head in the Canons is "Of the Death of Christ

---

9 Cf. Fred H. Klooster: "Arminianism is characterized by conditionalism." ("The Doctrinal Deliverances of Dort," in De Jong, *Crisis in the Reformed Churches*, 56).
10 Canons of Dordt 1.6, in *Confessions and Church Order*, 156.
11 Reprobation is especially taught in Canons 1.6, 10, 15, 16, 18; 1, error and rejection 8. For the French reformer's teaching on double predestination, see John Calvin, *Calvin's Calvinism*, ed. Russell J. Dykstra, trans. Henry Cole, 2nd ed. (1856; repr., Jenison, MI: Reformed Free Publishing Association, 2009).
12 The sixteenth-century Italian reformer Jerome Zanchius has an excellent treatment of God's eternal election and reprobation in *Absolute Predestination* (London: Silver Trumpet Publications, 1989).

and the Redemption of Man Thereby." The *L* for *limited* gets right to the key issue regarding Christ's death—that it is for the elect alone. Of course, we do not understand *limited* as if it implied any sort of deficiency in the cross or our Savior.[13]

Total depravity is called in the Canons "Of the Corruption of Man." Depravity and corruption mean the same thing. The *T* in total depravity is a most appropriate adjective, because fallen man is "wholly incapable of doing any good, and inclined to all wickedness" except he is "regenerated by the Spirit of God."[14] The little word *total* deliberately excludes man's free will.[15]

Next of the five points of Calvinism comes *I* for irresistible grace. This section is the second half of heads three and four. After "Of the Corruption of Man," the title continues, "His Conversion to God and the Manner Thereof." Irresistible grace in this section of the Canons refers to the grace of God in regenerating, calling, and converting his elect.[16] With *irresistible* grace, we have the right adjective, because this is the issue with Arminianism. Arminians believe that Jehovah earnestly wants and tries to convert everybody, but his grace is resistible. Arminians will say that God's grace is mighty and powerful, but not almighty. Thus, according to their teaching, the grace of the Most High is neutered, because, after all, it is resistible.[17]

---

13 Canons of Dordt 2.3, 4, 6; 3.9, in *Confessions and Church Order*, 163, 168. The classic work on Christ's particular atonement is John Owen, *The Death of Death in the Death of Christ*, rev. ed. (1852; repr., Edinburgh: The Banner of Truth Trust, 1989).
14 Heidelberg Catechism Q&A 8, in *Confessions and Church Order*, 86.
15 The 1525 magnum opus of Martin Luther forcefully teaches total depravity, especially against the Roman Catholic (and Arminian) notion of man's free will: *The Bondage of the Will,* trans. J. I. Packer and O. R. Johnston, rev. ed. (1957; repr., Grand Rapids, MI: Fleming H. Revell, 1998).
16 God's grace is also irresistible in its application of all the benefits of salvation, including justification, adoption, sanctification, preservation, and glorification.
17 Unlike the subjects covered in the other four heads of the Canons, there is no work on irresistible grace that is widely recognized as outstanding. For a moving, twentieth-century treatment that escapes the baleful influence of an ineffectual

Man's will is always decisive in salvation, according to Arminius and his disciples.

The titles of the first four heads of doctrine in the Canons give merely the broad subject of which they treat: "Of Divine Predestination"; "Of the Death of Christ and the Redemption of Men Thereby"; and "Of the Corruption of Man, His Conversion to God and the Manner Thereof." However, the corresponding names of the five points of Calvinism identify precisely the issue over against the Arminians: unconditional election (and reprobation) versus conditional election (and reprobation), limited atonement versus universal atonement (Jesus died for everybody head for head), total depravity over against partial depravity, and irresistible grace versus resistible grace.

Finally, we come to the fifth point of Calvinism. This time it is not presented in the form of an adjective followed by a noun (as in total depravity, unconditional election, limited atonement, and irresistible grace). The fifth point is the perseverance of the saints. The fifth head of the Canons is "Of the Perseverance of the Saints." They are exactly the same, apart from the little word *of* found in the title in the Canons.[18]

When was this helpful and penetrating acronym TULIP first used? According to the most current research available to me, TULIP goes back at least as far as 1905, when Dr. Cleland Boyd McAfee, an American Presbyterian minister, listed the five points of Calvinism as TULIP.[19]

---

desire of God to save the reprobate, see Herman Hoeksema, *Whosoever Will*, 2nd ed. (1945; repr., Jenison, MI: Reformed Free Publishing Association, 2002).

18 For an exhaustive treatment of the truth of the fifth point of Calvinism, see John Owen, "The Doctrine of the Saints' Perseverance Explained and Confirmed," in *The Works of John Owen*, 16 vols., ed. William H. Gould, rev. ed. (1850–53; repr., Edinburgh: The Banner of Truth Trust, 1966), 11:1–666.

19 Ed Sanders, "The Origin of the Acronym TULIP: The Five Points of Calvinism," accessed April 25, 2019, https://theologue.files.wordpress.com/2014/08/originoftheacronym-tulip.pdf.

McAfee used TULIP as a teaching device in a lecture in Newark, the most populous city in the state of New Jersey. Many people believe the name Newark to be a contraction of new ark (of the covenant) because it was settled by Connecticut Puritans in 1666. Newark is a very appropriate place for a lecture on the five points of Calvinism, because the ark with its mercy seat was sprinkled with blood of the Day of Atonement (Lev. 16) as a picture of God's grace in Christ crucified—the glorious subject of the Canons.

Dr. McAfee's TULIP is exactly the same as that known to us in four of its five points. However, for U (unconditional election), the Presbyterian pastor spoke of "universal sovereignty." I trust that he meant by this—and I have no indication to the contrary—that Jehovah is absolutely sovereign over the salvation or damnation of every individual person in the entire human race (Rom. 9:22–23). That is, God possesses and exercises "universal sovereignty" over all mankind (and the angels) with respect to election and reprobation.[20]

Head One: "Of Divine Predestination" (Unconditional Election)

The Canons start with "Of Divine Predestination." We have Dordt's own excellent definition of election in this pivotal article:

> Election is the unchangeable purpose of God whereby, before the foundation of the world, he hath out of mere grace, according to the sovereign good pleasure of his own will, chosen, from the whole human race, which had fallen through their own fault from their primitive state of rectitude into sin and destruction, a certain number of persons to redemption in Christ, whom he from eternity appointed the mediator and head of the elect, and the foundation of salvation.[21]

---

20 In 1 Timothy 5:21, we read of "the elect angels."
21 Canons of Dordt 1.7, in *Confessions and Church Order*, 156. This section's exposition of head one deliberately omits its teaching on reprobation because

The next four articles explain the truth of election.[22] First, there is *one* election, "both to grace and glory, to salvation and the way of salvation."[23] This is over against the various decrees of election as taught by the Arminians.[24]

Second, God's one election is *unconditional*, for it is "not founded upon foreseen faith, [or] the obedience of faith" or any "prerequisite, cause, or condition."[25] This opposes Arminianism's conditional election.[26]

Third, God's one, unconditional election is *sovereign*. Canons 1.10 cites Romans 9:11–13 regarding the twins in Rebecca's womb: "For the children being not yet born, neither having done any good or evil...it was said unto [Rebecca], The elder shall serve the younger. As it is written, Jacob have I loved, but Esau have I hated." The Canons polemicize here against the idea that election depends on the will of man and not on the will of the Almighty alone.[27]

Fourth, God's one, unconditional, sovereign election is *unchangeable*. Canons 1.11 states that divine election is as unchangeable as the immutable Jehovah himself. This truth is antithetical to Arminianism's changeable election.[28] The Canons teach that God's one, unconditional, sovereign, unchangeable election is like a "fountain."[29] What is the idea of a fountain? A pure spring that sends

---

this is the subject of chapter 7 in this book: "Illustrating and Recommending the Grace of Election: Dordt's Doctrine of Reprobation."

22 Canons of Dordt 1.8–11, in *Confessions and Church Order*, 156–57.
23 Canons of Dordt 1.8, in *Confessions and Church Order*, 157.
24 Canons of Dordt 1, error and rejection 2, in *Confessions and Church Order*, 160.
25 Canons of Dordt 1.9, in *Confessions and Church Order*, 157.
26 Canons of Dordt 1, error and rejection 2–5, 7, in *Confessions and Church Order*, 160–62.
27 Canons of Dordt 1, error and rejection 9, in *Confessions and Church Order*, 162.
28 Canons of Dordt 1, error and rejection 6, in *Confessions and Church Order*, 161.
29 Canons of Dordt 1.9, in *Confessions and Church Order*, 157. We read in the conclusion of the Canons that "election is the fountain and the cause of faith and good works." Of course, election is a "fountain" because the electing God

THE CANONS AS THE ORIGINAL FIVE POINTS OF CALVINISM

forth fresh, clear water. A fountain is a source of life-giving water that bubbles forth from beneath the earth where it was invisible to those above. The Canons state that "election is the fountain of every saving good, from which proceed faith, holiness, and the other gifts of salvation, and finally eternal life itself, as its fruits and effects."[30]

What a beautiful truth! Unconditional election is the fountain and source of every spiritual and saving good. Yea, unconditional election is the fountain and source of everlasting life itself.[31] Canons 1.9 quotes Ephesians 1:4 as proof: "He hath chosen [or elected] us [not because we were, but]…that we should be holy and without blame before him in love." Election is not only the sole fountain that issues forth in holiness and blamelessness; Ephesians 1 further explains that election is the source and fountain of our adoption (v. 5), our redemption (v. 7), the forgiveness of our sins (v. 7), our knowledge of God's will (v. 9), our inheritance in the new creation (vv. 10–11), and our sealing with the Holy Spirit (v. 13).

Other scriptures teach that God's unconditional election of us in Christ is the fountain and source of our faith, sanctification, and salvation (2 Thess. 2:13); our effectual calling, justification, and glorification (Rom. 8:30); and our "eternal life" (Acts 13:48).

But listen to the lies of the enemies of God's sovereign election. First, they proclaim, "Election is dead," meaning that election is irrelevant and has no connection to the Christian life. No, the truth is that election is the eternal fountain and source of living waters. How wrong can you get! Instead of being dead, election is the source of our spiritual and everlasting life in Jesus Christ: election is our

---

is "the overflowing fountain of all good" (Belgic Confession 1, in *Confessions and Church Order*, 23).
30 Canons of Dordt 1.9, in *Confessions and Church Order*, 157. In Canons 1.12, "a true faith in Christ, filial fear, a godly sorrow for sin, a hungering and thirsting after righteousness, etc.," are identified as "the infallible fruits of election pointed out in the Word of God," 157.
31 It is this too for the elect children of believers dying in infancy (Canons 1.17).

being "written in the book of life" (Rev. 17:8), so that we "bring forth fruit" unto God (John 15:16).

Second, election is charged with being "dry," as dry as dust, being merely a boring old doctrine that is of no practical relevance. But election is the fountain of fresh, invigorating, spiritual water. Election magnifies God's love (Deut. 7:7) and grace (Rom. 11:5). Our election is in Christ (Eph. 1:4), so that we are given to him (John 17:9). We are chosen to fellowship with the triune God (Isa. 41:8) in order that we "should shew forth the praises of him who hath called [us] out of darkness into his marvellous light" (1 Pet. 2:9).

Third, election, some profanely claim, "makes people into the 'frozen chosen.'" Yet the truth is that election is the fountain of flowing waters and not a block of ice![32] These waters of eternal life bubble over, so that "we love him, because he first loved us" (1 John 4:19). We are elected unto a glorious transformation: "to be conformed to the image of his [God's] Son" (Rom. 8:29).[33]

Thus we have two antithetical doxologies or praises. This is the damnably faint, nay, false, praise of cold and sterile Arminianism: "Blessed be the God who chose me because he foresaw that I would believe and choose him." This is not a caricature of Arminianism; this *is* Arminianism: God chooses those whom he foresaw

---

32 In keeping with the imagery of election as a "fountain" in Canons 1.9, W. Robert Godfrey, as well as others, accurately translates the Latin *profluunt* as "flow," stating that "faith, holiness, and all other saving gifts, even eternal life itself," "flow" from election, which "is the fountain of every saving good" (Godfrey, *Saving the Reformation*, 92).

33 Fools who utter blasphemies against God's election, such as those mentioned in the last three paragraphs, should hearken to the warning contained in the conclusion to the Canons of Dordt: "Moreover, the synod warns calumniators themselves to consider the terrible judgment of God which awaits them for bearing false witness against the confessions of so many churches, for distressing the consciences of the weak, and for laboring to render suspected the society of the truly faithful," 179–80.

would choose him.[34] In Arminianism, sinful man always possesses the whip hand. Yet holy scripture is clear that salvation "is not of him that willeth, nor of him that runneth, but of God that sheweth mercy" (Rom. 9:16).

On the other hand, with the apostle Paul, the Reformed believer exclaims, "Blessed be the God and Father of our Lord Jesus Christ, who hath blessed us with all spiritual blessings in heavenly places in Christ: according as he hath chosen [or elected] us in him before the foundation of the world, that we should be holy and without blame before him in love" (Eph. 1:3–4).[35]

These are two very different doxologies. The first one is essentially Pharisaism: "'God, I thank thee, that I am not as other men are' (Luke 18:11), because I believed by my free will!"

No wonder that John Calvin preached that the opponents of election and/or its preaching are "mortal enemies of God's praise":

> Now St. Paul immediately says that it is "to the praise of the glory of his grace" [Eph. 1:6]. Here he shows the final reason that moved God to elect us, namely, that his grace might be praised by it, yes, not after a common and ordinary manner, but with a certain glory. For he coupled those two things together so that we should be ravished when we see how God has drawn us out of the bottom of hell to open to us the gate of his kingdom and to call us to the heritage

---

34 Canons of Dordt 1.9; 1, error and rejection 5, in *Confessions and Church Order*, 157, 161.
35 Significantly, the positive section of head one also ends with a biblical doxology: "With holy adoration of these mysteries, we exclaim in the words of the apostle: O the depth of the riches both of the wisdom and knowledge of God! how unsearchable are his judgments, and his ways past finding out! For who hath known the mind of the Lord? or who hath been his counsellor? or who hath first given to him, and it shall be recompensed unto him again? For of him, and through him, and to him, are all things: to whom be glory for ever. Amen (Rom. 11:33–36)" (Canons 1.18), 159.

of salvation. Here we see once more the matter I dealt with previously, namely, that all who would do away with God's predestination or are loath to hear it spoken of, thereby show themselves to be mortal enemies of God's praise.[36]

Head Two: "Of the Death of Christ and the Redemption of Men Thereby" (Limited Atonement)

Next, we turn to head two, "Of the Death of Christ and the Redemption of Men Thereby," popularly known as limited atonement. The Canons teach not only that unconditional election is a "fountain," but also that Christ's limited (or particular) atonement is a "sacrifice."[37] The fathers of Dordt spoke biblically, for sacrifice is the dominant idea in scripture of our Savior's cross.[38] Jesus' atonement is nothing if it is not a sacrifice offered to God for our sins.

The five main Old Testament sacrifices are especially treated in Leviticus 1–7. Besides the unbloody meat or meal or grain or cereal offering (Lev. 2), there were the four bloody sacrifices of the burnt offering, the peace offering, the sin offering, and the trespass offering. Under the older covenant, one needed, first, an altar. In the early days, the altar was made of earth or stone (Ex. 20:24–25). Later, God commanded the building of a brazen altar at the tabernacle (Ex. 27:1–8) and the temple (2 Chron. 4:1). Second, a priest was required to serve at the altar. From Sinai onward, Israel's priests

---

36 John Calvin, *Sermons on the Epistle to the Ephesians* (Edinburgh: The Banner of Truth Trust, 1973), 42–43. Canons 1.14 advocates the faithful, reverent preaching of God's election, after the example of the prophets, the Lord Jesus himself, and his apostles.
37 Canons of Dordt 2.3, 6, in *Confessions and Church Order*, 163.
38 Cf. B. B. Warfield, "Christ Our Sacrifice," in *The Works of B. B. Warfield*, 2:401–35. Warfield is correct: "The New Testament writers, in employing this [sacrificial] language to describe the death of Christ, intended to represent that death as performing the functions of an expiatory sacrifice; wished to be understood as so representing it; and could not but be so understood by their first readers who were wonted to sacrificial worship," 434.

were adult males of the line of Levi through Aaron (Ex. 28–29). Third, bullocks, cows, rams, sheep, goats, lambs, pigeons, and doves were the stipulated sacrificial victims to be offered by the priests upon the altar.

Jesus Christ, the eternal Son of God and the sinless Son of man,[39] is our only high priest, "a priest for ever after the order of Melchizedek" (Ps. 110:4; Heb. 5:6). He is the Lamb of God (John 1:29, 36; 1 Pet. 1:19) who offered himself up to the Father (Eph. 5:2; Heb. 9:14) on the altar of the cross (Heb. 13:10), once and for all (Heb. 10:10).

It is no wonder, therefore, that the Canons call Christ's atonement "the only and most perfect sacrifice"[40] and describe his work in sacrificial terms. Jesus is our "surety"[41] and substitute "who was made sin, and became a curse for us and in our stead."[42] Our Lord thereby made full payment for our debt, the debt of our transgressions of the law of God, as a complete "satisfaction to divine justice on our behalf,"[43] a truth especially emphasized by his being our trespass offering (Isa. 53:10).[44]

By his sacrificial blood[45] and atoning death[46] under God's curse and wrath,[47] Christ propitiated or appeased God's wrath.[48] He

---

[39] Canons of Dordt 2.4, in *Confessions and Church Order*, 163.
[40] Canons of Dordt 2.3, in *Confessions and Church Order*, 163.
[41] Canons of Dordt 2.2; 2, error and rejection 2, in *Confessions and Church Order*, 163–65.
[42] Canons of Dordt 2.2, in *Confessions and Church Order*, 163.
[43] Canons of Dordt 2.2, in *Confessions and Church Order*, 163. Cf. Canons 2.1, 3; 2, rejection 3, in *Confessions and Church Order*, 162–63, 165.
[44] Canons of Dordt 2, error and rejection 1, in *Confessions and Church Order*, 164.
[45] Canons of Dordt 2.8–9; 2, error and rejection 2, in *Confessions and Church Order*, 163–65.
[46] Canons of Dordt 2.4, 7–8; 2, error and rejection 1–4, 6–7, in *Confessions and Church Order*, 163–66.
[47] Canons of Dordt 2.2, 4, in *Confessions and Church Order*, 163.
[48] Canons of Dordt 2, error and rejection 5, in *Confessions and Church Order*, 165.

expiated or blotted out our sins[49] and redeemed us from all iniquity.[50] He reconciled us to our heavenly Father[51] and purged us from all our transgressions.[52] Sacrificial terminology is found in the Canons because it is found in the Bible, for it is the language God wisely used to describe what Jesus did on the cross. Christ is "the only and most perfect sacrifice and satisfaction for sin."[53]

For whom did the Lord Jesus accomplish or achieve all this? This is the answer of God's word: his elect (Rom. 8:32–34)[54] and not the reprobate; his sheep (John 10:11, 15)[55] and not the goats (Matt. 25:33); his seed (Isa. 53:10)[56] and not the seed of the serpent (Gen. 3:15); his true church (Acts 20:28; Eph. 5:25) and not "the synagogue of Satan" (Rev. 2:9; 3:9). Our Savior shed his blood for those whom the Bible calls his people (Matt. 1:21; Heb. 2:17) and friends (John 15:13–14);[57] his sons, children, and brethren (Heb. 2:10–14) and not bastards, that is, the illegitimate (Heb. 12:8). Our Lord bore the iniquities of many (Isa. 53:11–12; Matt. 20:28; 26:28; Mark 14:24; Heb. 9:28), as opposed to everyone head for head—the Arminian heresy.

Remember the idea of substitution. Jesus, in his sacrifice, took the place of his own beloved people as our surety and representative. However, Arminianism does not have, and cannot have, despite all

---

49 Canons of Dordt 2.3, in *Confessions and Church Order*, 163.
50 Canons of Dordt 2.8; 2, error and rejection 1, 4, in *Confessions and Church Order*, 163–65.
51 Canons of Dordt 2, error and rejection 5, in *Confessions and Church Order*, 165.
52 Canons of Dordt 2.8, in *Confessions and Church Order*, 163–64.
53 Canons of Dordt 2.3, in *Confessions and Church Order*, 163. As such, neither Christ nor his sacrifice needs man's free will to make them effectual.
54 Canons of Dordt 2, error and rejection 7; 5, error and rejection 1, in *Confessions and Church Order*, 166, 176.
55 Canons of Dordt 2, error and rejection 1, 7, in *Confessions and Church Order*, 164, 166.
56 Canons of Dordt 2, error and rejection 1, in *Confessions and Church Order*, 164.
57 Canons of Dordt 2, error and rejection 7, in *Confessions and Church Order*, 166.

its protestations to the contrary, substitutionary atonement, because Arminianism tells every man that Christ died for him. But if Jesus truly bore the curse and wrath for every man as his substitute, then no man would or could perish everlastingly.

The truth regarding the extent of Christ's atonement is stated in Canons 2.8:

> This was the sovereign counsel and most gracious will and purpose of God the Father, that the quickening and saving efficacy of the most precious death of his Son should extend to all the elect, for bestowing upon them alone the gift of justifying faith, thereby to bring them infallibly to salvation; that is, it was the will of God that Christ by the blood of the cross, whereby he confirmed the new covenant, should effectually redeem out of every people, tribe, nation, and language all those, and those only, who were from eternity chosen to salvation and given to him by the Father.[58]

This is the crucial article in head two, because it expressly teaches the particularity of Christ's atonement, as being for "all those, and those only, who were from eternity chosen to salvation." The preceding seven articles lead up to it, and the next article clarifies it, by emphasizing that the elect's redemption is effectual.[59] Moreover, all seven of the rejection of errors in head two are related to Canons 2.8, making this article of unique significance in this reformed creed.[60]

Key biblical and Reformation truths are summed up by the five *solas* or alones: salvation is by faith alone, in Christ alone, through grace alone, to the glory of God alone, and according to scripture alone.[61] Here is another alone or only: the Lord Jesus died for his

---

58 *Confessions and Church Order*, 163.
59 *Confessions and Church Order*, 164.
60 Cf. Godfrey, *Saving the Reformation*, 237–38.
61 In Latin, the plural of *sola* is *solae*.

elect alone or only (this is an aspect of Christ alone). The Reformed Christian says, "I receive this gospel truth, that Jesus died for the elect alone, through grace alone, by faith alone, according to the scripture alone, and to the glory of God alone!"

Again, we have two contrasting doxologies, this time regarding Christ's cross. The Arminian sings, "Jesus was slain to make the redemption of everyone possible, and I used my free will aright."[62] But this is the new, and very different, song of the saints praising the Lamb: "Thou art worthy...for thou wast slain, and hast redeemed us to God by thy blood out of every kindred, and tongue, and people, and nation; and hast made us unto our God kings and priests: and we shall reign on the earth" (Rev. 5:9–10).[63]

Head Three: "Of the Corruption of Man" (Total Depravity)

The third head, "Of the Corruption of Man," is also known as total depravity. According to the Canons, man is "dead in sin"[64] and in "spiritual death."[65] As proof that the unregenerate are "really" and "utterly dead in sin," that is, "destitute of all powers unto spiritual good," the Canons quote Ephesians 2:1, 5: "Ye were dead through trespasses and sins."[66]

This biblical and Reformed teaching stands in sharp opposition to the semi-Pelagianism of Roman Catholicism, which teaches

---

62 The hymnals of many churches are filled with songs teaching the Arminian heresies of universal atonement and unregenerate man's free will, as well as resistible grace.
63 The last words of head two are also doxological, for Christ "laid down His life" for "His bride," so that she "may celebrate His praises here and through all eternity" (Canons of Dordt 2.9, in *Confessions and Church Order*, 164).
64 Canons of Dordt 3–4.3; 3–4, error and rejection 4, in *Confessions and Church Order*, 167, 171.
65 Canons of Dordt 3–4.16; 3–4, error and rejection 3, in *Confessions and Church Order*, 169–71. Cf. Canons 1.1; 3–4, error and rejection 1, in *Confessions and Church Order*, 155, 170.
66 Canons of Dordt 3–4, error and rejection 4, in *Confessions and Church Order*, 171. Cf. Canons 1, error and rejection 4, in *Confessions and Church Order*, 160.

that man is merely sick and not dead. The Canons also oppose the Arminianism of much of evangelicalism, which claims that man has free will and therefore is not dead. After all, whatever way you cut it, free will is surely a moral good in man, a little bit of life toward God. But that whole, rotten Arminian system of humanistic philosophy is false, because man is "dead in trespasses and sins" (Eph. 2:1).

Faithful to God's word, the fathers of Dordt, in the opening articles of their treatment of man's utter corruption, set forth man's fall,[67] original sin,[68] and total depravity.[69] In Adam, humanity is dead to the true God, dead to the biblical Christ, and dead to the gospel of grace. He is dead in sin with his body and his soul and in his heart, his mind, and his will.[70] Therefore, "without the regenerating grace of the Holy Spirit [fallen men] are neither able nor willing to return to God, to reform the depravity of their nature, nor to dispose themselves to reformation."[71] All loopholes are closed.

Here the Canons of 1618–19 reflect "The Counter Remonstrance of 1611." In this important document, six orthodox Dutch theologians describe the whole fallen human race as "lying dead in their trespasses so that there is within them no more power to convert themselves truly unto God to believe in Christ than a corpse has power to raise itself from the dead."[72]

This being the case, "the glimmerings of natural light" and "the law of the decalogue" are utterly insufficient to bring fallen man to salvation.[73] With these two ruled out as means of deliverance, the

---

67 Canons of Dordt 3–4.1, in *Confessions and Church Order*, 166.
68 Canons of Dordt 3–4.2, in *Confessions and Church Order*, 166.
69 Canons of Dordt 3–4.3, in *Confessions and Church Order*, 167.
70 Canons 3–4.11 characterizes the will of the unsaved as dead with respect to the good.
71 Canons of Dordt 3–4.3, in *Confessions and Church Order*, 167.
72 "The Counter Remonstrance of 1611" is included as an appendix in De Jong, *Crisis in the Reformed Churches*, 209–11.
73 Canons of Dordt 3–4.4, in *Confessions and Church Order*, 167. Cf. Canons 3–4, error and rejection 5, in *Confessions and Church Order*, 171–72. Through

Canons rightly state, "What therefore neither the light of nature nor the law could do, that God performs by the operation of the Holy Spirit through the Word or ministry of reconciliation, which is the glad tidings concerning the Messiah."[74]

This truth, taught by holy scripture and the Holy Spirit to the elect, makes every believer cry out from the heart, "God be merciful [or propitious] to me [the] sinner" (Luke 18:13). Why does each child of God make this heartfelt lamentation? "For I know that in me (that is, in my flesh) dwelleth no good thing" (Rom. 7:18). He does not add, as Arminianism requires, "except for my free will!"[75]

Even the section on total depravity ends with worship, for God "rescues them [elect but spiritually dead sinners] from the power of darkness," so "that they may show forth the praises of Him who hath called them out of darkness into His marvellous light, and may glory, not in themselves, but in the Lord, according to the testimony of the apostles in various places."[76]

Head Four: "Of [Man's] Conversion to God and the Manner Thereof" (Irresistible Grace)

The Canons' fourth head, "Of [Man's] Conversion to God and the Manner Thereof," is called irresistible grace in the five points of Calvinism. We have looked at the fountain of unconditional election, Christ's sacrifice on the cross (limited atonement), and our total depravity as spiritual death. Now we have another powerful biblical image used by the fathers at Dordt, this time for God's irresistible grace as it comes to wholly corrupted sinners. It is called a spiritual

---

natural light and the decalogue, the unregenerate only increase their sin (Canons 3–4.4, 5; Rom. 1:18–32; 7:5).
74 Canons of Dordt 3–4.6, in *Confessions and Church Order*, 167.
75 Man's alleged free will is especially the aspect of Arminianism opposed in the third and fourth heads of the Canons (cf. Canons 3–4.1, 3, 10–12, 14, 16; 3–4, error and rejection 2–4, 6–9, in *Confessions and Church Order*, 166–73).
76 Canons of Dordt 3–4.10, in *Confessions and Church Order*, 168.

"resurrection from the dead" (or a "making alive") in Canons heads 3–4.12:

> This is the regeneration so highly celebrated in scripture and denominated a new creation: a *resurrection from the dead*, a making alive, which God works in us without our aid. But this is in no wise effected merely by the external preaching of the gospel, by moral suasion, or such a mode of operation that after God has performed his part it still remains in the power of man to be regenerated or not, to be converted or to continue unconverted; but it is evidently a supernatural work, most powerful, and at the same time most delightful, astonishing, mysterious, and ineffable; not inferior in efficacy to creation or the resurrection from the dead, as the scripture inspired by the Author of this work declares.[77]

The Canons are following Ephesians 2, which describes God's regeneration of us as a resurrection from the dead: "And you hath he quickened [or made alive, or resurrected] who were dead in trespasses and sins" (v. 1); "Even when we were dead in sins, [God] hath quickened us together with Christ" (v. 5; cf. Rom. 6:4, 13).[78]

The explanation is simple: Those who are totally depraved (head three) can only be saved by irresistible grace (head four). Since man is "dead in sin,"[79] he needs a "resurrection from the dead,"[80] for the spiritually dead require a spiritual resurrection.

The grace that brings the elect to spiritual life is just as powerful and irresistible as the call of Jesus to his friend Lazarus, who had been dead for four days and was bound hand and foot with

---

77 *Confessions and Church Order*, 168 (emphasis added).
78 Likewise, Canons 3–4.16 teaches that God "spiritually quickens" the "will" (cf. Canons 3–4.11, in *Confessions and Church Order*, 168), 170.
79 Canons of Dordt 3–4.3; 3–4, error and rejection 4, in *Confessions and Church Order*, 167, 171.
80 Canons of Dordt 3–4.12, in *Confessions and Church Order*, 168–69.

grave clothes: "Lazarus, come forth" (John 11:43). This chapter of the gospel of John lays great emphasis on the fact that Jesus loved Lazarus (vv. 3, 5, 11, 35–36). Here God's wonder work of physical resurrection, like the spiritual resurrection of the elect (Ezek. 16:6, 8; Eph. 2:4–5; Titus 3:4–5), is the fruit of God's love.

Scripture is very clear that our new birth is the product of Jehovah's will: "Of his own will begat he us" (James 1:18). As with all things, God's will is sovereign in regeneration: "The wind bloweth where it listeth [or desires or wishes], and thou hearest the sound thereof, but canst not tell whence it cometh, and whither it goeth: so is every one that is born of the Spirit" (John 3:8). John 1:12–13 is, if anything, even stronger, explicitly excluding any role for man's will in effecting the new birth: "But as many as received him, to them gave he power to become the sons of God, even to them that believe on his name: which were born, not of blood, nor of the will of the flesh, nor of the will of man, but of God."

To the Arminian objection that this turns man into a robot, the Canons respond,

> But as man by the fall did not cease to be a creature endowed with understanding and will, nor did sin which pervaded the whole race of mankind deprive him of the human nature, but brought upon him depravity and spiritual death; so also this grace of regeneration does not treat men as senseless stocks and blocks, nor takes away their will and its properties, neither does violence thereto; but spiritually quickens, heals, corrects, and at the same time sweetly and powerfully bends it; that where carnal rebellion and resistance formerly prevailed, a ready and sincere spiritual obedience begins to reign, in which the true and spiritual restoration and freedom of our will consist.[81]

---

81 Canons of Dordt 3–4.16, in *Confessions and Church Order*, 169–70. Cf. Canons 3–4.11, in *Confessions and Church Order*, 168.

THE CANONS AS THE ORIGINAL FIVE POINTS OF CALVINISM

In Psalm 110, David speaks by the Holy Spirit's inspiration of Jesus Christ as our heavenly king (vv. 1–2) and Melchizedekian priest (v. 4). Nestled between these verses on two of our Lord's offices is the truth of his spiritual rule over his elect: "Thy people shall be willing in the day of thy power" (v. 3). This is the truth superbly expressed by our Reformed fathers in Canons 3–4.16.

Again, we have two antithetical thanksgivings. This is that of Arminian theology:

> I thank thee, O God, for saving me through my right use of my free will,[82] so that I did not resist[83] but consent[84] to thy "gentle…advising grace"[85] and "moral suasion,"[86] and "thus distinguish[ed]" myself "above others equally furnished with grace sufficient for faith and conversion."[87]

I am not putting words in the mouths of the Arminians, for this is their doctrine, ably summarized and refuted in our Canons of Dordt.

On the other hand, this is the confession of all Reformed believers:

> 20. Now unto him that is able to do exceeding abundantly above all that we ask or think, according to the power that worketh in us,

---

82 Canons of Dordt 3–4.10, 14, 16; 3–4, error and rejection 9, in *Confessions and Church Order*, 168–70, 173.
83 Canons of Dordt 3–4, error and rejection 8, in *Confessions and Church Order*, 172–73.
84 Canons of Dordt 3–4.14; 3–4, error and rejection 7, in *Confessions and Church Order*, 169, 172.
85 Canons of Dordt 3–4, error and rejection 7, in *Confessions and Church Order*, 172.
86 Canons of Dordt 3–4.12, in *Confessions and Church Order*, 168–69.
87 Canons of Dordt 3–4.10, in *Confessions and Church Order*, 168. Canons 3–4, error and rejection 9 quotes Paul's rhetorical question: "For who maketh thee to differ? and what hast thou that thou didst not receive?" (1 Cor. 4:7).

21. Unto him be glory in the church by Christ Jesus throughout all ages, world without end. Amen. (Eph. 3:20–21)[88]

Head Five: "Of the Perseverance of the Saints" (Perseverance of the Saints)

In the opening three sections of its final head, the Canons set forth the saints' depravity. Though we are delivered "from the dominion and slavery of sin in this life," we are still subject to "indwelling sin." Thus believers commit "daily sins of infirmity," and "spots adhere" to their best works.[89]

Through wickedly yielding to the temptations of the world, the flesh, and the devil, true Christians may fall into great, heinous, and enormous sins.[90] Yet Jehovah "certainly and effectually renews them to repentance, to a sincere and godly sorrow for their sins, that they may seek and obtain remission in the blood of the Mediator."[91]

Though "with respect to themselves," all believers "would undoubtedly" apostatize,[92] this cannot happen, because of our unchangeable election[93] and the irrevocability of the elements of our salvation, including regeneration,[94] adoption, and justification.[95] Article 8 makes a trinitarian argument. It refers to God the Father's

---

88 Head four ends with this praise of the living God who regenerates his own: "to whom alone all the glory, both of means and of their saving fruit and efficacy, is forever due. Amen" (Canons of Dordt 3–4.17, in *Confessions and Church Order*, 170.
89 Canons of Dordt 5.1–3, in *Confessions and Church Order*, 173.
90 Canons of Dordt 5.4–5, in *Confessions and Church Order*, 174.
91 Canons of Dordt 5.7, in *Confessions and Church Order*, 174. Cf. Canons 5.5, in *Confessions and Church Order*, 174.
92 Canons of Dordt 5.8, in *Confessions and Church Order*, 174. Cf. Canons 5.3, in *Confessions and Church Order*, 173.
93 Canons of Dordt 5.6, in *Confessions and Church Order*, 174.
94 Canons of Dordt 5.7; 5, error and rejection 8, in *Confessions and Church Order*, 174, 178.
95 Canons of Dordt 5.6; 5, error and rejection 3, in *Confessions and Church Order*, 174, 177.

counsel, promise, and call. It refers to God the Son's merit, intercession, and preservation. And it refers to God the Holy Spirit's sealing. Together, these ensure that the true believer will never perish.[96]

A beautiful, biblical image that the fathers at Dordt used here is that of God's hand. The comfort of Canons head five, error and rejection 3 is that "the Father's hand" envelops each and every elect child of God. We are secure in Jehovah's almighty yet gentle hand, with a grip that never fails and will not let us go. The hand of the triune God operates through Christ's hand, for the Father does all things through the Son (John 5:19–30). What a hand our Savior has, embracing all the elect members of his universal church, so that not one of his people is plucked out and none of his sheep are snatched away!

Thus Canons head five, error and rejection 3 quotes the wonderful teaching of Jesus in John 10:28–29: "I give unto them eternal life; and they shall never perish, neither shall any man pluck them out of my hand. My Father, which gave them me, is greater than all; and no man is able to pluck them out of my Father's hand."

The biblical truth of the fifth point of Calvinism could be summed up in the following pithy statements: God preserves all his saints, so that every one of them perseveres in holiness;[97] the true believer falls, but he never falls away;[98] the regenerate may fall into sin, but he cannot fall into hell.[99]

The Arminian heresy of the falling away of true saints includes the terrifying thought that one may have everlasting life one day but

---

[96] Articles 9–13, etc., of head five on the assurance of God's preservation of all true believers and the saints' perseverance, as well as other references to assurance in the Canons, especially regarding election in head one, are wholly untreated in this chapter, for they are covered later in chapter 8 of this book: "Assurance: Sovereign Grace's Speech to the Heart."
[97] Canons of Dordt 5.9, in *Confessions and Church Order*, 175.
[98] Canons of Dordt 5.6, in *Confessions and Church Order*, 174.
[99] Canons of Dordt 5, error and rejection 4, in *Confessions and Church Order*, 177.

lose it the next.[100] Arminianism also embraces the "absurd" notions that "one having lost his first regeneration" can be born again, and again, and again; and that the "[incorruptible] seed" of regeneration can be corrupted (1 Pet. 1:23)![101]

This is the gratitude that flows from the Arminian theology opposed in the fifth head of the Canons: "Father, I thank thee that not only did I use my free will aright in accepting salvation in the first place, but also that I have kept the 'condition of the new covenant'[102] and, unlike many who were true believers, I have not fallen from salvation[103] nor committed the unpardonable sin...so far. Amen." [104]

The true doxology, regarding Jehovah's preservation of all his elect saints, comes right at the end of the penultimate book of the Bible: "Now unto him that is able to keep you from falling, and to present you faultless before the presence of his glory with exceeding joy, to the only wise God our Saviour, be glory and majesty, dominion and power, both now and ever. Amen" (Jude 24–25).

It is wholly appropriate that the last positive article in our Canons of Dordt ends with adoration of the holy Trinity: "Now, to this one God, Father, Son, and Holy Spirit be honor and glory forever. AMEN."[105]

The Golden Chain of Our Salvation

We have used a phrase from the Canons to summarize each truth of the five petals of TULIP (or ULTIP, as arranged in the five heads drafted at Dordt):

---

100 Canons of Dordt 5, error and rejection 3, in *Confessions and Church Order*, 177.
101 Canons of Dordt 5, error and rejection 8, in *Confessions and Church Order*, 178.
102 Canons of Dordt 5, error and rejection 1, in *Confessions and Church Order*, 176.
103 Canons of Dordt 5, error and rejection 3, in *Confessions and Church Order*, 177.
104 Canons of Dordt 5, error and rejection 4, in *Confessions and Church Order*, 177.
105 Canons of Dordt 5.15, in *Confessions and Church Order*, 176.

Unconditional election—"the fountain of every saving good"[106]

Limited atonement—"the only and most perfect sacrifice"[107]

Total depravity—"dead in sin"[108]

Irresistible grace—"a resurrection from the dead"[109]

Perseverance of the saints—"the Father's hand"[110]

Do we also have an expression from the Canons that can be used to bring together the five points of Calvinism? Yes, the fathers at Dordt employed another delightful phrase: "this golden chain of our salvation,"[111] appealing to Romans 8:30: "Moreover whom he did predestinate, them he also called: and whom he called, them he also justified: and whom he justified, them he also glorified."[112]

Let us see how Romans 8:30 unites the Canons' five points of Calvinism. Beginning with the first clause, "whom he did predestinate" is a reference to God's unconditional election (head one). Second, those who are predestinated are called, and the effectual call is, of course, a blessing obtained by the cross of Christ for his elect, so this presupposes limited atonement (John 10:15–16),[113] which is treated in head two. After mentioning predestination and calling, Romans 8:30 refers, third, to justification; and the effectual call and

---

[106] Canons of Dordt 1.9, in *Confessions and Church Order*, 157.
[107] Canons of Dordt 2.3, in *Confessions and Church Order*, 163.
[108] Canons of Dordt 3–4.3; 3–4, error and rejection 4, in *Confessions and Church Order*, 167, 171.
[109] Canons of Dordt 3–4.12, in *Confessions and Church Order*, 168–69.
[110] Canons of Dordt 5, error and rejection 3, in *Confessions and Church Order*, 177.
[111] Canons of Dordt 1, error and rejection 2, in *Confessions and Church Order*, 160.
[112] Romans 8:30 is one of the most cited texts in the Canons; it is also quoted in Canons 1.7; Canons 1, error and rejection 6.
[113] Cf. Canons of Dordt 1.7; 5.8; 5, error and rejection 1, in *Confessions and Church Order*, 156, 174, 176.

justification are works of God's irresistible grace (head four). When our text states that the predestinate are not only called and justified, but also glorified, this last word presupposes that Jehovah preserves all his saints so that they persevere by his power unto the end (1 Cor. 1:8; Phil. 1:6; 1 Pet. 1:5), as head five explains.

The heads of the Canons of Dordt are set forth in a trinitarian order.[114] Head one treats especially the Father in unconditional election (and reprobation). Head two covers the Son's limited (or particular) atonement. Then comes the Holy Spirit's work in irresistible grace (head four) and the preservation (and therefore the perseverance) of the saints (head five). Truly, "salvation is of the LORD" (Jonah 2:9)—all of it![115]

The Canons are also chronologically arranged. The golden chain of our salvation began with our unconditional election in eternity past (head one). The next link in the chain was added some two thousand years ago, when the good shepherd laid down his life for the sheep (head two), who are, of themselves, totally depraved (head three). Other links are added during the lifetime of those predestinated, including their justification and effectual calling by irresistible grace (head four), and their preservation and perseverance (head five), so that all are certainly glorified.[116]

The golden chain of our salvation, being made of metal, is strong and cannot be broken, as the imagery of Canons head one, error and rejection 2 requires. This chain is spoken of as golden because our salvation is exceedingly precious, more valuable than "the whole world" (Mark 8:36–37). Yet our spiritual deliverance,

---

114 Cf. Heidelberg Catechism Q&A 24, in *Confessions and Church Order*, 92.
115 Man's "contribution" is his total depravity (Canons 3).
116 Head three is not mentioned in the previous three paragraphs, because total depravity is not an element of God's work of saving us, but the occasion and presupposition of his grace in Jesus Christ.

and the faith that receives it, comes to us entirely freely:[117] "For by grace are ye saved through faith; and that not of yourselves: it is the gift of God: not of works, lest any man should boast" (Eph. 2:8–9).

What about Arminianism? Arminianism does not have a golden chain that starts with unconditional election in heaven and bends down to our Savior's efficacious and redeeming cross on earth (limited atonement). Arminianism lacks a powerful chain that grips us with irresistible grace and embraces and preserves us, so that we enter heaven—the new creation.

Salvation, according to Arminianism, depends on man's fulfilling prerequisites and conditions,[118] such as rightly using "the light of nature,"[119] consenting to the gospel, performing good works, and not apostatizing but continuing in obedience unto the end—all performed by his own free will, assisted by sufficient (but not irresistible) grace.[120]

If the doctrines of God's sovereign and efficacious grace in Jesus Christ constitute the beautiful and invincible golden chain of our salvation, what would be an appropriate metaphor for Arminianism? A paper chain![121] The Arminian scheme is a mere paper chain, for it easily breaks, even with a little pull. In fact, Arminianism is even weaker than a paper chain and has none of its decorative value, for salvation by man's free will is utterly useless to totally depraved sinners.

Like children, much of the church world is entranced by a paper chain, the paper chain of Arminianism. This paper chain is flimsy;

---

[117] Canons of Dordt 1.5, in *Confessions and Church Order*, 155.
[118] Canons of Dordt 1.9, in *Confessions and Church Order*, 157.
[119] Canons of Dordt 3–4, error and rejection 5, in *Confessions and Church Order*, 171–72.
[120] Canons of Dordt 3–4.10; 3–4, error and rejection 5, 7; 5, error and rejection 2, in *Confessions and Church Order*, 168, 171–72, 176–77.
[121] Englishman Christopher Ness used another image for Arminianism, that of poison (*An Antidote Against Arminianism*, rev. ed. [1700; repr., USA: Still Waters Revival Books, 1988]).

it is merely for show; it is manmade. Picture a little girl, upon completing her paper chain, running to her mother with the words: "Look what I have done!" This is a fitting illustration of Arminianism: "With my free will, I have completed the links of the paper chain, consisting of God's conditional election, Christ's universal atonement, and the Spirit's resistible grace!"

Psalm 115 involves a sharp contrast. There are the useless idols who can do nothing at all (vv. 4–7), and their followers can do absolutely nothing good (v. 8). Over against them, the true church exclaims, "But our God is in the heavens: he hath done whatsoever he hath pleased" (v. 3). Thus we bow our heads in adoration: "Not unto us, O LORD, NOT UNTO US, BUT UNTO THY NAME GIVE GLORY, for thy [covenantal] mercy, and for thy truth's sake" (v. 1).[122]

We need a firm grasp of the true gospel of sovereign grace. We require not only the few short phrases of TULIP, though they are useful memory aids, designed to lead us into the original of the five points of Calvinism. We need the full Canons of Dordt, stated in all ninety-three articles, including the thirty-nine Rejections of Errors.[123]

This is the creedal gospel, the Reformed gospel, the biblical gospel, the only saving gospel of our Lord Jesus Christ. The truths of

---

[122] John Owen deals with the idolatry of Arminianism in his 1642 work, "A Display of Arminianism," in *The Works of John Owen*, 16 vols., 10:1–137. The subtitle of this book is *A Discovery of the Old Pelagian Idol Free-Will, With the New Goddess Contingency, Advancing Themselves Into the Throne of the God of Heaven, to the Prejudice of His Grace, Providence, and Supreme Dominion Over the Children of Men*. Also on the cover page is Isaiah 45:9: "Woe unto him that striveth with his Maker! Let the potsherd strive with the potsherds of the earth" (1).

[123] It was a grievous error of the Reformed Church in America (RCA) only to adopt the positive articles of the Canons of Dordt and not to accord confessional status to the rejection of errors, which are sharply antithetical and thoroughly biblical. Sadly, this glaring omission facilitated further departure from Christ's truth.

the Canons of Dordt open up the scriptures and comfort the child of God in all his afflictions in this world. Jehovah's almighty grace will sustain us against all hellish opposition, until we stand triumphant at the day of Jesus Christ. May this book be used as a means to these holy ends.[124]

---

124 Canons of Dordt 1.16; 3–4.17; 5.14, in *Confessions and Church Order*, 158–59, 170, 176.

Chapter 3

WARRING A GOOD WARFARE WITH THE CANONS

Brian Huizinga

Introduction

On one side of the battlefield were the soldiers of Arminianism, a theological position about which the soldiers on the other side of the battlefield cried, "This is the Pelagian error brought out of hell!"[1] On the side of the battlefield opposite of Arminianism were the soldiers of the theology of the Confession and Catechism of the Belgic Churches, that is, the theology of scripture, the theology that has its origin in heaven, the theology of salvation by sovereign grace alone.

In order to understand and appreciate the war of 1618–19, one ought to read the historical foreword that the Synod of Dordt appended to its Acts as a recounting of the history leading up to the synod.[2] One also ought to read the summary of the daily work of the synod written by Douglas Kuiper.[3]

The synod convened in 1618. Jacob Arminius, the man at the

---

1 Of Arminianism, the Canons state, "For these adjudge too contemptuously of the death of Christ, do in no wise acknowledge the most important fruit or benefit thereby gained, and bring again out of hell the Pelagian error" (Canons of Dordt 2, error and rejection 3, in *Confessions and Church Order*, 165).
2 The historical foreword can be found in Hoeksema, *Voice of Our Fathers*, 567–624, and "Historical Forward" at dordt400.org.
3 This summary is included in Appendix 1 of this book.

center of the controversy, had been ordained a preacher in Amsterdam in 1588. From the ordination of Arminius to the convening of the synod was a period of thirty years. Can you imagine unrest in the church for thirty years?

Yet there was trouble prior to Arminius, for Reformed ministers were controverting the doctrine of sovereign predestination taught by Calvin and Beza and also were objecting to the binding authority of the Belgic Confession and Heidelberg Catechism. However, the trouble intensified with the more capable and influential Arminius, who not only was sympathetic to the objections of these ministers, but from his pulpit in Amsterdam also began to undermine election and teach the good of the will of fallen man.

There was a crisis in the Reformed churches when Arminius was appointed seminary professor in Leiden in 1602 and started spreading his views among his students. But Arminius died in 1609, and many hoped that his death signaled the end of controversy. Greater trouble came, for one year later, in 1610, some forty of the disciples of Arminius expanded and advanced his false doctrine by formulating it into five doctrinal statements known as the Five Articles of the Remonstrants. During this time, there were many Arminian preachers in the churches, many brazen attacks against the confessions, and so much craft and deceit as the Arminian preachers refused to explain their concerns and differences with the confessions.[4]

Finally a national synod was held in 1618 to weigh and pass judgment on the doctrine of Arminianism. It was war. Even though the Arminians came to the Synod of Dordt trying to convince the delegates that the synod was a conference for brotherly theological discussion, everyone at the synod knew it was war. The Reformed knew it was war between two hostile and irreconcilable positions—one from hell and one from heaven. The Arminians also knew it was

---

[4] In addition to the historical foreword, one can find a recounting of this history in De Jong, *Crisis in the Reformed Churches*, 22–37.

war, and they used their tactics of deception and delay to try to win the war.

When the Reformed believer reads this history and the decades of unrest caused by all the Arminian errors and wrangling, he becomes exasperated and infuriated and wants to shout, "Why? If you so hate the doctrine of sovereign double predestination, which is the doctrine in which you were trained from your youth, why not be honest enough to say so? Why cannot you say, 'We hate election, and we hate reprobation'? Why all this diabolical and troublesome maneuvering in God's precious church?"

At the Synod of Dordt, five Canons were assembled and used as the mighty weapons of God to pull down the Arminian strongholds in the church of Jesus Christ. By *canon* we do not refer to a large, loud, smoking cylinder that hurls physical projectiles across enemy lines, but to an ecclesiastical rule, a standard, a written definition of the truth of scripture. The synod formulated and adopted five heads or five chapters of doctrine we know as the Canons of Dordt, and with those Canons the synod waged the kind of warfare unto which the inspired apostle Paul exhorted the young pastor Timothy according to 1 Timothy 1:18, "This charge I commit unto thee, son Timothy, according to the prophecies which went before on thee, that thou by them mightest war a good warfare." The synod warred a good warfare by vindicating the name of God, defending the gospel of his Son, laboring for the restoration of a measure of peace in his church, and giving to us who stand four hundred years later an enduring monument of theological struggle that defines the soul-comforting truth that salvation is of God and of God alone.

The Arminian Error

With the Canons, the synod rejected Arminianism as *error*. The distinctive feature of the Canons as a confessional statement is that each chapter or head is divided into two sections. First there is a positive statement of the truth, and then there is a rejection of errors. For example, in the first head, which is called "Of Divine Predestination," the first section consists of eighteen articles that positively define and explain the truth of predestination. The second section then explains nine errors and rejects them.

The synod warred a good warfare with the Canons by explicitly identifying the Arminian position as *error*. The term *error* is biblical. It is found, for example, in 1 John 4:6, "We are of God: he that knoweth God heareth us; he that is not of God heareth not us. Hereby know we the spirit of truth, and the spirit of error." There are two kinds of spirits, the spirit of truth and the spirit of error. Error is departure from the truth. Error is not truth. Error militates against the truth. Of Arminianism, the Canons declare: "Error! Departure from truth! Not the truth! Against the truth! Not of God and not for God, but against God! Not right, but wrong!"

Note, then, how the synod did *not* identify Arminianism. First of all, it did not call Arminianism a different way of expressing the truth. The Arminians insisted that they were orthodox, that they were brethren in the church, that their differences were in nonessentials, and that their differences were merely matters of terminology and therefore should be tolerated in the church. They could not understand why anyone would object to and put up a fuss about their teaching.

The Arminians hated nothing more than sovereign predestination. They hated reprobation and they hated election as God's eternal, sovereign, and particular decree unto salvation. However, they said they believed in election, they used the term *election*, and they preached sermons on the doctrine of election, even as they used the terms *grace* and *faith* but gave to them different meanings. In so doing, they convinced many people in the pews that while they may have had some different formulations to express the truth, they were fundamentally orthodox.

A conference was held in Delft in 1613 so that three representatives from each side of the battlefield could come together and discuss their differences in a brotherly spirit. In the historical foreword we read that the Arminians said that "the articles in question were of little importance and did not concern the fundamentals of salvation, and for this reason people ought to be tolerant."[5]

Many were sympathetic to the Arminians. Even today when some read the Five Articles of the Remonstrants for the very first time they typically do not see the kind of blatantly egregious expressions of gross error that they were expecting. They think, "War was waged over these few phrases that don't even sound all that bad?" The Arminians were so careful to sound Reformed and insisted that they believed the truth but only had different ways of expressing the truth.

Referring to this tactic of the Arminians, the Presbyterian theologian Samuel Miller says of heretics in general, "But when taxed with deviations from the received faith, they complain of the unreasonableness of their accusers, as they 'differ from it only in words.' This has been the standing course of errorists ever since the apostolic age."[6]

The Synod of Dordt warred a good warfare with the Canons when it studied the Arminian position and declared, "Error!" In identifying Arminianism as *error* the synod was expressing its conviction that the difference between Arminianism and the orthodox, confessional Reformed faith was *not* mere quibbling about words or acceptable phrases as if each side confessed the truth, but the Arminians only had a different way of expressing it. Error!

Second, with the Canons the synod did not identify Arminianism as doctrinal confusion. To be sure, Arminianism *is* confusion. *Necessarily*, Arminianism is confusion. Arminianism is error, and all error is departure from the clear truth of God's word; and as soon as

---

5 Hoeksema, *Voice of Our Fathers*, 608.
6 Samuel Miller, "Introductory Essay," in *The Articles of the Synod of Dort*, by Thomas Scott (Harrisonburg, VA: Sprinkle Publications, 1993), 16.

teaching departs from the clear word of God it becomes murky and increasingly murkier. *Deliberately* Arminianism is confusion, since the goal of errorists is always to disguise the error.

Consider only the Arminian doctrine of election as condemned in the Canons head one, error 2, which states,

> Who teach that there are various kinds of election of God unto eternal life: the one general and indefinite, the other particular and definite; and that the latter in turn is either incomplete, revocable, non-decisive and conditional, or complete, irrevocable, decisive and absolute. Likewise: that there is one election unto faith, and another unto salvation, so that election can be unto justifying faith, without being a decisive election unto salvation.[7]

Imagine coming to catechism class and receiving instruction on election from an Arminian preacher. You are taught that one election is general and indefinite and another is particular and definite. One is incomplete, the other complete. One is revocable, the other irrevocable, and so on. What does that mean?

The orthodox Reformed catechism teacher probably introduces the doctrine of election to children who are around ten years old when he teaches Paul's first missionary journey and that according to Act 13:48, "As many as were ordained to eternal life believed." The fundamental idea of election as taught in scripture is simple, simple enough for a ten-year-old to understand. Election is God's choosing. From eternity God chose certain people whom he would save by giving them faith to believe the gospel. However, there is not a seminary professor who can clearly understand the Arminian doctrine of election with its various kinds of election and all of its distinctions.

---

7 *Confessions and Church Order*, 160.

As confusing as Arminianism is, the synod did not identify Arminianism as confusion. The synod said, "It is wrong; it is error." You see, it is possible to be an orthodox preacher who believes the truth, but who is at the same time a very poor preacher and makes the truth confusing so that people walk out of church saying, "Everything he said was true, but I do not know what point he was trying to make. He does not follow a clear line; he muddles everything together." The Arminians were not like that. They were not orthodox preachers who made the truth confusing with ambiguous expressions, convoluted explanations, and illogical presentations.

To say that Arminianism is doctrinal confusion or the introduction of a confusing theology that could lead to error is not warring a good warfare. Arminianism is error. It is wrong. It is against the truth. It is not of God or for God, but against God. The Synod of Dordt warred a good warfare with the Canons, by identifying Arminianism as *error*.

Rejection of the Arminian Error

Having identified Arminianism as error, the synod took the only proper course of action before the face of God. The synod rejected Arminianism.

While the second section of heads two through five of the Canons is introduced with the formula, "The true doctrine having been explained, the synod *rejects* the errors of those," the second section of the *first* head uses a slightly different formulation in which the doctrine explained in the first part is explicitly stated. We read, "The true doctrine concerning *Election* and *Rejection* having been explained, the synod *rejects* the errors of those…" God rejects.[8] In election God chooses, and in reprobation God rejects. Regardless of why and how he rejects, God rejects. How could the synod identify

---

8 *Confessions and Church Order*, 159.

Arminianism as error and not reject it before the face of the God of rejection? Explicitly, in the second section of the Canons, the synod rejected Arminianism as error and subsequently censured the errorists.

Notice four characteristics of this rejection. First, the synod warred a good warfare with the Canons by rejecting the Armininian error *authoritatively*. There is no confession like the Canons that incorporates into its body so many proof texts. Many confessions include scriptural references, and many confessions have scriptural references attached as footnotes. But no confession includes within its body so many biblical quotations and citations. Strikingly, most of the scriptural quotations and citations are found in the rejection of errors section. Not on the authority of a persuasive Bogerman or Gomarus, but on the authority of the word of God synod rejected Arminianism.

This appeal to the authority of scripture and *not* to the Belgic Confession and Heidelberg Catechism should not be misunderstood as a concession to the Arminians who were agitating against the binding nature of the confessions and the requirement to preach the Catechism. For, first of all, the States General required that synodical decisions touching Arminianism be made on the basis of scripture alone. But second, the synod itself expressed its commitment to the two confessions when in the conclusion to the Canons, the synod stated, "This doctrine the synod judges to be drawn from the Word of God, and to be agreeable to the confessions of the Reformed Churches."[9] Additionally, in drawing up the Formula of Subscription, the synod called the Canons "an explanation of some points of the aforesaid doctrine,"[10] referring to the Belgic Confession and Heidelberg Catechism. Synod believed that the Canons were no new formulation of doctrine, but rather a further explanation of the

---

9 *Confessions and Church Order*, 179.
10 *Confessions and Church Order*, 326.

doctrine, particularly the doctrine of predestination, contained in the existing creeds. Standing on the authority of scripture and with their eye on and hand pointed toward the Belgic Confession and Heidelberg Catechism, the synod rejected Arminianism.

Second, the synod warred a good warfare with the Canons by rejecting the Arminian error *comprehensively*. The Canons demonstrate that the synod clearly understood that Arminianism is not a collection of stray statements but a system. We speak of the solar system and refer to that massive, interconnected network consisting of the sun and a host of bodies that orbit the sun forming a unified whole. The Calvinistic doctrine of salvation, which is positively explained by the Canons, is a system in which various truths of salvation orbit and find their significance in the sun that is God's sovereign election. God is at the center of the system. All of salvation proceeds from the almighty and gracious will of God. This doctrine of salvation is the doctrine taught by the inspired apostle Paul in Romans 9:16: "So then it is not of him that willeth, nor of him that runneth, but of God that sheweth mercy."

Arminianism is a system, and in the final analysis, in spite of all Arminian denials to the contrary, everything moves around the will of man. What is election? It is God's will to save those who exercise their so-called free will and choose to believe. Salvation does not depend upon the electing will of God, but is ultimately conditioned upon man's willing and running. What is the cross? It is Christ's sacrificial death for all human beings, which sacrifice is made effectual by those who exercise their so-called free will and choose to accept it. Salvation does not depend upon the effectual work of the Savior, but is ultimately conditioned upon man's willing and running. The whole system begins with and revolves around man.

What created trouble in the Amsterdam congregation where Arminius preached was his departure from orthodoxy on exactly this matter of the source of salvation. Arminius was sympathetic to denials of sovereign election, and so with one hand he robbed God of his sovereign will in the matter of salvation. At the same time, Arminius was using his other hand to give to the will of the dead sinner power in salvation. For Arminius was explaining Romans 7 so as to teach that Paul was crying, "The good that I would" as an unregenerate man, meaning, unregenerate Paul was capable of willing what was good in his natural condition as a fallen sinner. What Arminius took from the sovereign will of the electing God he gave to the will of the dead sinner. The disciples of Arminius developed his errors into the full-blown Arminianism rejected by the Canons. Upon reading the Canons it is plain to everyone that the synod did not reject a handful of stray statements, but it *comprehensively* rejected an entire soteriological system that was essentially built on the erroneous statement, "It *is* of him who willeth and runneth and *not* all of God who sheweth mercy."

Third, the synod warred a good warfare with the Canons by rejecting the Arminian error *honorably*. The delegates of the synod were some of the most valiant and courageous soldiers ever to take the field of battle in the history of the church. They were also honorable men of God.

How honorable was their carefulness? The synod was not rash or hasty in its business; neither did it operate on hearsay or even on the basis of some private notes some student of Professor Arminius took in the classroom at Leiden. The synod carefully studied the Five Articles that the Remonstrants drew up as their official, written position. Then at synod, the president repeatedly asked the Arminians to explain further their convictions. Finally on December 17 at the 34th session, the Arminians delivered a written document, which was an elaboration of their Five Points and is known as "The Opinions of the Remonstrants."[11] When it came time to write the

---

11 See Hoeksema, *Voice of Our Fathers*, 628–34.

Canons, the synod used these two documents to understand the Arminian position and gave all the delegates opportunity to express their convictions on every point of doctrine. When on Wednesday, January 30, some delegates voiced their concern that the pace was too tedious, synod decided to continue with its careful, methodical pace.[12] The synod displayed the same honorable carefulness in the positive formulation of the Canons by taking opinions from all the delegates and then drafting concept canons and revising them multiple times after getting feedback from the body.

How honorable also was their patience with the Arminians. The Arminians employed one tactic after another to delay the synod. They disobeyed the orders of President Bogerman, they would not appear when called upon, they were evasive and dodged pointed questions, they lied, and they tried to solicit the favor of the States General. Yet the synod continued to give them time to defend themselves and prepare written objections to the confessions. They were not expelled until January 14, 1619. The synod put up with their shenanigans for two months! Two weeks would have been an uncommon act of patience. Two *months*! The synod expelled the Arminians after dealing with them honorably, carefully, patiently, and judiciously.

Fourth, the synod warred a good warfare with the Canons by rejecting the Arminian error *sharply*. To show how serious the error was, synod used a sharp tongue throughout the Canons, a tongue sharp like that of the apostle Paul and our Lord himself. For example, the Canons say that the Arminians "deceive the simple"[13] and that their doctrine is "gross error,"[14] "bring(s) again out of hell the

---

12 Douglas Kuiper, "The Sessions of the Synod of Dordt, Week Twelve: Sessions 68–72," in Appendix 1 of this book, 253–54.
13 Canons of Dordt 1, error and rejection 1, in *Confessions and Church Order*, 159.
14 Canons of Dordt 1, error and rejection 6, in *Confessions and Church Order*, 161.

Pelagian error,"[15] "seek[s] to instill into the people the destructive poison of the Pelagian error,"[16] is to be equated with "the proud heresy of Pelagius,"[17] and does "as did the wicked Socinius."[18]

The synod also warred a good warfare with the Canons in rejecting Arminianism because in so doing it left for us four hundred years later a monument and model for polemics in the church. There is no greater distaste in the church world at large and even in reputedly conservative Reformed and Presbyterian churches than the distaste for calling the doctrinal teaching of another man or church "error" and then "rejecting" it. In the name of loving tolerance and out of a fear of hurting feelings, rejecting error is absolutely reprehensible in the eyes of man. We learn from Dordt that the defense of the truth demands rejecting error. Error is against the truth and against God and against the church and her communion. Error is not dead or static but a spirit that lives and poisons, divides and conquers.

Bound by our vow before God and man in the Formula of Subscription, let us as officebearers "exert ourselves in keeping the church free from such errors."[19] Let us strive to keep the uncommon spirit of Dordt alive after four hundred years and reject all errors repugnant to God's holy word, doing so authoritatively, comprehensively, honorably, and if necessary, sharply. And may all the brethren from around the world who attended the Dordt400 conference and joined the Protestant Reformed Churches in America (PRCA) in celebrating the spirit of truth at the Synod of Dordt go back to their homelands with the same conviction the delegates brought to Dordt four hundred years ago. As the devil ceases not to assault the church

---

15 Canons of Dordt 2, error and rejection 3, in *Confessions and Church Order*, 165.
16 Canons of Dordt 2, error and rejection 6, in *Confessions and Church Order*, 166.
17 Canons of Dordt 3–4.10, in *Confessions and Church Order*, 168.
18 Canons of Dordt 2, error and rejection 4, in *Confessions and Church Order*, 165.
19 Formula of Subscription, in *Confessions and Church Order*, 326.

in every land with error, may we all be willing and bold to reject error, and as true friends says, "Friends, if we ever maintain error, then love God, love the gospel of Jesus, and love us enough to show us and demand that we reject it wholeheartedly."

Defining Truth Positively

As critically important and necessary as the rejection of errors is, good polemics involves the rejection of errors for the sake of a sharp and positive definition of the truth. The outstanding contribution of the Canons as a polemical document is its positive section in each of the five heads. Generally speaking, when most people think of the Canons as a polemical document they think of the rejection of errors section, and that is understandable and even proper, for that feature of the Canons is distinctive. Nevertheless, the great wonder that is the Canons is the marvelous first section of every head, which gives positive expression to the glorious truth of salvation.

It is important that we be positive. While from one point of view it is very difficult to be negative and reject what must be rejected, from another point of view it is not difficult at all to be negative. It is not so difficult to be a parent and say, "No, you may not do that; you may not go here or there; you may not engage in this entertainment or listen to that music, or pursue that career; no, no, no." But it is more difficult to be positive and to explain what *is* permissible and to teach children how they can develop and use their abilities positively in all the areas of life. It is not so difficult to be a preacher and preach against sin and make people feel guilty and condemn false doctrine and wicked living, but it is much more difficult to formulate a positive explanation and application of the truth of God's word. It is not always so difficult to see and condemn doctrinal error, or even to sense that something is amiss without being able to lay the finger on exactly what is wrong. But it is more difficult to formulate sharply and clearly the positive truth. Ecclesiastes 3:3 says there is "a time to break down, and a time to build up." Nebuchadnezzar can break down the temple in a day. But the Jews told Jesus it took their fathers forty and six years to build it up (John 2:20). Destruction is not so difficult. Construction is painstakingly strenuous and time-consuming.

While it may be easy to be negative and to reject, the church is not negative as a response over against something. The church is positive as the pillar and ground of God's truth in the world. God is not a response to something; he is the I AM. Christ is not a reaction to something; he is the heart of God's counsel, the firstborn of every creature by whom and for whom all things consist. The truth is not a reaction to something but its own absolute and everlasting principle. Error, like Arminianism, is always a reaction to the truth and cannot exist apart from the truth. Truth can stand alone, and it will into all eternity.

Very often when people first encounter the PRCA, and after having done a little reading, they say, "So doctrinally, you are *against* common grace right from the inception of your denomination in 1924, and you are *against* the well-meant offer, and you are *against* conditionality in the covenant." We help them by saying, "That is correct, but please understand that we are *for* sovereign, particular, efficacious, saving grace. Our fundamental purpose of existence is not to be *against* error but to be *for* God's truth." Or they say, "I have read a number of the pamphlets off the rack in the church. So, practically speaking, I see you are *against* labor unions, and *against* remarriage after divorce, and *against* public education in the state schools for your children, and *against* mothers leaving their children to pursue a career." We help them by saying, "That is correct, but please understand that we are *for* submission to God and the employer he puts over us, and we are *for* the lifelong bond of marriage, and we are *for* covenantal education, and we are *for* the home and family." The church of Jesus Christ is positive.

The brilliance of the Canons as a polemical document that arose out of bitter conflict and as a confession that was written with contributions from delegates all over Europe—delegates who did not always agree on precisely every doctrinal point—is the Canons' robust, positive definition and explanation of the truth. Unanimously it was adopted.

The Canons are positive, and in being positive, they are beautifully harmonious from beginning to end so that you find the preservation of the saints already in head one and you find election all the way back in head five. Furthermore, in the positive definition of the truth, the Canons are so doctrinally profound and pastorally heart-warming.

How easy it is to aim a canon at the Arminian doctrine of free will and obliterate it with doctrinal fire. But do we have anything positive to say about the sinner's will? How profound and lovely are the Canons in the positive definition of God's salvation of us even as to our will:

> So also this grace of regeneration does not treat men as senseless stocks and blocks, nor takes away their will and its properties, neither does violence thereto; but spiritually quickens, heals, corrects, and at the same time sweetly and powerfully bends it; that where carnal rebellion and resistance formerly prevailed, a ready and sincere spiritual obedience begins to reign; in which the true and spiritual restoration and freedom of our will consist.[20]

What pastor, friend, or family member has not prayed regarding the will of a husband who mistreats his wife, or a wife who is untrustworthy with other men, or a rebellious young man who is stiff-necked in his slanderous opposition to his consistory, or a young

---

20 Canons of Dordt 3–4.16, in *Confessions and Church Order*, 169–70.

woman who is against all advice and admonition dating an unbeliever? He has a will. She has a will. Who does not pray, "Lord God of salvation, take his will as thou alone art able, and sweetly bend it. Carnal rebellion and resistance prevail! This is war. We grieve. We are powerless. O Lord, sweetly bend his will unto the fear of thy name, so that a ready and sincere spiritual obedience begins to reign!"

How easy it is to rail against the Arminian system, but look at how the Canons so beautifully expresses the Reformed system in positive language: "Therefore election is the fountain of every saving good; from which proceed faith, holiness, and the other gifts of salvation, and finally eternal life itself, as its fruits and effects."[21] The Reformed system has a source from which everything flows and upon which everything depends, the electing will of God. To God be the glory.

It must have been because of a shared love for these positive truths of God's grace in Jesus Christ that when Bishop Hall fell ill and reluctantly had to return home to Great Britain he said, "There was no place on earth so like heaven as the Synod of Dordt."[22] I hope all of the foreign guests who attended the Dordt400 conference, having returned home, would say something similar, having a shared love for the truth of salvation by grace alone as celebrated at the conference.

The Synod of Dordt was war, intense war. But the synod warred a good warfare with the Canons, because out of the warfare came what must and according to the good will of God will come out of every controversy in the church: an advancement of our understanding of, expression of, and appreciation for the positive, heavenly truth of sovereign grace. The rejection of errors is *for* the defining and magnifying of truth, the truth embodied in this anthem of heaven, "Salvation to our God which sitteth upon the throne, and unto the Lamb" (Rev. 7:10).

---

21 Canons of Dordt 1.9, in *Confessions and Church Order*, 157.
22 Miller, "Introductory Essay," *Articles of the Synod of Dort*, 33.

Chapter 4

DORDT'S UNFEIGNED CALL OF THE GOSPEL

Mark Shand

Introduction

"As many as are called by the gospel are unfeignedly called. For God hath most earnestly and truly shown in his word, what is pleasing to him, namely, that those who are called should come to him. He, moreover, seriously promises eternal life, and rest, to as many as shall come to him, and believe on him."[1] The Canons of Dordt explicitly declares that those who are called by the gospel are unfeignedly or seriously called. Nonetheless, controversy has surrounded precisely what the Canons mean when they speak of the call of the gospel as being unfeigned.

The controversy that has a long history concerns whether the call of the gospel as envisaged by the fathers of Dordt is expressive of a desire on the part of God for the salvation of all who come to hear it. This doctrinal controversy goes by several names: "the well-meant offer of the gospel," "the sincere offer of the gospel," "the free offer of the gospel," as well as "the gracious offer of the gospel." All four terms refer essentially to the same thing. The terms *well-meant offer* and *sincere offer* are intended by those who utilize them to emphasize

---

1 Canons of Dordt 3–4.8, in *Confessions and Church Order,* 168.

God's sincerity in offering salvation to all who hear the gospel and, moreover, his earnest desire to save all that come under the preaching of the gospel; the term *free offer* is intended to emphasize that the external call of the gospel is unrestricted in its scope, salvation being graciously offered to all who hear the gospel; and the term *gracious offer* is designed to reflect that God has an attitude of favor toward all men in the preaching of the gospel.[2]

What is the Well-Meant Offer of the Gospel?

The proponents of the well-meant offer maintain that in the preaching of the gospel, God evidences an earnest and sincere desire to save all who come under the preaching. They contend that the preaching of the gospel is an offer or invitation of salvation to all, to both the elect and the reprobate. In the preaching of the gospel, God calls upon and invites all men to repent and believe on Jesus Christ in order to receive the benefits and blessings of salvation. Behind this offer or invitation, it is contended, there lies an earnest desire or intention on the part of God that his offer of salvation should be accepted by all who hear it. In other words, in the offer of the gospel, there is an expression of God's love for every sinner. However, it should be added that this love is not a saving love. Even the proponents of the well-meant offer acknowledge that not all who hear the gospel come to faith and salvation in Jesus Christ.[3]

---

2 In this chapter, the phrase *the well-meant offer of the gospel* will be utilized.

3 The Free Church of Scotland (Continuing) minister Maurice Roberts defines the "Free Offer" as "the invitation given by a Christian preacher to all sinners to believe in Jesus Christ, with the promise added that if they do believe they will receive at once forgiveness of all sins and eternal life. Implied in the concept of this 'Free Offer' are these ideas: The 'Offer' made is for all who hear it, whether they be elect or not; The 'Offer' is not to be restricted or modified by the preacher in his presentation; The 'Offer' is an expression of love and grace on God's part towards sinful, unbelieving men; The 'Offer' is sincere on God's part and it is genuinely well-meant; The 'Offer' is addressed to sinners as they are and requires of them repentance and faith." Maurice Roberts, "The

In their majority report to the Fifteenth General Assembly of the Orthodox Presbyterian Church in 1948, John Murray and Ned B. Stonehouse, professors at Westminster Theological Seminary in Philadelphia, provided the following insights into the meaning of the well-meant offer:

> The question then is: what is implicit in, or lies back of, the full and free offer of the gospel to all without distinction? The word "desire" has come to be used in the debate, not because it is *necessarily* the most accurate or felicitous word but because it serves to set forth quite sharply a certain implication of the full and free offer of the gospel to all. This implication is that in the free offer there is expressed not simply the bare preceptive will of God but the disposition of lovingkindness on the part of God pointing to the salvation to be gained through compliance with the overtures of gospel grace. In other words, the gospel is not simply an offer or invitation but also implies that God delights that those to whom the offer comes would enjoy what is offered in all its fullness...Again, the expression "God desires," in the formula that crystallizes the crux of the question, is intended to notify not at all the "seeming" attitude of God but a real attitude, a real disposition of lovingkindness inherent in the free offer to all, in other words, a pleasure or delight in God, contemplating the blessed result to be achieved by compliance with the overture proffered and the invitation given.[4]

Free Offer of the Gospel," accessed April 26, 2019, https://mauriceroberts.org/blog/2018/4/5/the-free-offer-of-the-gospel.

4   John Murray, *The Free Offer of the Gospel* (Edinburgh: The Banner of Truth Trust, 2001), 4 (emphasis added). John Murray was professor of systematic theology in Westminster Theological Seminary in Philadelphia, Pennsylvania (1937–1966), and Ned B. Stonehouse was professor of New Testament in Westminster Theological Seminary in Philadelphia, Pennsylvania (1929–1962).

Murray and Stonehouse's report concludes:

> There is in God a benevolent lovingkindness towards the repentance and salvation of even those whom he has not decreed to save. This pleasure, will, desire is expressed in the universal call to repentance…The full and free offer of the gospel is a grace bestowed upon all. Such grace is necessarily a manifestation of love or lovingkindness in the heart of God. And this lovingkindness is revealed to be of a character or kind that is correspondent with the grace bestowed. The grace offered is nothing less than salvation in its richness and fullness. The love or lovingkindness that lies back of that offer is not anything less; it is the will to that salvation. In other words, it is Christ in all the glory of his person and in all the perfection of his finished work whom God offers in the gospel. The loving and benevolent will that is the source of that offer and that grounds its veracity and reality is God's will to the possession of Christ and the enjoyment of the salvation that resides in him.[5]

The fundamental issues raised by the well-meant offer include:

- Whether the preaching of the gospel is expressive of the will of God to save all those who hear it;
- Whether the preaching of the gospel is to be viewed as an expression of God's love and sincere desire for the salvation of all men; and
- Whether in the preaching of the gospel God graciously invites all men to repent and believe on Jesus Christ in order that they might be saved.

---

5 Murray, *The Free Offer*, 27.

To these propositions, the proponents of the well-meant offer respond with a resounding, "Yes."

The Battle for Confessional Support

Within Reformed and Presbyterian circles there has been and is an ongoing struggle over whether the well-meant offer is orthodox or heterodox. At the heart of that struggle, for those churches that hold to the three forms of unity, is whether confessional support for the well-meant offer can be elicited from the Canons of Dordt. The all-important questions are: What do the Canons of Dordt have to say, if anything, on the call of the gospel? Can the Canons be called in aid of the well-meant offer of the gospel? Do the Canons support the notion that there is in God a desire for the salvation of all men? And does that desire come to expression in the preaching of the gospel? The same essential battle is waged within Presbyterianism with respect to the Westminster Confessional Standards. The stakes are unquestionably high. What is at stake is Reformed orthodoxy. Therefore, it comes as no surprise to discover that proponents of the well-meant offer repeatedly and confidently appeal to the Canons in support of their views.

The following examples are certainly not exhaustive, but they are illustrative and they reflect the longstanding nature and currency of the battle.

In 1924, the controversies that led to the formation of the Protestant Reformed Churches revolved around the doctrine of common grace. Embedded within the Christian Reformed Church's support for common grace was an adoption of the well-meant offer. In the first of the three doctrinal statements approved by the synod of the Christian Reformed Church, reference is made to the well-meant offer, and an appeal is made to the Canons for support.

> Concerning the first point, with regard to the favorable disposition of God toward mankind in general, and not only to

the elect, Synod declares that according to the Scripture and confessions it is determined that besides the saving grace of God, shown only to the elect unto eternal life, there is a *certain kind of favor or grace of God which He shows to His creatures in general.* This is evidenced by the quoted Scripture passages and from the *Canons of Dort 2.5 and 3–4.8–9*, which deals with *the general offer of the Gospel*; whereas the quoted declarations of Reformed writers from the golden age of Reformed theology also give evidence that our Reformed fathers from of old have advocated these opinions.[6]

The Christian Reformed Church maintained that the three points adopted by the synod contained nothing new but were "merely further interpretations of what [was] clearly implied or expressed in the forms of unity."[7] Louis Berkhof, referring to the three points, declared:

> In the first place we would call attention to the fact, that in these points we have no material in addition to our Confessional Standards...Our people may be assured that the Synod of 1924 by adopting the three points added nothing to the essential contents of our Confessions. She only brought forward and formulated a triplet of truths that are clearly implied in our Confessional Standards and that are partly emphatically expressed therein.[8]

---

[6] *1924 Acts of Synod of the Christian Reformed Church*, trans. Henry De Mots (Grand Rapids, MI: Calvin College, Archives of the Christian Reformed Church), 145–46 (emphasis added).

[7] Herman Hoeksema, *A Triple Breach in the Foundation of the Truth* (Grandville, MI: Evangelism Committee of Southwest Protestant Reformed Church, 1992), 2.

[8] Louis Berkhof, *De Drie Punten in Alle Deelen Gereformeerd* [The three points, Reformed in all their parts] (Grand Rapids, MI: Wm. B. Eerdmans Publishing Co., 1925), 5. Louis Berkhof was a professor in Calvin Theological Seminary from 1906 to 1944.

A second illustration is afforded by Professor Anthony Hoekema.[9] In his book *Saved by Grace*, Hoekema under the heading "The Gospel Call Is Seriously Meant" lends his support to the well-meant offer.

> The Christian Reformed Church of North America maintains, in agreement with the majority of Reformed theologians, that the preaching of the gospel is a well-meant offer of salvation, not just on the part of the preacher, but on God's part as well, to all who hear it, and that God seriously and earnestly desires the salvation of all to whom the gospel call comes.[10]

With that acknowledgment, Hoekema goes on to assert under the heading "The Canons of Dort on the Well-Meant Offer" that the Canons affirm what he styles as "the well-meant gospel call."[11] He grounds his assertion in Canons 2.5, and heads 3–4.8. Having referenced those portions of the Canons, Hoekema proceeds to place into the mouths of the divines of Dordt his own interpretation of what they were saying to the Remonstrants.

> In reply to what the Arminians had said, the theologians at Dort stated: "We quite agree with you that God seriously, earnestly, unhypocritically, and most genuinely calls to salvation all to whom the gospel comes. In stating this, we even use the very same words you used in your document: *serio vocantur* ('are seriously called'). But we insist that we can hold to this well-meant gospel call while at the same time maintaining the doctrines of election and limited or definite atonement. We do not feel the need for rejecting the

---

9 Anthony Hoekema (1913–1988) was professor of systematic theology at Calvin Theological Seminary in Grand Rapids, Michigan, from 1958 to 1978.
10 Anthony A. Hoekema, *Saved by Grace* (Grand Rapids, MI: William B. Eerdmans Publishing Company, 1994), 73.
11 Hoekema, *Saved by Grace*, 78.

doctrine of election and repudiating the teaching of definite atonement in order to affirm the well-meant gospel call."[12]

Significantly, Hoekema goes on to say with respect to the call of the gospel: "The gospel call can be defined as follows: The offering of salvation in Christ to people, together with an invitation to accept Christ in repentance and faith, in order that they may receive the forgiveness of sins and eternal life."[13] He then proceeds to identify and distinguish three elements that combine to make up the call of the gospel.

First, he says there must be "a presentation of the facts of the gospel and of the way of salvation. The work Christ has done for our salvation must be clearly and carefully set forth."[14] Second, he says that the gospel call must include "an invitation to come to Christ in repentance and faith. The gospel call must be more than a presentation; it must include an earnest invitation. Jesus himself invites people to come to him in repentance and faith: 'Come unto me, all ye that labour and are heavy laden, and I will give you rest (Matt. 11:28).'"[15]

Furthermore, Hoekema observes:

> The gospel invitation is, however, at the same time a command, like a summons which comes from a king. Note how Jesus expresses this point in the Parable of the Great Banquet: "And the lord said unto the servant, Go out into the highways and hedges, and compel them to come in, that my house may be filled." (Luke 14:23) The gospel invitation is not one a person may feel free to accept or decline, as one might with an invitation to go bowling, but it is an order from the sovereign Lord of all creation to come to him for

---

12 Hoekema, *Saved by Grace*, 78.
13 Hoekema, *Saved by Grace*, 68.
14 Hoekema, *Saved by Grace*, 68.
15 Hoekema, *Saved by Grace*, 69.

salvation—an order that can be ignored only at the cost of one's eternal perdition.[16]

Third, Hoekema contends that the gospel call must also include a promise of forgiveness and salvation. The gospel call must also include the promise that those who respond properly to this call will receive the forgiveness of sins and eternal life in fellowship with Christ. This promise is, however, conditional: you will receive forgiveness and salvation if you repent and believe.[17]

A third illustration is provided by Dr. Joel Beeke.[18] In two recently published books, Beeke draws on different articles in the Canons to support the well-meant offer of the gospel. In his book on experiential preaching, writing under the heading, "Preaching Makes a Sincere Offer of Christ to All Men," he writes:

> God's election remains a secret until it bears fruit in conversion. Therefore, the preacher must proclaim the gospel to all who hear him. The canons read: "Moreover, the promise of the gospel is, that whosoever believeth in Christ crucified, shall not perish, but have everlasting life. This promise, together with the command to repent and believe, ought to be declared and published to all nations, and to all persons promiscuously and without distinction, to whom God out of his good pleasure sends the gospel" (2.5). The phrase "promiscuously and without distinction" is a pleonasm, meaning the gospel is to be proclaimed to any person and to

---

16 Hoekema, *Saved by Grace*, 69.
17 Hoekema, *Saved by Grace*, 70.
18 Dr. Joel Beeke is the president and professor of systematic theology and homiletics at the Puritan Reformed Theological Seminary and a pastor of the Heritage Reformed Congregation in Grand Rapids, Michigan.

all alike, and applies to both the promise and the command of the gospel. It implies that the minister has no business trying to guess which unconverted people may or may not be elect, but must press upon all his hearers their *duty* to turn from sin and trust in Christ.[19]

Having noted that the proclamation of the gospel involves both a promise and a command, Beeke then goes on to comment on Canons 2.5, noting, "Here the canons teach both the redemption of a particular people and the gospel invitation for all to come to Christ."[20] He then proceeds to lend his full support to the well-meant offer of the gospel.

> The gospel call expresses God's sincere invitation for all sinners to come to Christ. The canons say: "As many as are called by the gospel, are unfeignedly called. For God hath most earnestly and truly shown in his Word, what will be acceptable to Him, namely, that those who are called *should comply with the invitation*. He, moreover, seriously promises eternal life, and rest to as many as shall come to Him, and believe on Him" (3–4.8). Christ is truly "offered" in the gospel, though many men who are "called by the ministry of the Word" nevertheless reject him (3–4.9). Thus, the preacher proclaims a sincere call from God that all men should repent, offering Christ to them as the only Savior of sinners.[21]

---

19 Joel Beeke, *Reformed Preaching: Proclaiming God's Word from the Heart of the Preacher to the Heart of His People* (Wheaton, IL: Crossway, 2018), 259 (emphasis is Beeke).
20 Beeke, *Reformed Preaching*, 260.
21 Beeke, *Reformed Preaching*, 260 (emphasis added). It is noteworthy that Beeke chooses to quote Canons 3–4.8 from an English translation of the Latin original adopted by the Reformed (Dutch) Church in America in which the words "should comply with the invitation" appear, though subsequently he acknowledges in his footnotes that a better translation of the Latin would be "should come to him."

It is of interest to note that though Beeke declares that the call of the gospel, as described in Canons 2.5, involves both a promise and a command, he, without explanation or justification, goes on in his commentary on that same article to assert, "Here the canons teach both the redemption of a particular people and the *gospel invitation* for all to come to Christ."[22] Note the change of terminology. What Beeke had initially described as a command and a promise, he recasts as a gospel invitation. He reinforces that view when he adds, "The gospel call expresses God's sincere invitation for all sinners to come to Christ."[23]

The command and promise are suddenly and inexplicably transformed into a gospel invitation, and what Beeke envisages by a "gospel invitation" becomes evident when he goes on to say:

> God personally, earnestly, sincerely, and seriously calls all men to come unto him and find salvation by trusting in his Son…A Reformed preacher of predestination should offer Christ to everyone who hears the gospel, giving heartfelt calls for them to come to Christ and be saved.[24]

In his book titled *A Puritan Theology*, Beeke is equally explicit:

> The Canons of Dort explain the international Puritan and Reformed perspective [on the gospel call] well in head 3–4, articles 8–9…The Canons make plain that there is no insufficiency in God's willingness to save sinners. *The invitation does not lie or deceive; it is a true, rich, full, free invitation. The gospel is a well-meant offer.* Christ has declared Himself ready and willing to receive all who to come to Him and to save them…The call is based on the condition of faith, but it is

---

22 Beeke, *Reformed Preaching*, 260 (emphasis added).
23 Beeke, *Reformed Preaching*, 260.
24 Beeke, *Reformed Preaching*, 261.

a true invitation...Judgement day will confirm this truth. No one will stand before God on the last day and say..."I received the invitation, but I did not think it was sincere." The call to come to Christ is a well-meant offer of salvation addressed to every human being.[25]

It is also significant to note the language that Beeke employs with respect to the preaching of the gospel and the role of the preacher in relation to the presentation of the well-meant offer. The language is confusing and internally contradictory.

> How does the offer of Christ function in experimental preaching? If Christ is the preeminent subject of preaching, and his righteousness is at the center of salvation, we must freely offer his righteousness and this savior to sinners. We must call and command men to come to him. We must *allure* sinners to him by presenting Christ in his beauty, sufficiency, and mercy.[26]

Furthermore, he writes,

> Do not be surprised that there is little experiential knowledge in congregations where the ministers do not often preach Christ. But where Christ is faithfully preached and freely offered, you will often find that, over a period of time, the Spirit cultivates rich Christian experience in those who hear. Thus, the Dutch sometimes ask about a minister, "*Is hij een Christus prediker?*" ("Is he a Christ-preacher?") They are not asking merely whether he preaches the doctrines of Christ. They are asking, "Does he offer the

---

[25] Joel R. Beeke and Mark Jones, *A Puritan Theology: Doctrine for Life* (Grand Rapids, MI: Reformation Heritage Books, 2012), 510 (emphasis added).
[26] Beeke, *Reformed Preaching*, 63 (emphasis added).

riches of Christ and *woo* sinners to him?" There is no more important question.[27]

The Remonstrants and the Call of the Gospel

Not surprisingly, in light of the Remonstrants' universalistic conception of the atonement, whereby salvation was made available and possible for all, the call of the gospel was a matter that came up for consideration at Dordt.[28] Naturally, the primary focus of the synod centered upon a refutation of the five points of the Remonstrants; nonetheless, in the Canons, the synod also expressed its views, both directly and indirectly, as regards the call or offer of the gospel.[29] Though the heresies that the synod condemned were concerned primarily with the *content* of the gospel, nonetheless, in light of the position advanced by the Remonstrants with respect to the preaching of the gospel, the synod also expressed its views on the *way* in which the gospel was to be proclaimed. In other words, the errors of the Remonstrants raised not only the *substance of the gospel*, but also the *way* in which the gospel was to be preached.[30]

Consistent with their understanding of the atonement, the Remonstrants advocated a particular view of the preaching of the

---

27 Beeke, *Reformed Preaching*, 63 (first emphasis is Beeke; second emphasis is Shand).
28 It should be appreciated that though the Remonstrants taught that Christ made atonement for all men on the cross, and thereby made salvation possible for all, they also taught that the benefits of salvation accrued only to those who accepted the offer of salvation according to the freedom of their own will.
29 Herman Hanko and Mark Hoeksema opine that "in the defense of their position, the Arminians raised many of the identical issues that repeatedly have been raised in discussions of the well-meant offer. Especially in their views of the preaching and the relationship between the preaching and the atonement, the Arminians set forth ideas that have been inextricably woven into the well-meant offer concept." Herman Hanko and Mark H. Hoeksema, *Corrupting the Word of God: The History of the Well-Meant Offer* (Jenison, MI: Reformed Free Publishing Association, 2016), 41.
30 Ronald Cammenga, "Dordt's Rejection of the Well-Meant Gospel Offer," *Standard Bearer* 95, no. 3 (November 1, 2018): 71.

gospel. Their convictions were recorded in the "Opinions of the Remonstrants [*Sententiae Remonstrantium*],"[31] and this is what the Remonstrants asserted:

> Whomever God calls to salvation, he calls *seriously* (*serio vocat*), that is, *with a sincere and completely unhypocritical intention and will to save*; nor do we assent to the opinion of those who hold *that God calls certain ones externally whom He does not will to call internally*, that is, as truly converted, even before the grace of calling has been rejected.[32]

The sincerity of the call of the gospel was a point of contention between the Remonstrants and the Calvinists at Dordt. The Remonstrants contended that the Calvinists could not maintain a sincere gospel call, that is, they could not assert, in light of their views on predestination and the atonement, that God in the preaching of the gospel seriously called (*serio vocat*) all who came under the preaching of the gospel.

The position of the Remonstrants was that whenever God called men through the external call of the gospel, whoever they were, he did so seriously or sincerely (*serio vocat*); by that the Remonstrants meant that God called all men with a genuine desire and intention to save them, God having a sincere and unhypocritical intention and will to save all who came under the preaching of the gospel. In accord with that view, the Remonstrants rejected the suggestion that God, in the external call of the gospel, called men to faith and salvation, though he did not will to save them.

---

[31] As part of the preparations for the synod, the Remonstrants were required to provide a statement of their convictions on the points in dispute, and those statements became known as the "Opinions of the Remonstrants." The Canons of Dordt need to be read and understood in the light of these official opinions submitted by the Remonstrants.

[32] "Opinions of the Remonstrants," trans. Anthony A. Hoekema, in De Jong, *Crisis in the Reformed Churches*, 226–27 (emphasis added).

There is *not in God a secret will which so contradicts the will of the same revealed in the Word* that according to it (that is, the secret will) *He does not will the conversion and salvation of the greatest part of those whom He seriously calls and invites by the Word of the Gospel and by His revealed will*; and we do not here, as some say, acknowledge in God a holy simulation, or a double person.[33]

The Remonstrants insisted that there was no contradiction or conflict between God's secret and revealed wills. According to both wills, he seriously desired and willed the salvation of all men. In their judgment, for God to call men to faith and salvation, without a genuine or sincere desire on his part for their salvation, would have amounted to a deception on God's part and have revealed in him an inconsistent internal duality. Therefore, the Remonstrants rejected the notion that according to God's revealed will, he seriously called and invited men unto salvation, while at the same time, according to his secret will, he had no such desire.

As evident from their own statements, the Remonstrants held to a position not altogether dissimilar from that espoused by the proponents of the well-meant offer. Indeed, it ought not to pass unnoticed that the statements and concerns expressed by the Remonstrants are echoed in many respects, though not all, by those who hold to the well-meant offer. Note the following similarities:

- In the preaching of the gospel, God sincerely offers salvation to every man; the offer of the gospel is a well-meant offer.
- The preaching of the gospel is expressive of a genuine desire and intention in God for the salvation of all men.
- The preaching of the gospel is an offer or invitation in the sense that, by means of it, God personally, earnestly,

---

33 De Jong, *Crisis in the Reformed Churches*, 227 (emphasis added).

sincerely, and seriously calls all men to come unto him and to find salvation in Jesus Christ.

The Canons and the Call of the Gospel

Not only did the Synod of Dordt reject the Remonstrants' view of the call of the gospel, but it also rejected their contention that in the preaching of the gospel there is evidenced a desire in God for the salvation of all mankind. In Canons 2.5, the fathers of Dordt declared:

> Moreover, the promise of the gospel is, that whosoever believeth in Christ crucified, shall not perish, but have everlasting life. This promise, together with *the command to repent and believe, ought to be declared and published to all nations, and to all persons promiscuously and without distinction,* to whom God out of his good pleasure sends the gospel.[34]

The Remonstrants contended that, if the atonement was not universal, there could be no general proclamation of the gospel. To call all men to repentance and faith when not all were encompassed by the atoning work of Jesus Christ was, said the Remonstrants, to render the call of the gospel insincere and hypocritical.

Canons 2.5 declares that the call of the gospel includes not only a promise, but also a command to repent and believe. This serves to highlight the authoritative nature of the call of the gospel. The gospel at its heart is not an offer in the sense of an invitation or entreaty. It is the proclamation of a command, coupled with a promise. According to the Canons, the command together with the promise must be proclaimed promiscuously or indiscriminately.

The command, along with the promise, must be preached to all—to all nations and to all persons. No distinction is to be made. The church of Jesus Christ must diligently preach the gospel

---

34 *Confessions and Church Order*, 163 (emphasis added).

wherever God in his good pleasure opens a door. This demands that the church be actively engaged in evangelism and missions. It should be the church's delight to be used of God in the gathering of the elect.

Furthermore, the article indicates that though the promise is to be "declared and published to all nations, and to all persons promiscuously and without distinction," nonetheless, it is particular, that is, it is only for those who believe in Christ crucified. The promise is not for all; it is only for those who believe on Jesus Christ. The article advocates the general proclamation of a particular promise.

Significantly, proponents of the well-meant offer contend that this article lends support to their contentions by reading into it a desire on the part of God for the salvation of all who come under the preaching of the gospel. In particular, they draw encouragement from the fact that the promise of the gospel must be "declared and published to all nations, and to all persons promiscuously and without distinction, to whom God out of his good pleasure sends the gospel." However, it should be carefully noted that the article says nothing about God's intention or desire with respect to the salvation of all those who come under the call of the gospel. Nowhere does the article suggest a desire on the part of God that all to whom the command and promise are communicated should be saved.

Undoubtedly, God is serious when he calls men to repent and believe and to embrace the promise of the gospel, but that does not mean that God desires the salvation of all who hear the call of the gospel. The command is to be preached promiscuously, as is the promise that accompanies it. However, as the parable of the wedding feast in Matthew 22 makes plain, the promise is only for those who obey the command, and it is only the elect who will obey the command, though the external call of the gospel is heard by many. As Jesus himself says in his explanation of that parable, "For many are called, but few are chosen" (Matt. 22:14).

Next, it should be noted that the synod in head two, error and rejection 6 of the Canons explicitly rejected the errors of those

> Who use the difference between meriting and appropriating, to the end that they may instill into the minds of the imprudent and inexperienced this teaching, *that God, as far as he is concerned, has been minded of applying to all equally the benefits gained by the death of Christ;* but that, while some obtain the pardon of sin and eternal life, and others do not, this difference depends on their own free will, which joins itself *to the grace that is offered without exception,* and that it is not dependent on the special gift of mercy, which powerfully works in them, that they rather than others should appropriate unto themselves this grace.[35]

The Canons reject the proposition that God ever intended to apply the promises secured by Jesus Christ on the cross to all. In other words, the Canons deny that God ever intended that all men should be the recipients of his grace and of the benefits of the salvation purchased by Jesus Christ. Yet that is what the proponents of the well-meant offer assert is expressed in the call of the gospel. The very thing that the Canons reject, they assert.

The Canons reject the Remonstrants' contention that in the preaching of the gospel, grace is offered to all. Grace, say the divines of Dordt, is not offered to all in the preaching without exception. Yet that also is an integral component of the well-meant offer.

Another article in the Canons that warrants consideration is 3–4.8.

> As many as are called by the gospel, are *unfeignedly called.* For God hath most earnestly and truly shown in his Word, *what is pleasing to him, namely, that those who are called should come*

---

35 *Confessions and Church Order,* 166 (emphasis added).

to him. He, moreover, seriously promises eternal life, and rest, to as many as shall come to him, and believe on him.[36]

It should be noted that the words *unfeignedly*, *earnestly*, and *seriously* all translate the same Latin word (*serio*).[37] "As many as are called by the gospel, are unfeignedly [*seriously*] called. For God hath most earnestly [*seriously*] and truly shown in his Word, what is pleasing to him, namely, that those who are called should come to him. He, moreover, *seriously* promises eternal life, and rest, to as many as shall come to him, and believe on him."

Notice that the synod picked up the language of the Remonstrants with respect to the fact that the call of the gospel was a serious call, but they did not accept the Remonstrants' requirements for such a call, namely, that God must sincerely intend and will to save all who hear it.[38] Indeed, it is evident from Canons 1.6 and 15 that the synod rejected the notion that God wills or intends to save all.

Nonetheless, the Canons plainly assert that the call of the gospel is a serious and unquestionably sincere call. "As many as are called by the gospel, are unfeignedly called." In Canons 3–4.8, the synod explains how the call of the gospel is truly a serious call, notwithstanding that God does not intend or will the salvation of every man. The article affirms that those who are called by the preaching of the gospel are seriously called. This affirmation is then followed by a twofold explanation as to how that is the case. This twofold explanation is based on the distinction between the decretive and perceptive wills of God, sometimes also described as the secret and revealed wills of God. The decretive or secret will of God refers

---

36 *Confessions and Church Order*, 168 (emphasis added).
37 Martyn McGeown, *Grace and Assurance: The Message of the Canons of Dordt* (Jenison, MI: Reformed Free Publishing Association, 2018), 231.
38 Raymond A. Blacketer, "The Three Points in Most Parts Reformed: A Re-examination of the So-Called Well-Meant Offer of Salvation," *Calvin Theological Journal* 35, no. 1 (2000): 42.

to God's eternal counsel, whereby whatever he has decreed always comes to pass. The preceptive or revealed will of God refers to those things that God commands or requires of men, but which are frequently disobeyed by men.

The Canons maintains that the call of the gospel is an unfeigned or serious call to all who hear it because it corresponds to the twofold distinction between the will of God's decree and the will of his precept or command. The Canons make that plain when they declare, "For God hath most earnestly [seriously] and truly shown in his Word, what is pleasing to him, namely, that those who are called should come to him." The external call of the gospel is unfeigned, it is sincere, it is serious in that it truly reflects what God requires of men, namely, that men should come to him in repentance and faith. This command comes to all who hear the gospel.

However, it is a vast overreach on the part of those who maintain the well-meant offer to assert that the Canons here teaches or implies a will or intention on the part of God to save all who come under the preaching. The words of this article are directed only to the obligation of sinners to come unto God. They do not express anything regarding God's desire for the salvation of all men.

Undoubtedly, the call of the gospel is a serious call; God seriously commands every man through the call of the gospel to repent and believe, just as he was serious when he said to Pharaoh through Moses, "Let my people go."

The call of the gospel is absolutely sincere. God sincerely calls all who hear the gospel to come to him. But the reality is that many who hear refuse to obey. The issue is not that they are unable to come; rather the issue is that they will not to come. Nonetheless, the call of the gospel contains a serious and sincere promise of salvation for all who do repent and believe. Those who do come and do believe are those whom God has chosen before the foundation of the world in Jesus Christ; and they will receive the life and the rest that God has promised.

Canons 3–4.9 also warrants consideration.

It is *not the fault of the gospel*, nor of Christ *offered* [*oblato*] therein, nor of God, who calls men by the gospel, and confers upon them various gifts, *that those who are called by the ministry of the Word refuse to come and be converted: the fault lies in themselves*, some of whom when called, regardless of their danger, reject the Word of life; others, though they receive it, suffer it not to make a lasting impression on their heart; therefore their joy, arising only from a temporary faith, soon vanishes, and they fall away; while others choke the seed of the Word by perplexing cares, and the pleasures of this world, and produce no fruit. This our Savior teaches in the parable of the sower (Matt. 13).[39]

The advocates of the well-meant offer seize upon the Canons' reference to offer in this article. "It is not the fault of the gospel, nor of Christ, offered therein." The word translated "offered" is the Latin word *ablato*, which appears in the Latin original of the Canons. The word *ablato* is a participial form of the Latin word *offero*, translated here in the English as *offered*. The primary meaning of *oblato* is "to present" or "to set forth." What the Canons simply states is that Jesus Christ is presented or set forth in the preaching of the gospel.[40] This is the natural and primary meaning

---

39 *Confessions and Church Order*, 168, (emphasis added).
40 It is of interest to note that the use of the term *offered* with respect to the preaching of the gospel is not confined to the Canons. The Westminster Confession of Faith, which was approved by the Church of Scotland approximately thirty years after the formulation of the Canons, also employs that term. For example, in chapter 7, which is titled "Of God's Covenant with Man," section 3 reads, "Man by his fall having made himself incapable of life by that covenant, the Lord was pleased to make a second, commonly called the covenant of grace: wherein *he freely offered unto sinners life and salvation by Jesus Christ*, requiring of them faith in him, that they may be saved, and promising to give unto all those that are ordained unto life, his Holy Spirit, to make them willing and able to believe" (emphasis added), Westminster Confession of Faith 3.7, in

of the word. It is unwarranted to make the reference to "Christ, offered therein" as referring to a gracious invitation on the part of God, expressive of his desire that all who hear the gospel should be saved.[41]

Yet this is the section of the Canons to which appeal is frequently made in support of the well-meant offer of the gospel. The proponents of the well-meant offer, without justification, contend that the reference to "Christ, offered therein" is to a well-meant offer of the gospel. Beeke adopts that view. Commenting on the suggestion that "to offer" means to present or set forth, he continues, "To offer often means to put something before someone for his acceptance or rejection, as in offering food or a gift."[42] On that basis, he proceeds, as do other proponents of the well-meant offer, to import into the Canons the concept of a gracious offer and invitation on the part of God, grounded in his desire to save all mankind.[43] But where is the justification for doing so?

It is undeniable that Jesus Christ is offered in the preaching of

---

Philip Schaff, ed., *The Creeds of Christendom with a History and Critical Notes*, 6th ed., 3 vols. (New York: Harper and Row, 1931; repr., Grand Rapids, MI: Baker Books, 2007), 3:617. Also in the Westminster Larger Catechism Q&A 32: "How is the grace of God manifested in the second covenant? Answer: The grace of God is manifested in the second covenant, in that *he freely provides and offers to sinners a Mediator, and life and salvation by him*; and requiring faith as the condition to interest them in him, promises and gives his Holy Spirit to all his elect, to work in them that faith, with all other saving graces; and to enable them unto all holy obedience, as the evidence of the truth of their faith and thankfulness to God, and as the way which he has appointed them to salvation" (emphasis added), https://www.ligonier.org/learn/articles/westminster-larger-catechism, accessed August 30, 2019.

41 Blacketer, "The Three Points," 44–45.
42 Beeke, *Reformed Preaching*, 261 (emphasis is Beeke).
43 As Raymond Blacketer observes, "To interpret this article as teaching that all persons who hear the gospel are *confronted* with Christ, or that they encounter Christ in the gospel, is at least as plausible as the assertion that such persons are *offered* Christ and salvation through Christ in the preaching of the gospel" (Blacketer, "The Three Points," 45).

the gospel, that is, the salvation to be found in Jesus Christ is set forth or presented to all who hear the preaching. And that is precisely what the Canons asserts in this article: "It is not the fault of the gospel, nor of Christ offered therein…that those who are called by the ministry of the Word refuse to come."[44] But it is quite another thing to say that in the preaching of the gospel there is to be found an expression or desire on the part of God for the salvation of all men. To assert such a thing involves an unwarranted soteriological leap. The suggestion infers that in some respect Jesus Christ died for all men and that he made atonement for every human being. Yet that is precisely what the Canons repudiate under the second head.

In response the proponents of the well-meant offer say, "a paradox." Maurice Roberts in his "The Free Offer of the Gospel" blog states:

> Put simply, it is this: God has fixed the number of the elect from eternity past; yet God desires every sinner who hears his gospel offer to receive it and be eternally blessed in Christ. If the question is now asked, "How can both things be harmonised?", we answer: "In this life we do not know." Here we face Paradox or Antinomy, i.e. it is an apparent contradiction. But to us in this life it seems to be so. God cannot really have two contradictory wills. But so it now seems to us.[45]

John Murray in his book *The Free Offer of the Gospel* states:

A mystery!

We have found that God himself expresses an ardent desire for the fulfilment of certain things which he has not

---

44 Canons of Dordt 3–4.9, in *Confessions and Church Order*, 168.
45 Maurice Roberts, "The Free Offer of the Gospel," accessed June 10, 2019, https://mauriceroberts.org/blog/2018/4/5/the-free-offer-of-the-gospel.

decreed in his inscrutable counsel to come to pass. This means that there is a will to the realization of what he has not decretively willed, a pleasure towards that which he has not been pleased to decree. This is indeed mysterious, and why he has not brought to pass, in the exercise of his omnipotent power and grace, what is his ardent pleasure lies hid in the sovereign counsel of his will. We should not entertain, however, any prejudice against the notion that God desires or has pleasure in the accomplishment of what he does not decretively will. [46]

Summation

Despite the repeated claims that the Canons support the well-meant offer of the gospel, those claims cannot be substantiated. Indeed, not only do the Canons not support the well-meant offer, they repudiate it. It is evident that the Canons teach the following concerning the call of the gospel:

- The call of the gospel is an unfeigned or serious call to all who hear it. It reflects what God commands and requires of men, namely, that men should come to him in repentance and faith, in and through Jesus Christ.
- The call of the gospel consists of a command and a promise. The command is to repent and believe, and the promise is the promise of everlasting life and rest in and through Jesus Christ.
- The command, together with the promise, must be proclaimed promiscuously or indiscriminately.

Those who faithfully preach the gospel will call all who come under the preaching to repent of their sins and to believe on Jesus

---

[46] Murray, *The Free Offer*, 29.

Christ. There will be no attempt to tailor or confine the call to the elect. How can it be? The preacher does not know who are and who are not the elect of God in his audience! The gospel must be preached promiscuously. This is the plain teaching of Canons 2.5.

The Canons say nothing about God's intention or desire with respect to the salvation of all who come under the preaching of the gospel. However, the Canons do categorically deny that God intends that all men should be the recipients of his grace and of the benefits of the salvation purchased by Jesus Christ. Not all men are saved, nor has God ever purposed to save all mankind.

The call of the gospel, as is asserted by the Canons, is unfeigned. Indeed, it is a divine summons. "The times of this ignorance God winked at; but now commandeth all men everywhere to repent" (Acts 17:30). What was John the Baptist's message to Israel? "Repent ye: for the kingdom of heaven is at hand" (Matt. 3:2). Jesus himself issued that same call of the gospel. "From that time Jesus began to preach, and to say, Repent: for the kingdom of heaven is at hand" (4:17).

That the call of the gospel is both a command and a promise, as opposed to an invitation or a plea, is repeatedly indicated in the scriptures. By way of illustration: "Again, he sent forth other servants, saying, Tell them which are bidden, Behold, I have prepared my dinner: my oxen and my fatlings are killed, and all things are ready: come unto the marriage" (Matt. 22:4). "[He] sent his servant at supper time to say to them that were bidden, Come; for all things are now ready" (Luke 14:17). "Come unto me, all ye that labour and are heavy laden, and I will give you rest. Take my yoke upon you, and learn of me; for I am meek and lowly in heart: and ye shall find rest unto your souls. For my yoke is easy, and my burden is light" (Matt. 11:28–30).

> 1. Ho, every one that thirsteth, come ye to the waters, and he that hath no money; come ye, buy, and eat; yea, come, buy wine and milk without money and without price.

2. Wherefore do ye spend money for that which is not bread? and your labour for that which satisfieth not? hearken diligently unto me, and eat ye that which is good, and let your soul delight itself in fatness.

3. Incline your ear, and come unto me: hear, and your soul shall live; and I will make an everlasting covenant with you, even the sure mercies of David. (Isa. 55:1–3)

Those who propound the well-meant offer conveniently glide over the explicit references to "promise" and "command" and recast the external call of the gospel as an invitation. In that way, they subtly transform God's summons and command into an offer to treat or an invitation. But nowhere do the Canons speak of the external call of the gospel in those terms. Yet that is the language that is consistently employed by those who maintain the well-meant offer.

Consistent with their styling of the call of the gospel as a gracious invitation, as opposed to a command coupled with a promise, those who propound the well-meant offer tend in the direction of a soul-winning, pleading ministry. They speak as though the gospel needs to be presented in such a way as to cajole, allure, or woo men into the arms of the Savior.

Such ministry is inconsistent with a sovereign God who has chosen a people unto himself in Jesus Christ and who works irresistibly in the hearts of men by his Spirit; who regenerates them, gives them a new heart, and thereby enables them to believe. To suggest that God needs to allure or woo sinners through the preaching is a subtle watering down and attack upon the Canons' teaching on irresistible grace and unconditional election.

For the call of the gospel to be sincere, vibrant, warm, comforting, and urgent does not require the adoption of the well-meant offer. In fact, the well-meant offer is a hindrance to the preaching of the gospel. The sad irony is that it fosters the very doctrines to which the Canons stand opposed. Those within the Reformed camp who defend the well-meant offer repudiate the free will of man, but nonetheless, "The teaching of free will is necessarily implied in the doctrine of the offer."[47] Fundamental to the well-meant offer is the idea that in the preaching of the gospel there is set before every sinner an offer or invitation that requires either acceptance or rejection; and the implication is that every sinner has the ability to make such a choice.

Unquestionably, the Reformed preacher must call sinners, all sinners, to repentance and faith, and he must do so having a genuine concern for the souls of men. Men must hear Jesus Christ's words through him, "Come unto me, all ye that labour and are heavy laden, and I will give you rest. Take my yoke upon you, and learn of me; for I am meek and lowly in heart: and ye shall find rest unto your souls" (Matt. 11:28–29). The command and the promise.

The Reformed preacher ought to exhibit the tenderness and concern of the apostle Paul when he says, "I say the truth in Christ, I lie not, my conscience also bearing me witness in the Holy Ghost, that I have great heaviness and continual sorrow in my heart. For I could wish that myself were accursed from Christ for my brethren, my kinsmen according to the flesh" (Rom. 9:1–3). But that does not require a Reformed preacher to embrace the well-meant offer of the gospel. Quite the contrary.

Those who propound the well-meant offer seek to ground themselves in the teachings of the Canons. However, the truth is that they are undermining, if not demolishing, the very truths taught in the Canons.

On the occasion of the four hundredth anniversary of the Synod of Dordt, Reformed preachers would do well to remind themselves of what the Canons actually teach about the unfeigned call of the gospel.

---

47 David J. Engelsma, *Hyper-Calvinism and the Call of the Gospel* (Grand Rapids, MI: Reformed Free Publishing Association, 1994), 48.

Chapter 5

THE DOCTRINE OF THE COVENANT IN THE CANONS OF DORDT

Douglas J. Kuiper

Introduction

The Canons of Dordt explicitly sets forth the Reformed confessional position regarding five fundamental doctrines: God's unconditional and eternal election, Christ's efficacious atonement for the elect only, the total depravity of the human nature, God's irresistible grace in salvation, and God's preservation of his saints. In the Canons, on the basis of scripture, Reformed churches and believers confess that God is sovereign in every aspect of salvation.

Imbedded in the Canons are other doctrines that the Canons does not develop at length. Because the Canons does not develop them, some might conclude that they are secondary. In fact they are not secondary in their significance for Reformed theology or for a right understanding of scripture. Nor are they truly secondary in the Canons; each serves a significant function relating to and undergirding the five doctrines that the Canons treats explicitly. A right understanding of these other doctrines is necessary for a right understanding of the doctrines of sovereign grace.

One doctrine embedded in the Canons is that of divine revelation. Although no single head is devoted to this doctrine, the Canons teaches the means by which God reveals himself and the purpose of his revelation.[1] God's purpose in the preaching of the gospel is another secondary doctrine.[2] A third, differing from the first two in that it is a false doctrine, is the notion of common grace as the Remonstrants (Arminians) taught it. In this instance, what undergirds the Canons is not the teaching of common grace but the rejection of common grace.[3] The doctrine of assurance, treated elsewhere in this book, is a fourth. And a fifth is the doctrine of the covenant. The Canons does not ignore the doctrine of the covenant; it is referred to eight times in six articles. However, no head of doctrine in the Canons is devoted to the covenant. The Reformed doctrine of the covenant undergirds the five primary doctrines of the Canons.

In brief, God's covenant is the bond of friendship and fellowship between him and his people in Jesus Christ, according to which he is our God (Gen. 17:7) and we are his people (Ex. 19:5–6; see also Jer. 31:31–34; Hos. 1:9–10; Rom. 9:26; Heb. 8:7–13; 1 Pet. 2:9–10). In this covenant God calls us his friends (Isa. 41:8; James 2:23) and causes us to walk with him as our chief friend (Gen. 5:22, 24; 6:9; 17:1; Gal. 5:16; Eph. 5:8; 1 Thess. 2:12; 1 John 1:7). The covenant is not merely a promise; it is a relationship. God establishes his covenant by promise, and in the covenantal bond he makes promises to us and we to him.

From every viewpoint, this covenantal relationship relates to God's sovereign grace. By establishing and maintaining his covenant with sinners, God manifests his grace (undeserved favor). He establishes his covenant by sovereign grace (in his power) apart from the will or aid of humans. His covenant puts the wonder of his sovereign grace on display for all to see.

---

1 Canons of Dordt 3–4.4, 6; 3–4, error and rejection 5, in *Confessions and Church Order*, 167, 171–72.
2 Canons of Dordt 1.3–4; 1, error and rejection 9; 2.5, in *Confessions and Church Order*, 155, 162–63.
3 Canons of Dordt 3–4, error and rejection 5, in *Confessions and Church Order*, 171–72.

This chapter explores the relationship of the doctrine of the covenant to the five doctrines that the Canons treats explicitly.[4] Although the Canons does not explain and develop the idea of the

---

4 I have found no book devoted entirely to this subject, and only a few chapters or articles. In two hundred pages, and writing in the Dutch language, C. Graafland examines the development of two different strands of covenantal thought among the Dutch Reformed in the later sixteenth century, just prior to the Synod of Dordt: that of the "orthodox Reformed" (represented by Theodore Beza, Jerome Zanchius, and Francis Gomarus, out of which strand the Canons developed) and the "humanist Reformed" (represented by Dirk Coornhert, Joannes Veluanus, Gellius Snecanus, Cornelis Wiggertsz—all precursors of Arminianism—and Jacob Arminius himself). In this connection, see C. Graafland, *Van Calvijn tot Comrie: Oorsprong en ontwikkeling van de leer van het verbond in het Gereformeerde Protestantisme* [From Calvin to Comrie: Origin and Development of the Doctrine of the Covenant in Reformed Protestantism] (Zoetermeer: Boekencentrum, 1996), volume 3, part 5. In treating the covenantal thought of Gomarus, who was a delegate to the Synod of Dordt, Graafland devotes eight pages to the doctrine of the covenant in the Canons of Dordt (3:80–87), but his purpose here is to show how the doctrine of the covenant in the Canons relates to that of Beza, Zanchius, and Gomarus. A second noteworthy resource, also in Dutch, is Klaas Schilder's *Het Verbond in De Gerformeerde Symbolen: Collegeverslagen Symboliek*, 5d Druk [The Covenant in the Reformed Symbols (or Confessions): College Reports Symbolism] (Kampen: Berg-Broederweg, 1977). In English, there is David Engelsma's fourth chapter, "Covenant and Election in the Canons," in *Covenant and Election in the Reformed Tradition* (Jenison, MI: Reformed Free Publishing Association, 2011), 63–72. Not surprisingly, Engelsma's presentation of the matter is significantly different from Schilder's. Engelsma opposes the conditional covenant presentation of Schilder and the Liberated. Commentaries on the Canons refer to the doctrine of the covenant in explaining the various passages in the Canons that use the word. Church controversies have arisen that relate directly to the idea of the covenant as the Canons present it. One instance is the conditional covenant controversy in the PRC in the 1940s and 1950s. Interdenominational discussions regarding the covenant in the confessions have been held, particularly between the United Reformed and Canadian Reformed Churches. The interested reader can confer with John A. Bouwers and Theodore G. VanRaalte, eds., *The Bond of the Covenant Within the Bounds of the Confessions: A Conversation Between the URCNA and CANRC* (St. Catharines, ON: Church Unity Publications, 2015). Appeal has been made in these conversations and controversies to the doctrine of the covenant in the Canons, but apparently there has been little scholarly development of the use of the doctrine of the covenant in the Canons of Dordt.

covenant, the writers of the Canons had a definite conception of what God's covenant was, and they used the doctrine in the service of the five doctrines of sovereign grace. How they did so will be demonstrated, and why they did so will be explained.

The first section of this chapter is a survey of the use of the term *covenant* in the Canons. Next comes a demonstration of how the Canons relates the covenant to the five primary doctrines. Third, the reason why the Canons touches on the covenant is explained. The chapter concludes by noting why it is significant that the Canons touch on this doctrine.

The Use of *Covenant* in the Canons of Dordt

The Canons of Dordt was originally written in Latin.[5] Two Latin words, both found in the Canons, can be translated *covenant*. One of them, *testamentum*, relates to covenant in a general way. It refers to a last will and testament, and particularly to the death of the testator as the way in which one receives the bequest (Heb. 9:16).

This word is commonly translated *testament* in reference to the Old Testament and the New Testament of the scriptures, that is, to God's covenant as revealed and administered both before and after Christ died. Christ's death, fulfilling the Old Testament ceremonial laws, marked the transition from Old to New. On the basis of Christ's death, God no longer administered his covenant by using types and pictures, but by giving his people the fuller knowledge of himself and writing his law on our hearts by his Holy Spirit. That

---

5 Recently a new translation of the Canons has been published. See "Part II: The Canons of the Synod of Dort—A Pastoral Translation" in Godfrey, *Saving the Reformation*, 33–77. Godfrey explains that the goal of his translation is to make the Canons understandable for Reformed believers: "The translation does not simplify the vocabulary. Its main difference from earlier translations is to break the long Latin sentences of the original into shorter English sentences. A little of the precision of the Latin is lost in this process, but the result is a faithful translation that is much easier to read and understand for contemporary readers of English" (Godfrey, *Saving the Reformation*, 3).

this word refers to God's covenant with his people from the viewpoint of its ratification by Christ's death is clear from Hebrews 7, Hebrews 9, and Christ's own words when he instituted the Lord's supper ("this is my blood of the new testament," Matt. 26:28). In the Latin original the Canons uses the word *testamentum* in head one, article 8; head two, error and rejection 2; heads three and four, articles 6 and 7; and head five, error and rejection 6.[6] In all but one of these instances, the Canons uses the word to refer to the Old and/or New Testaments. The one exception is found in Canons head two, error and rejection 2. There the Canons refers to scripture to explain that Christ, on the basis of his death, "has become the Surety and Mediator of a better, that is, the new covenant, and that a testament is of force where death has occurred (Heb. 7:22; 9:15, 17)."[7] This article represents the only use of *testamentum* that is relevant to the purpose of this chapter.

The second Latin word for *covenant* is *foedus*, from which comes the word *federal*, referring to a league or federation. In Latin this word originally referred to a treaty or agreement between two parties—something that God's covenant is *not*. However, this was the best Latin word to use in reference to God's sovereign, unilateral, unconditional covenant of grace. The Canons uses this word eight times.[8] It is found three times in head two, error and rejection 2, part of which was quoted above, the only article in which both *testamentum* and *foedus* are used. It is also used one time each in head one, article 17; head two, article 8; head two, errors and rejections 4 and 5; and head five, error and rejection

---

6 *Confessions and Church Order*, 156, 164–65, 167, 178.
7 *Confessions and Church Order*, 164–65.
8 Godfrey's new translation uses the word "covenant" ten times. In the process of making the translation simpler by breaking up longer sentences into shorter, Godfrey adds the word twice to make the meaning of the sentences clear (Canons of Dordt 1.17; 2, error and rejection 4). He never uses the word in a context in which the Latin *foedus* was not used.

1. These articles will be quoted in whole or in part in the second section of this chapter.

Regarding the doctrine of the covenant in the Canons, two general observations are in order. First, the covenant to which the Canons refers is the covenant of grace that God has established with elect sinners, with Adam after the fall, and with everyone who is included in the seed of the woman (Gen. 3:15). On this point, the Canons is explicit: it is the "covenant of grace"[9] and the "new covenant."[10]

In other words, in speaking of the "new covenant" the Canons does not refer to the New Testament in distinction from the Old, but to the covenant of grace in distinction from the covenant that God had established with Adam as the head of the human race before the fall. When the Canons was written in 1619, Reformed and Presbyterian theologians had already begun developing the doctrine of a covenant of God with Adam before the fall, popularly but unfortunately known as the "covenant of works."[11] This pre-fall covenant with Adam was known as the old covenant; the covenant of grace with the elect in Christ, revealed after the fall, is the new covenant.

---

9 Canons of Dordt 1.17, in *Confessions and Church Order*, 159.
10 Canons of Dordt 2.8; 2, error and rejection 2; 5, error and rejection 1, in *Confessions and Church Order*, 163–65, 176.
11 "Covenant of works" is an unfortunate name because it suggests that Adam's obedience would earn or merit some reward. A brief history of the development of the doctrine of the covenant can be found in various works, all of which demonstrate that the idea of a pre-fall covenant of God with Adam was developed in the last decades of the 1500s, and that Zacharius Ursinus was influential in developing the idea. See D. A. Weir, *The Origins of the Federal Theology in Sixteenth-Century Reformation Thought* (Oxford: Clarendon Press, 1990); Andrew A. Woolsey, *Unity and Continuity in Covenantal Thought: A Study in the Reformed Tradition to the Westminster Assembly* (Grand Rapids, MI: Reformation Heritage Books, 2012); and Geerhardus Vos, "The Doctrine of the Covenant in Reformed Theology," in *Redemptive History and Biblical Interpretation: The Shorter Writings of Geerhardus Vos*, ed. Richard B. Gaffin Jr. (Phillipsburg, NJ: Presbyterian and Reformed Publishing Co., 1980), 234–67.

That the Canons refers always and exclusively to this covenant is in harmony with its purpose to defend the sovereign, particular, irresistible character of God's grace. At every turn, the Remonstrant error regarding the covenant touched on the work of God to save sinners in Jesus Christ. In the Canons, our Reformed fathers limited themselves to responding to that error.

That the Canons refers to this covenant of grace is of special interest to members of the Protestant Reformed Churches in America (PRCA) and to our friends and fellow believers elsewhere. We love the doctrine of God's covenant of grace and have come to see that it is central to a right understanding of scripture and Reformed doctrine. Our ministers and theologians endeavor to preach, teach, write about, and defend the doctrine of the covenant of grace. It was this doctrine, particularly the unconditional character of God's covenant, that our forefathers defended in the controversy that convulsed the PRCA in the 1950s. At that time, those who defended God's sovereign grace in the covenant appealed to the teaching of the Canons of Dordt. We desire to grow in our understanding of what the Canons teaches about this doctrine.

The second observation is that several features of the doctrine of the covenant of grace, although reflected in the Canons, are not relevant to our immediate purpose. One such feature is the unity of the covenant of grace throughout all history. Inherent in the Canons' use of the familiar terms *Old Testament* and *New Testament* is the unity of the covenant: it is one covenant.[12] A second feature, also suggested by the terms *Old Testament* and *New Testament*, is the difference in the way in which God administered the covenant in the Old Testament and the New Testament.[13] A third such feature is that God continues his covenant with elect believers in the line

---

12 Canons of Dordt 1.8; 5, error and rejection 6, in *Confessions and Church Order*, 156, 178.
13 Canons of Dordt 3–4.5–7, in *Confessions and Church Order*, 167.

of generations. The Canons treats this truth in head one, article 17. Because God continues his covenant with godly believers in the line of generations, "godly parents have no reason to doubt of the election and salvation of their children whom it pleaseth God to call out of this life in their infancy."[14]

A fuller explanation of the Canons' doctrine of the covenant might explain these points in more detail. However, these are not the fundamental ways in which the Canons use the doctrine of the covenant to undergird the five doctrines of sovereign grace. The Canons relates the doctrine of the covenant to God's sovereign grace in four particular ways.

Election Governs God's Covenant

First, the use of the term *covenant* in the Canons underscores that the covenant of grace is governed by God's eternal decree of election. The two articles that refer to God's covenant in the positive section of the Canons in head one, article 17, and head two, article 8, both speak explicitly of God's covenant and election. These articles read:

> Since we are to judge of the will of God from his Word, which testifies that the children of believers are holy, not by nature, but in virtue of the covenant of grace in which they, together with the parents, are comprehended, godly parents have no reason to doubt of the election and salvation of their children whom it pleaseth God to call out of this life in their infancy [Gen. 17:7; Acts 2:39; 1 Cor. 7:14].[15]

> For this was the sovereign counsel and most gracious will and purpose of God the Father, that the quickening and saving efficacy of the most precious death of His Son should

---

14 *Confessions and Church Order*, 159.
15 *Confessions and Church Order*, 159.

extend to all the elect, for bestowing upon them alone the gift of justifying faith, thereby to bring them infallibly to salvation; that is, it was the will of God that Christ by the blood of the cross, whereby he confirmed the new covenant, should effectually redeem out of every people, tribe, nation, and language all those, and those only, who were from eternity chosen to salvation and given to him by the Father; that he should confer upon them faith, which, together with all the other saving gifts of the Holy Spirit, he purchased for them by his death; should purge them from all sin, both original and actual, whether committed before or after believing; and having faithfully preserved them even to the end, should at last bring them free from every spot and blemish to the enjoyment of glory in his own presence forever.[16]

In sum, Canons 1.17 teaches that godly parents are not to doubt the election of their children who die in infancy because these children are holy by virtue of God's covenant, and Canons 2.8 teaches that Christ, by his blood by which he confirmed the new covenant, redeemed the elect.

That election governs the covenant means three things. First, it means that only the elect are members of the covenant. It is true that God places some reprobate close to the covenant. A phrase commonly used to make this point is that they are "in the sphere of the covenant." They were baptized and raised in the same manner as elect children and heard the gospel preached. But that God does not regard them as his friends they make plain by their own hatred of him. God works a new heart in all whom he views as his friends, so that they live as though he is their friend. Only the elect are truly members of God's covenant. Esau was born to Isaac, Abraham's

---

16 *Confessions and Church Order*, 163–64.

covenantal seed; but evidently God did not consider Esau to be his friend (Rom. 9:11–13), nor did Esau view God as his friend (Gen. 25:29–34).

Second, that election governs the covenant means that God will certainly, without fail, bestow all the blessings of salvation on the elect members of the covenant. Canons 2.8 indicates that God's decree of election included the decree to bless his covenantal people with all the blessings that are reserved for the elect.

Third, that only the elect are members of the covenant means that Christ is and must be the mediator of the covenant. The elect alone are those for whom Christ has died. If the elect are members of the covenant, that can only be due to the fact that Christ has died for them.

The relationship between covenant and election, that election governs the covenant, is clearly the teaching of the Canons. The Canons will allow no other view. To be sure, the Canons presents covenant and election as distinct realities, not identical or synonymous, just as scripture also presents them. Election is the eternal decree of God to save some sinners in Jesus Christ (Rom. 9:11–18; Eph. 1:4–6). The covenant of grace is the relationship of friendship between God and his people, whereby he is their God and they are his people (Jer. 31:33; Heb. 8:10; 1 Pet. 2:10).

Nor can one read the Canons as teaching that God's covenant of grace governs election, as though God determined to elect those who fulfilled certain conditions of the covenant. If this were true, election would not be an eternal decree of God; it would be reduced to a work of God in time only. And if this were true, membership in God's covenant would be the reason for one's election. The questions regarding how one enters God's covenant and why one is elect would be raised, and the way opened to answer those questions by saying that election and covenant are both conditional.

However, neither Canons 1.17 nor Canons 2.8 can be understood this way. They can be understood only to teach that election governs the covenant. In formulating its statement, Canons 1.17 begins with the reality of the covenant and then moves to the reality of election: being in the covenant, we do not doubt the election of infants of believing parents. This is not because the covenant determines who are elect, but because election determines who are in the covenant. Those who are genuinely members of God's covenant are elect, because only the elect are in the covenant. Likewise, Canons 2.8 suggests that the explanation for membership in God's covenant is that Christ shed his blood in order to confirm, or ratify, or put the seal of genuineness on, God's covenant. Canons 2.8 also teaches that Christ did so for the elect only. He is therefore the head and mediator of the covenant.

Christ the Head and Mediator of the Covenant

Christ is the head of the covenant inasmuch as he is the head of the elect. All the elect were chosen to salvation in Christ (Eph. 1:4). In determining from eternity whom he would save, God chose Christ as the elect and determined to save all whom he saw as united to Christ. Scripture refers to Christ as the elect, in Isaiah 28:16 as quoted in 1 Peter 2:6: "Behold, I lay in Sion a chief corner stone, elect, precious," and in Isaiah 42:1: "Behold my servant, whom I uphold; mine elect, in whom my soul delighteth." Accordingly, the Canons say in head one, article 7,

> Election is the unchangeable purpose of God whereby, before the foundation of the world, he hath out of mere grace, according to the sovereign good pleasure of his own will, chosen, from the whole human race, which had fallen through their own fault from their primitive state of rectitude into sin and destruction, a certain number of persons to redemption in Christ, whom he from eternity appointed the Mediator and Head of the elect, and the foundation of

salvation. This elect number…God hath decreed to give to Christ, to be saved by him.[17]

The article does not use the word *covenant*, but if Christ is the mediator and head of the elect, and if election governs the covenant, then Christ is the head of the covenant. God demonstrated this by indicating that he had a special covenantal relationship with Christ (Isaiah 42:1: "in whom my soul delighteth"), and Christ was devoted to his heavenly Father in all his work. As the head of the covenant, Christ is the mediator of the covenant. Christ's death provided the basis for God to establish his covenant with sinners. Christ's resurrection and ascension demonstrated that he had the power and authority to make this covenant a reality by bestowing covenantal blessings on all the elect. As the mediator of the covenant Christ is our chief prophet, only high priest, and eternal king.[18] Accordingly, when our fathers at Dordt rejected the Remonstrant notion regarding what Christ accomplished in his death, they said: "For this is repugnant to scripture, which teaches that *Christ has become the Surety and Mediator of a better, that is, the new covenant,* and that *a testament is of force where death has occurred* (Heb. 7:22; 9:15, 17)."[19]

Christ's Death Confirmed the Covenant

Christ did not establish God's covenant; the triune God did and does that. Rather, the ascended Christ, by his Holy Spirit, brings into the covenant, in the process of time, all whom God has chosen in Christ, and Christ applies to the elect all the blessings of salvation. Christ's death on the cross relates to the covenant in three ways.

---

17 *Confessions and Church Order*, 156.
18 Heidelberg Catechism Q&A 31, in *Confessions and Church Order*, 95–96.
19 Canons of Dordt 2, error and rejection 2, in *Confessions and Church Order*, 165 (emphasis added).

First, Christ's death on the cross provided the legal basis for God to establish his covenant with sinners. As sinners, we have no right to covenantal fellowship with God. Moreover, God will not have covenantal fellowship with any whom he declares to be guilty of sin. Christ, in dying on the cross, bore the sins and guilt of God's elect and earned for them righteousness. In this way he satisfied God's justice, so that God could establish his covenant with humans.

Second, Christ's death on the cross showed that God's covenant as he had established and maintained it in the past, in the Old Testament, was genuine. By prescribing the sacrifices that Israel was to bring, God repeatedly pointed the Old Testament saints to the shedding of the blood of the Lamb as that act on which his covenant was founded. In this respect too, the death of Christ was a confirmation of the covenant.

Third, Christ's death showed that all the promises that God made to his covenantal people regarding covenantal blessings were genuine promises. For one thing, Christ's coming in our flesh and his dying on the cross was a central aspect of the covenantal promises, and God fulfilled those promises in Christ's death. For another, the complete atoning work of Christ is the basis for God to bestow every blessing on his people, to fulfill every promise.

Because of this, Canons 2.8 says that "Christ by the blood of the cross…confirmed the new covenant." The Latin verb translated *confirm* means to ratify or to make certain. Christ was the testator whom God pictured in the sacrifices and ceremonies of the law and whose death was necessary for God's people to receive covenantal blessings as our inheritance (Heb. 7:22; 9:15, 17).

So far we have seen that the concept of covenant relates both to God's electing work (head one) and to Christ's atoning work (head two). Only the elect are in covenant with God. Only those for whom Christ died are in covenant with God. Only on the basis of Christ's death can we be in covenant with God. And on the basis of

Christ's death, we shall certainly receive every covenantal blessing. All of this leads to the final way in which the Canons use the doctrine of covenant.

God's Covenant of Grace is Unconditional

That God's covenant of grace is unconditional means that God requires nothing of humans in order to establish his covenant, maintain his covenant, or bring his covenant to its final perfection in heaven. God does not require people to choose for or agree to this covenant. Nothing in the human will is a condition. The activities of believing and of obeying are not prerequisites. God alone establishes his covenant, God alone maintains it, and God alone brings it to its highest realization. In God's covenant, we have the calling to live as God's covenantal friends, showing our thankfulness to him by obeying his law and praying. Our carrying out that calling, however, is the fruit and effect of his bringing us into the covenant and of his maintaining the covenant; it is not the reason or basis for God to establish or maintain or finally realize his covenant with us.

The defense of this unconditional character of God's covenant is prominent in the Canons, which devotes several articles to making this point explicit. Four articles, in particular, set forth this truth clearly. The first of these articles is head one, article 9, which reads:

> This election was not founded upon foreseen faith, and the obedience of faith, holiness, or any other good quality or disposition in man, as the prerequisite, cause, or condition on which it depended; but men are chosen to faith and to the obedience of faith, holiness, etc. Therefore election is the fountain of every saving good, from which proceed faith, holiness, and the other gifts of salvation, and finally eternal life itself, as its fruits and effects, according to that of the apostle:

He hath chosen us (not because we were, but) *that we should be holy, and without blame before him in love* (Eph. 1:4).[20]

The other three articles that drive home this point are found in the rejection of errors section of the first head. Canons head one, error and rejection 3 rejects the idea that God "chose out of all possible conditions (among which are also the works of the law), or out of the whole order of things, the act of faith which from its very nature is undeserving, as well as its incomplete obedience, as a condition of salvation."[21] Canons head one, error and rejection 4 opposes the notion "that in the election unto faith this condition is beforehand demanded, namely, that man should use the light of nature aright, be pious, humble, meek, and fit for eternal life, as if on these things election were in any way dependent."[22] And Canons head one, error and rejection 5 rules out the idea that

> the complete and decisive election occurred because of foreseen perseverance unto the end in faith, conversion, holiness and godliness; and that this is the gracious and evangelical worthiness for the sake of which he who is chosen is more worthy than he who is not chosen; and that therefore faith, the obedience of faith, holiness, godliness, and perseverance are not fruits of the unchangeable election unto glory, but are conditions which, being required beforehand, were foreseen as being met by those who will be fully elected, and are causes without which the unchangeable election to glory does not occur.[23]

Of course, these articles speak of divine election as unconditional, not of God's covenant as unconditional. But election governs

---

20 *Confessions and Church Order*, 157.
21 *Confessions and Church Order*, 160.
22 *Confessions and Church Order*, 160.
23 *Confessions and Church Order*, 161.

the covenant. If election is unconditional, the covenant must be unconditional also. As if anticipating the objection, the Canons includes a fifth article that explicitly rejects conditions in the covenant. In the first article in the rejection of errors section of head five, the Synod of Dordt rejected as error the idea "that the perseverance of the true believers is not a fruit of election, or a gift of God gained by the death of Christ, but a condition of the new covenant, which (as they declare) man before his decisive election and justification must fulfill through his free will."[24]

In addition to these articles that explicitly reject the idea of conditions in the covenant, the Canons rejects this notion by emphasizing that Christ's death on the cross was a confirmation of the covenant and an effectual redemption of all the elect.[25] An explanation of the word *confirm* has already been given. The point for the moment is that the word is entirely out of place if the death of Christ served only to make salvation *possible* but not to make it a *reality*. If his work did not actually save the elect, and if humans have yet to do something in order to make the covenant a reality, then the covenant is not founded on or confirmed by his death.

Where in the world can one find another instance of a covenant that required the death of one covenantal member in order to make something only *possible*, but not *actual*, for the other? Never does a covenant between two or more human parties require the death of one in order to bestow blessing on the other; in earthly covenants, the death of one is a punishment for not keeping the terms of the covenant, and that death ends the covenant. But suppose that there was a covenant in which one party promised to die as part of the covenantal stipulations. In such a case, would not that person promise to die *after* the obedience of the other? Death makes it impossible

---

24 *Confessions and Church Order*, 176.
25 Canons of Dordt 2.8, in *Confessions and Church Order*, 163–64.

for one ever again to experience the benefits of an earthly covenant. Certainly one would not agree to die and *then* expect obedience of the other.

The closest analogy is that of a testament, that is, a bequest or inheritance that a father leaves his child, which becomes the child's after the father dies. But what father leaves such a bequest on the condition that the child obeys *after* the father's death? A father might disinherit his child while he yet is alive, but he cannot do so after he dies. Yet those who teach that God requires our obedience in addition to the work of Christ on the cross speak of the covenant in such terms: Christ died to do his part, and now we must do ours. What if no one ever fulfilled the conditions? The reality is that totally depraved humans are unable to do so. Was Christ's death, then, in vain?

That the Canons speaks of Christ's death as confirming the covenant is, then, further indication that it teaches that God's covenant is unconditional. For this reason, in the rejection of errors section of head two, the Canons rejects conditions in respect to the matter of the efficacy of Christ's death. The fathers of Dordt rejected the erroneous teaching:

> That the new covenant of grace, which God the Father, through the mediation of the death of Christ, made with man, does not herein consist that we by faith, inasmuch as it accepts the merits of Christ, are justified before God and saved, but in the fact that God, having revoked the demand of perfect obedience of the law regards faith itself and the obedience of faith, although imperfect, as the perfect obedience of the law, and does esteem it worthy of the reward of eternal life through grace.
>
> For these contradict the scriptures: *Being justified freely by his grace through the redemption that is in Christ Jesus: whom God hath set forth to be a propitiation through faith*

in his blood (Rom. 3:24, 25). And these proclaim, as did the wicked Socinus, a new and strange justification of man before God, against the consensus of the whole Church.[26]

The Remonstrants' Erroneous Covenantal View

Why did the Canons embody this covenantal view? Why did our Reformed fathers sense the need to refer at all to the doctrine of the covenant?

The answer is not that our Reformed fathers were trying explicitly and consciously to develop the doctrine of the covenant. This point is worth making, because the Canons of Dordt was written in 1619, during which time the doctrine of the covenant was being developed in Reformed and Presbyterian churches. The study of the historical development of this doctrine is a fascinating study (see footnote eleven. But the fathers at the Synod of Dordt did not treat the doctrine of the covenant in the Canons because of such a desire. Any contribution of the Canons to the development of this doctrine was the result and effect of, not the motive or purpose for, relating the doctrine of the covenant to the doctrines of sovereign grace.

In short, the answer to the question is that the Remonstrants based their teachings regarding election, atonement, and grace on a wrong covenantal view. As Graafland documents, two covenantal views had been developing in Reformed circles, and each covenantal view implied, resulted from, or led to different theological outlooks.[27]

Especially three characteristics of the Remonstrant view of covenant are worthy of note.[28]

---

26 Canons of Dordt 2, error and rejection 4, in *Confessions and Church Order*, 165.
27 Graafland, *Van Calvijn tot Comrie*, 3:80–87.
28 Those interested in reading more about the Remonstrant doctrine of the covenant can read any survey of Arminius' thought. In particular, one general work and two specific works are recommended. The general work, covering more than just Arminius' doctrine of covenant, is Richard Muller's *God, Creation,*

The first of these is that the covenant is identical to election. The Remonstrants did not explicitly state that they viewed the covenant as essentially the same as election. However, such is the consensus of scholars. Graafland notes that the Remonstrant covenantal theologians gave the covenant a central place in their theology and that they did not develop the doctrine of election in distinction from covenant; for them election was the eternal dimension of the covenant.[29]

Graafland's general observation was based on a survey of Remonstrant theologians in distinction from orthodox Reformed theologians. On the basis of a survey of Jacob Arminius' writings, William den Boer has made the same observation. He writes, "God's covenant, as the way in which He has determined now to deal with humankind, here appears to be the same as God's decree (*decretum*). For Arminius, therefore, the decree does not concern the 'final result' but the 'rules', and is synonymous with the covenant."[30] Later Den Boer says, "It also becomes clear that the content of the doctrine of predestination is the same as what Arminius ascribes to the covenant, the *foedus* that God established on the basis of his *pactum* with

---

and Providence in the Thought of Jacob Arminius: Sources and Directions of Scholastic Protestantism in the Era of Early Orthodoxy* (Grand Rapids, MI: Baker Book House, 1991). Two journal articles that are devoted more specifically to the Arminian doctrine of the covenant are Raymond A. Blacketer, "Arminius' Concept of Covenant in its Historical Context," *Dutch Review of Church History* 80, no. 2 (2000): 193–220, and Richard Muller, "The Federal Motif in Seventeenth Century Arminian Theology," *Dutch Review of Church History* 62, no. 1 (1982): 102–22.

29 "4. Het verbond krijgt hierdoor een zodanige centrale positie, dat daarnaast de verkiezing geen eigen plaats inneemt…Verkiezing is de eeuwigheids-dimensie van het verbond, die gegrond is in God's rije besluit" (Graafland, *Van Calvijn tot Comrie*, 3:209).

30 William den Boer, *God's Twofold Love: The Theology of Jacob Arminius (1559–1609)*, trans. Albert Gootjes (Göttingen, Germany: Vandenhoeck & Ruprecht, 2010), 67. Den Boer made this comment after surveying James Arminius' "Orations."

God the Son."[31] W. Stephen Gunter's words are also worth noting, because whereas Graafland was not sympathetic to Arminius, and Den Boer presents his material objectively, Gunter is an Arminian sympathizer. He writes:

> In Arminius' Evangelical Theology, even when he uses words like election and predestination, we read him wrongly if we think he is referring to those topics discretely. He is constantly weaving a theological coat of many colors and threads. He is writing theology in which twofold love, covenant, decree, election, predestination, divine will, and multi-dimensional freedom come together in such a way that if any single one of them should be isolated from the other, we would no longer be talking about the gospel. All of these together…narrate the sum of the gospel.[32]

Arminius failed to make important distinctions in his theological terms and failed to define his terms carefully. This served his theological purpose: by making covenant identical to election, Arminius removed God's final decree of election (God's last word regarding the everlasting salvation of a particular individual) from eternity and placed it into time. Because it was a work of God in time, it could be—and it was—conditioned on the person's own activity.

The second characteristic of the Arminian view of the covenant is that it is conditional. Regarding this and the next point regarding the Remonstrant view of covenant, ample quotes from Arminius and his followers can be made. In rejecting the idea that faith,

---

31 Den Boer, *God's Twofold Love*, 149. Den Boer made this comment after surveying Arminius' response to William Perkin's treatise regarding predestination and grace.
32 W. Stephen Gunter, *Arminius and His Declaration of Sentiments: An Annotated Translation with Introduction and Theological Commentary* (Waco, TX: Baylor University Press, 2012), 179.

incomplete obedience, the right use of the light of nature, piety, humility, meekness, and being fit for eternal life are conditions of election,[33] and in opposing the notion that the perseverance of true believers is a condition of the new covenant,[34] the Canons refers specifically to the writings of the Remonstrants.

The Remonstrants had informed the Synod of Dordt that they viewed the covenant as conditional. The synod had asked them to submit their opinions regarding the five controverted points of doctrine. On December 13, 1618 (session 31), the Remonstrants presented their opinion regarding divine predestination, in which they wrote, "The election of particular persons is decisive, out of consideration of faith in Jesus Christ and of perseverance; not, however, apart from a consideration of faith and perseverance in the true faith as a condition prerequisite for electing."[35] Four days later (session 34) they presented their opinions regarding the extent of Christ's death, in which they said, "Though Christ has merited reconciliation with God and the remission of sins for all men and for every man, yet no one, according to the pact of the new and gracious covenant, becomes a true partaker of the benefits obtained by the death of Christ in any other way than by faith; nor are sins forgiven to sinning men before they actually and truly believe in Christ."[36]

In speaking of conditions, the Remonstrants were not merely speaking of faith as the necessary instrument by which the blessings of salvation are bestowed on the elect, and by which the elect experience them; rather, the Remonstrants were speaking of a decisive

---

[33] Canons of Dordt 1, error and rejection 3–4, in *Confessions and Church Order*, 160.
[34] Canons of Dordt 5, error and rejection 1, in *Confessions and Church Order*, 176.
[35] The quotation is from the translation of the "Opinions of the Remonstrants" in Hoeksema, *Voice of Our Fathers*, 629. The Dutch version can be found in *Acta of Handelingen*, 120.
[36] Hoeksema, *Voice of Our Fathers*, 630; *Acta of Handelingen*, 130.

act that must arise out of the human will. God has done his part to begin the work of salvation, but until humans perform their part, they are not saved. Because the Remonstrants confused election, covenant, and divine love, this conditionality applied to every aspect of the Remonstrant theology of salvation.

What, then, of the death of Christ, if salvation is conditional? What did Christ do in dying on the cross?

The third characteristic of the Arminian view of the covenant is that Christ's death did not confirm the new covenant, as the orthodox taught and the Canons of Dordt stated.[37] That Christ's death confirmed the new covenant accords with an unconditional covenantal view. That Christ's death satisfied God's justice completely, provided the foundation of the covenant, and assured God's people that the blessings of the covenant would be theirs accords with an unconditional covenant. One who teaches a conditional covenant must necessarily explain Christ's death differently.

The position of the Remonstrants was that, rather than confirming the new covenant, Christ's death gave God the right to establish yet another covenant with humans. In their "Opinions" the Remonstrants said, "Christ has, by the merit of his death, so reconciled God the Father to the whole human race that the Father, on account of that merit, without giving up his righteousness and truth, has been able and has willed to make and confirm a new covenant of grace with sinners and men liable to damnation."[38] In keeping with this, our Dordt fathers rejected the teachings of the Remonstrants that Christ's death did nothing more than "acquire for the Father the mere right to establish with man such a covenant as he might please, whether of grace or of works"[39] and that in dying Christ

---

37 Canons of Dordt 2.8, in *Confessions and Church Order*, 163–64.
38 Hoeksema, *Voice of Our Fathers*, 105; *Acta of Handelingen*, 130.
39 Canons of Dordt 2, error and rejection 2, in *Confessions and Church Order*, 164.

merited for the Father only the authority or the perfect will to deal again with man, and to prescribe new conditions as he might desire, obedience to which, however, depended on the free will of man, so that it therefore might have come to pass that either none or all should fulfill these conditions.[40]

The Remonstrants and the orthodox Reformed alike referred to God's covenant with humans after the fall of Adam as a "covenant of grace" and a "new covenant," in distinction from that before the fall. However, the Remonstrants viewed the covenant of grace in the Old Testament as an essentially different covenant of grace than that which is established in the New Testament. According to them, in the Old Testament covenant of grace God required perfect obedience. In the New Testament covenant of grace God requires imperfect obedience and faith. Christ's death served the purpose of providing a just reason for God to nullify the covenant of grace in the Old Testament and make a second new covenant of grace in the New Testament—a second new covenant of grace that would actually be a covenant of works, requiring humans to believe and attempt—do their best—obedience.[41]

These were the Remonstrant teachings regarding the covenant that led our fathers at Dordt to speak of the covenant as they did. It ought to be clear to all that the Remonstrant view of covenant affected their view of grace and salvation. Because the Remonstrants had the view of covenant that they did, they had the view of election and salvation that they did. The fathers at Dordt could not ignore this aspect of the teaching of the Remonstrants; they had to respond to it.

---

40 Canons of Dordt 2, error and rejection 3, in *Confessions and Church Order*, 165.
41 See Hoeksema's commentary on Canons 2, error and rejection 2–3, in *Voice of Our Fathers*, 221–29, for a more detailed commentary regarding this.

Only eight times in six articles does the word *covenant* appear in the Canons, and only twice in the positive section of the Canons. However, the importance and significance of these references in the Canons cannot be overstated. By using this term, the Reformed fathers were insisting that Christ, as the mediator and head of the covenant, confirmed the covenant of grace, thereby demonstrating that it is unconditional.

Significance of the Canons' Covenantal Doctrine

The Canons' doctrine of the covenant is significant, first, because it demonstrates that a right understanding of sovereign grace and a right understanding of the covenant of grace must go together. To err in either one of these two areas will result in error in the other. This is true because both covenant and election are rooted in grace.

The Arminian understanding of the covenant of grace demonstrates that one's understanding of covenant and one's understanding of the doctrines of grace are inextricably intertwined. To use the words of one scholar, Arminius "employs and develops the covenant concept in a manner that is amenable to his more synergistic soteriology."[42] Even Arminius' view of the relationship between the Old and New Testaments, which view this chapter does not develop at length, is put in the service of his conditional theology. Arminius finds more dissimilarity than unity between the two,[43] paving the way for speaking of human activity as a condition in the covenant.

The Canons' presentation of the doctrine of the covenant, by contrast, undergirds the Canons' presentation of the doctrines of grace. A right understanding of the covenant of grace goes hand-in-hand with, and leads to, a right understanding of election, Christ's death, irresistible grace, and the preservation of the saints.

---

42 Blacketer, "Arminius' Concept of Covenant," 194.
43 Blacketer, "Arminius' Concept of Covenant," 212–20.

From all this, it ought to be clear that the Remonstrants, and Arminian theology in general, do not present an orthodox covenantal doctrine. To classify Arminius as a covenantal theologian on the ground that he worked the doctrine of the covenant into his theology, and even structured his theology around the doctrine of the covenant, is misleading. That he spoke of the covenant is not the point; what he said about the covenant is the point. Arminius also spoke of predestination, but he was not a friend of sovereign predestination. Likewise, he referred to the doctrine of the covenant—but understood it wrongly.

In light of the Arminian controversy and the decisions of the Synod of Dordt, Reformed believers must be wary of any presentation of the covenant of grace in which the covenant is viewed as conditional. The covenantal view of the Liberated, which view the PRCA rejected in adopting the Declaration of Principles in 1951, is a conditional covenantal view. This is also true of the covenantal view of those promoting the federal vision. The covenant of the federal vision is a conditional covenantal view at every stage and ultimately dependent on man's fulfillment of the conditions of the covenant. It is accurate to say that the Synod of Dordt condemned the conditional covenantal view.

Second, the Canons' doctrine of the covenant is significant because it sets forth a distinct view of the covenant as the official, creedal position of Reformed churches. Granting that the doctrine of the covenant has been developed further since Dordt, and that more could be said about the covenant than Dordt said, no true development may go contrary to what Dordt said. Dordt said the covenant is unconditional and is governed by election. Reformed churches are not free to think otherwise. David Engelsma does not overstate the matter when he writes:

> Reformed officebearers and Reformed churches, therefore, are not at liberty, and never have been at liberty, to teach a

doctrine of the covenant that liberates the covenant from election.

A denomination of Reformed churches that confesses that election governs the covenant is not outside the mainstream of the Dutch Reformed tradition. On the contrary, it is the contemporary representative of the tradition—the *confessional* tradition.[44]

Engelsma applies the truth of the unconditionality of the covenant to three controversies. First, he applies Dordt's unconditional covenantal view to the controversy between the Protestant Reformed Churches in America and the Liberated Churches in the Netherlands in the 1940s; second, to the schism in the PRCA in the 1950s; and third, to the federal vision theology that has more recently arisen.[45] Engelsma's argument is simply that the Canons of Dordt speaks to the issue of the unconditionality of the covenant. All who advocate a conditional covenant are in conflict with the Canons of Dordt. Indeed, they are! For Reformed churches, there may be no question! Those who desire to teach a conditional covenant must be honest and admit that they have departed from the position of the Canons.

This leads us to the third point of significance of the Canons' doctrine of the covenant: a study of the Canons' use of the doctrine of the covenant makes clear that the PRCA, in adopting the Declaration of Principles in 1951, added nothing to the doctrine of the covenant that the Canons did not make clear.[46] Anyone who reads the Declaration will observe that it is little more than a series of quotations from the Belgic Confession, Heidelberg Catechism, and

---

44 Engelsma, *Covenant and Election*, 72.
45 Engelsma, *Covenant and Election*, 15–31.
46 For a more in-depth study of the history and issues involved in the adoption of the Declaration of Principles, see David J. Engelsma, *Battle for Sovereign Grace in the Covenant: The Declaration of Principles* (Jenison, MI: Reformed Free Publishing Association, 2013).

Canons of Dordt, with some explanatory statements. The Declaration is not extra-confessional but is confessionally based. Several times the Declaration makes statements regarding the doctrine of the covenant, but always its statements accord with the doctrine set forth in the Canons.

This can be demonstrated by noting the various instances in which the Declaration refers to the covenant. First, after quoting Canons 2.8, the Declaration makes three brief comments.

This article very clearly teaches:

1. That all the covenant blessings are for the elect alone.
2. That God's promise is unconditionally for them only: for God cannot promise what was not objectively merited by Christ.
3. That the promise of God bestows the objective right of salvation not upon all the children that are born under the historical dispensation of the covenant, that is, not upon all that are baptized, but only upon the spiritual seed.[47]

Second, the Declaration later refers to Canons head one, article 10, and head one, errors and rejections 2, 3, and 5, to show that "the election of God, and consequently the efficacy of the death of Christ and the promise of the gospel, is not conditional."[48] Later the Declaration of Principles repudiates the teaching "that the promise of the covenant is conditional and for all that are baptized."[49]

Why refer to these statements in the Declaration of Principles after surveying the Canons' use of the doctrine of election? Simply to show that the statements of the Declaration are based on the doctrine of the covenant that the Canons make explicit.

---

47 *Confessions and Church Order*, 418.
48 *Confessions and Church Order*, 421.
49 *Confessions and Church Order*, 424.

In only six of its ninety-three articles does the Canons use the word *covenant* (*foedus*), and it uses the word only eight times. However, the doctrine of the covenant is no mere afterthought of the Canons, and its references to the doctrine are not casual. The Canons gives evidence of an orthodox Reformed and biblical understanding of the doctrine of the covenant of grace and makes use of that doctrine both to undergird its presentation of the doctrines of sovereign grace and to oppose a wrong Remonstrant system of theology. May members of God's covenant everywhere, praising him for his sovereign grace, hold fast to the covenant view expressed in the Canons.

Chapter 6

The Polity of Dordt: Om Goede Orde in de Gemeente Christi te Onderhouden (To Maintain Good Order in the Church of Christ)

William A. Langerak

Introduction

This chapter is devoted to a study of the church order or polity of the Synod of Dordt. Any anniversary commemorating the venerable synod that produced the Canons of Dordt that does not also acknowledge the Church Order it produced would do grave injustice to the work of that synod. And it would only add to the relative ignorance about Dordt's polity in comparison to Dordt's theology. Mention Dordt to any Reformed Christian who takes their faith seriously and they immediately think of the synod, then the Canons, and rightly so. Far less often are they likely to think also of the Church Order of Dordt, which ought not to be so. It is my hope that this chapter will not only do justice to this aspect of the work of the synod, but foster greater interest and appreciation for this heritage of the Lord so that at least when the Synod of Dordt is next mentioned, more church members will think also of its church polity.

When we refer to polity, we mean the form or process by which an organization is governed. It is related to the English words *politics*, *political*, *policy*, and *police*, which are all derived from two Greek words, *polites*, which means citizen, and *polis*, which means city. We could say church polity is simply the policy by which the *polis*, or city of God, the church, is policed. More often when referring to church polity, we mean specifically the church order that contains the policies by which the church is governed.

Background to the Church Order of Dordt

Good church polity is a blessing from God. And the polity of Dordt is not just good; it is magnificent. For it is the beautiful, mature expression of Protestant church polity as it developed out of the Reformation. As such, I would argue that it deserves at least an equal (if not a greater) place of respect with the Canons for its use in maintaining and promoting the Reformed faith—both in doctrine and practice. For the church is "the pillar and ground of the truth" (1 Tim. 3:15). Without good polity, the foundation would crumble and the pillars collapse, and with it the truth. The Belgic Confession makes this inter-dependence of the truth, the church, and good church polity a matter of faith when it states: "We believe that this true church must be governed by that spiritual policy…that by these means the true religion may be preserved and the true doctrine everywhere propagated."[1] It is also exemplified by the calling of the great synod itself. The truth was at stake. It was good church polity

---

1 De Ridder, *Ecclesiastical Manual*, 161. For a more accurate translation of some of this same material, see *The Church Orders of the Sixteenth Century Reformed Churches of the Netherlands Together with Their Social, Political, and Ecclesiastical Context*, trans. Richard R. De Ridder with the assistance of Peter H. Jonker and Rev. Leonard Verduin (Grand Rapids, MI: Calvin Theological Seminary, 1987), 546–57. This later work is a translation of material in C. Hoijer, *Oude Kerkordeningen der Nederlandsche Gemeente (1563–1638)* (Zalt-Bommel: Joh. Noman en Zoon, nd.)

that explained the necessity and desire to have something called a synod to deal with the matter, that then governed how the synod conducted its business, and therefore contributed to the outcome, the preservation of the truth. And, we might add, it was problematic polity that contributed to the inability to call that synod earlier.

This opinion about church polity in general, and the polity of Dordt in particular, is not just my own opinion. It is that of the synod itself. For when the synod refers to the Church Order, it uses the very same word for it as the doctrinal confession it had just produced, the Canons (session 156).[2] Then, the Church Order itself opens with these words: "*Om goede orde in de Gemeente Christi te onderhouden*," i.e., "to maintain good order in the Church of Christ"; and then adds, "It is necessary to have in it offices, assemblies, supervision of doctrine, sacraments and ceremonies, and Christian discipline, concerning [which matters the following articles] shall appropriately deal with."[3] This exact statement appears in every edition of the Church Order after 1581, and it is based on the opening line of the first recognized form of Dutch Reformed church polity, the 1568 Articles of Wesel, which states: "All things must be done decently and in order so that unanimous agreement may be established and maintained *not only in doctrine but also in the polity* [of the church]…and for the benefit of the church."[4]

The great synod consciously labored for the benefit of the church. The final day of synod, Balthasar Lydius preached that their efforts were "for the best interests of the churches."[5] After him, the president of the commissioners, Hugo Muijsius, said that it was "to

---

[2] The original Dutch is "*De (Canones) Artikelen van de Kerkenordening zijn… deze (Canones) Artikelen te versterken.*" See *Acta of Handelingen*, 935. In his translation, De Ridder omits the parenthetical *Canones* of the original (*Ecclesiastical Manual*, 156).

[3] De Ridder, *Ecclesiastical Manual*, 225.

[4] De Ridder, *Ecclesiastical Manual*, 20 (emphasis added).

[5] De Ridder, *Ecclesiastical Manual*, 201.

maintain and promote the Reformed religion together with the edification of the churches."[6] And although the delegates would have agreed that the Canons were their primary focus, they considered the polity of the synod equally important for the churches. One proof of this attitude is that, after adopting the Church Order, the synod delivered an overture to the government by a delegation of a professor, Polijander, and officers, Bogerman (president), Faukelius (assessor), and Hommius (clerk). It states: "The National Synod, in the fear of the Lord, has given attention to both *the doctrine and order* of these churches…[and] requests that your High Majesty…establish *them* with your…approval…and by your…authority to cause *them* to be observed *for the rest, peace, and edification of the churches everywhere in these lands*."[7] Then, after speaking about the doctrine of Dordt, it adds: "be pleased [also] to approve and to order that *the church order*, as reviewed in this synod and expanded in some points for greater edification and peace, should be uniformly maintained everywhere in the churches of these lands as much as possible."[8]

The process of adopting the Church Order of Dordt began formally during the 155th session of the synod, on Monday, May 13. Only Dutch delegates were present, the foreign delegates having returned home since the doctrinal matters for which they had been summoned were completed. The main matters left on the agenda were church political. And the first order of business was to receive a report from the political commissioners that they "agreed that the church order regulations…should be received and examined" by the synod.[9]

That same morning another significant event occurred nearby. As the church order was placed on the floor of synod at the *Kloveniersdoelen* in Dordt, thirty miles away at the *Binnenhof* in The

---

6   De Ridder, *Ecclesiastical Manual*, 202.
7   De Ridder, *Ecclesiastical Manual*, 196 (emphasis added).
8   De Ridder, *Ecclesiastical Manual*, 196–97 (emphasis added).
9   De Ridder, *Ecclesiastical Manual*, 176.

Hague, Johan Oldenbarnevelt was beheaded for treason. One can only imagine the discussions during coffee break at synod that day. The story is worth telling because it illustrates the partisan political milieu and intertwined church-state relations at the time the synod was called. Besides, church polity, some would say, is boring. And since this chapter is about church polity, a good story thrown in might liven it up a bit.

Oldenbarnevelt was arrested in August 1618, three months before the synod first convened. He was arrested under order of Prince Maurice, son of William the Silent, of the House of Orange. Twenty years Maurice's senior, Oldenbarnevelt was a highly regarded lawyer, statesman, and after William the Silent, is largely considered the second founding father of the Republic of the Netherlands. This was due to his assistance in helping the besieged cities of Haarlem and Leiden during the time of Spanish oppression, and because he was an architect of the Union of Utrecht that federated the seven provinces of the Lowlands into a republic.

The careers of Maurice and Oldenbarnevelt first crossed in 1586, two years after William was assassinated. Oldenbarnevelt recommended that eighteen-year-old Maurice be appointed to his father's post as *statholder*. A *statholder* was one who was charged with maintaining provincial peace and order, primarily as head of the national armed forces. Oldenbarnevelt was appointed *landsadvocaat* of Holland, basically prime minister, secretary to the nobility, and chief legal counsel of the richest and most influential of the provinces. By virtue of their positions and ambitions there were bound to be differences. Maurice had a national perspective in defending the provinces against the Spanish and maintaining unity in the federation. He was a brilliant military man, credited with being the first European general to incorporate coordinated musket volley fire into the infantry and with whipping the Dutch army into a formidable fighting force against the Spanish. Oldenbarnevelt was a politician with a provincial perspective and interested in increasing the wealth and political clout of Holland within the union. He was credited with negotiating an alliance with England and France against Spain in 1596, and in 1602 with brokering the formation of the Dutch East India Company, which would bring "an embarrassment of riches" to the provinces, especially Holland.[10]

Their first conflict occurred in 1600 when Oldenbarnevelt convinced the States General to order Maurice to lead a military expedition by land and sea into Flanders to stop pirates based in Dunkirk from disrupting Holland's lucrative trade. Maurice considered the plan of little military value and dangerous because it left the Dutch republic vulnerable to counterattack. Then, throughout the campaign, Oldenbarnevelt and the States General meddled in military strategy, which almost resulted in a catastrophic loss of Dutch forces at the battle of Nieuwpoort.

In 1609 the rift widened when Oldenbarnevelt negotiated the Twelve Years Truce with Spain against the opposition of Maurice, who thought it would only allow the Spanish time to regroup and return with a vengeance. The great irony is that, although the truce originally strengthened the political hand of Oldenbarnevelt and weakened Maurice's, it ultimately led to a reversal of their political fortunes. This is largely because the truce gave the provinces motive and opportunity with Maurice's support to pass, albeit by a slim margin, the resolution calling for the national synod that would eviscerate the Arminian cause with which Oldenbarnevelt had cast his lot to become their "big fish" politically.[11]

---

10 Simon Schama, *The Embarrassment of Riches: An Interpretation of Dutch Culture in the Golden Age* (Berkeley, CA: The Regents of the University of California, 1988), 289.

11 Joke Spaans, "Imagining the Synod of Dordt and the Arminian Controversy," in Goudriaan, *Revisiting the Synod of Dordt*, 346.

During the Arminian controversy Oldenbarnevelt actively helped the Remonstrant cause, especially by stymying calls for a national synod unless revision of the Belgic Confession or loose subscription to it were also on the agenda. Maurice was noncommittal until July 1617. Then he openly sided with the Calvinists and did so in a way that humiliated his political rival—with his entourage Maurice walked by Oldenbarnevelt's house to worship next door at the *Kloosterkerk*, which recently had been seized back by Calvinists from Remonstrant squatters against the express order of Oldenbarnevelt. Oldenbarnevelt responded by convincing Holland and West Friesland to adopt the Sharp Resolution, which gave them sovereign right to form their own militias. Maurice viewed this as a thinly disguised declaration of civil war and responded by arresting Oldenbarnevelt, along with officials of three prominent cities, Hugo Grotius (Rotterdam), Rombout Hogerbeets (Leiden), and Gilles van Ledenberg (Utrecht).

Grotius and Hoogerbeets were sentenced to life in prison. Grotius would eventually be smuggled out in a chest of books. Hoogerbeets would be released after the death of Maurice. Oldenbarnevelt, at seventy-one years old, was sentenced to death. The following day, he knelt down in the public square of The Hague, and after his final words, "*Maak het kort,*" that is, "Make it short," was beheaded. Diodati, a Genevan delegate to the Synod of Dordt, is said to have quipped that he had his head shot off by the Canons.[12] Ledenberg committed suicide but was sentenced posthumously to death. And on Wednesday, two days after the execution of Oldenbarnevelt, and the same day that synod made its first revisions to the Church Order, his body was hung in a lead coffin from a gibbet, where it remained

---

12 Nicolas Fornerod, "The Canons of the Synod Had Shot Off the Advocates Head: A Reappraisal of the Genevan Delegation at the Synod of Dordt," in Goudriaan, *Revisiting the Synod of Dordt*, 185.

until after synod.[13] Likely that was another interesting day at synod during coffee break.

Development of the Church Order of Dordt

It is relatively easy to tell the immediate history of the Dordt Church Order because the synod did not formulate a new order but adopted an existing one, to which it made only fourteen changes. On Monday morning, May 13, 1619, the political commissioners reported their desire that "the church order adopted by the last-held National Synod be received and examined."[14] This was the Church Order adopted thirty-three years earlier by the Synod of The Hague (1586). That Church Order was read. After lunch, synod decided: "The articles (canons) of the church order are in substance approved by all the delegated ministers and elders from every province."[15] And that is all. Although synod would go on during the course of the week to add seven new articles and revise seven others, in its main substance, the Church Order of The Hague is now the Church Order of Dordt.

Because Dutch church polity was forged during intense religious persecution, a war for national independence, and constitutional creation of a new republic, with all the political intrigue, secrecy, hardship, chaos, and mass migration that such things entail, the deeper historical origins of the Church Order are more complicated, and mysteries still remain. As noted, the Church Order of Dordt (1619) is basically that of The Hague (1586), which in turn is derived from church orders revised and adopted by two national synods, Middelburg (1581) and Dordt (1578), and a provincial synod, also in Dordt (1574), which in turn has its roots in the Articles of Wesel (1568) and Emden (1571)—generally regarded as the official

---

13 Joke Spaans, "Imagining the Synod of Dordt and the Arminian Controversy," in Goudriaan, *Revisiting the Synod of Dordt,* 340.
14 De Ridder, *Ecclesiastical Manual,* 176.
15 De Ridder, *Ecclesiastical Manual,* 176. See also footnote 2 of this chapter.

organization of the Dutch Reformed churches. Historians have also traced Dutch church polity back to John Calvin's Ecclesiastical Ordinances of 1541, the church orders of the French Reformed churches (1559), the Scots (1560), and Hungarians (1567), with influences from the Dutch refugee churches in England and Germany and men such as Valerand Poullain, John a'Lasco, Peter Datheen, and Marten Macron.[16]

Influences on the Development of the Church Order of Dordt

Historians sometimes overlook the obvious, and in my opinion, this has been done with regard to the development of the Church Order in two respects: the influence of the Belgic Confession, and the Church Order's origins in gravamina considered at the Synod of Dordt. We will consider the latter of these first.

The origin and development of the Church Order in gravamina is significant and contributed greatly to its attractive organic and practical character. It also is an example of a Reformed church political principle—that assemblies consider only concrete cases, not abstractions, even when formulating church polity. Basically a gravamen (singular form of gravamina) is a grievance, complaint, or plea directed to a synod by an individual or minor assembly about the confessions, liturgical forms or church order.[17] In the earliest days,

---

16 In 1551 a'Lasco wrote a rough church order in Latin for use in the London refugee churches. In 1554 Macron published his *De Christlicke ordinancien*, which is considered a modified form of a'Lasco's work, and because it was in Dutch it would become more widely used in these churches. In 1555, a'Lasco published in Frankfort, again in Latin, a more extensive church order known as *Forma ac Ratio*. A French edition appeared in 1556. Macron and a'Lasco both acknowledge they relied upon and collaborated with each other. See Brian D. Spinks, *From the Lord and the Best Reformed Churches: A Study of the Eucharistic Liturgy in the English Puritan and Separatist Traditions, 1550–1633* (Eugene, OR: Wipf & Stock Publishers, 2004), 100–102.

17 *Gravamen* and *gravamina* are recognized legal terms in civil courts. Official pronunciation is with a schwa in the first syllable, then a long "a" sound and accent on the second syllable. In ecclesiastical circles, especially those of Dutch

they also came as concerns or questions about practical problems for synod to address. Few gravamen are written today, but hundreds were written in the decades prior to Dordt, and synodical rulings on them frequently became articles in the church order or impetus for revision. Such was also the case at Dordt. In fact, on Monday, May 13, right after receiving the agreement of the political commissioners that the Church Order (of 1586) should be received and examined, but before getting into the business of doing so, synod considered a request from the South Holland delegates to treat certain gravamina first. Bogerman assured them that these gravamina would be considered in conjunction with the Church Order. In this, Bogerman was not being novel, for this was how previous synods had handled gravamina. And so also at Dordt, almost every subsequent addition and revision to the Church Order would originate in a gravamen.

On Tuesday, May 14, 1619, the day after the Church Order was adopted in principle, six gravamina were presented. On Wednesday morning, synod considered committee advice on them. The first gravamen concerned the previously numbered article 40, which allowed classis to authorize one minister to supervise the doctrine and life of the other ministers and the condition of the churches in the classis. In response to that gravamen, synod revised the article to require classis to appoint "at least two of the oldest, most experienced, and most prudent [ministers], who shall visit all the churches…annually, and diligently take note whether the pastors, elders, and schoolmasters faithfully perform their duties, adhere to soundness of doctrine, maintain in all its parts the accepted Church Order, etc."[18] This would become article 44 of the Church Order of Dordt.

The second gravamen concerned the question of how provincial synods were to execute decisions between the convening of synods.

---

origins, the common pronunciation is with a short "a" sound in both first and second syllables (accent also on the second syllable).

[18] De Ridder, *Ecclesiastical Manual*, 178.

The problem is that a synod is not a permanent body and ceases to exist when it adjourns. In response, Dordt required each synod to appoint official delegates "to carry out all that the synod has decided with reference to both the government and the respective classis resorting under it, etc."[19] This would be a new article 49 of the Church Order of Dordt.

The third gravamen concerned correspondence between particular provincial synods. Synod's response became the new article 48.

The fourth gravamen concerned admission into the ministry of *ongeletterden* ("illiterates," i.e., those who had not received a higher education).[20] In response, synod added article 8, which prescribes that "[n]o schoolmaster, artisans, or others who have not [followed the regular course of studies] shall be admitted to the ministry, unless people are assured of their exceptional gifts, godliness, humility, modesty, common sense, and discretion, together with the gift of public speaking."[21]

The fifth gravamen concerned whether or not all ministers from a church with more than one minister could vote, if they attended the classis meeting. The problem is that this could have given some churches disproportionate representation at classis. In response, synod added article 42, which states that "they shall be allowed to attend the classis together and have the right to vote, except in matters which concern their persons or churches in particular."[22] In 1914, this article would be revised to grant such ministers only advisory vote and then extended this right to all non-delegated ministers who attended the meetings of classis.

Treatment of the sixth gravamen did not result in any change

---

19 De Ridder, *Ecclesiastical Manual*, 179.
20 *The Ecclesiastical Manual* incorrectly translates *ongeletterden* as "insane." See page 178 in *Ecclesiastical Manual*.
21 De Ridder, *Ecclesiastical Manual*, 179.
22 De Ridder, *Ecclesiastical Manual*, 179.

to the Church Order, but it deserves mention because it led to the adoption of the Formula of Subscription. Such a formula was already implied by articles 53 and 54, which required ministers, professors, and schoolmasters to "subscribe to…the Confession of Faith."[23] Subscribing to a creed was not new but goes back to the Council of Nicaea (325). In the Dutch churches, the articles of Wesel (1568) required a minister declare his "complete agreement" to the French Confession, Belgic Confession, and Heidelberg Catechism; the church orders of Emden (1571) and Dordt (1574) required them to "subscribe," i.e., to sign the confessions directly.[24] But there was no standard formula of subscription or universal use of one until Dordt (1618–19). In it the synod would articulate precisely what it believed the Confession, Catechism, and the new Canons to be: "We heartily believe and are persuaded that all the articles and points of doctrine…do fully agree with the Word of God."[25] Over against the opinion of the by-now-deceased Oldenbarnevelt and soon-to-be-deposed Remonstrants, no loose subscription would be tolerated in the Dutch Reformed churches.[26]

Later Wednesday morning, six more gravamina were presented for future consideration. In the meantime, a debate ensued on a proposal prescribing the call of new ministers according to article 4.

---

[23] Synod also considered whether or not elders should be required to subscribe, but decided to leave it to the discretion of each classis.

[24] De Ridder, *Ecclesiastical Manual*, 24, 43, 63. Credit to Dr. Karlo Janssen for this point of research on Classis Walcheren.

[25] De Ridder, *Ecclesiastical Manual*, 188.

[26] Noteworthy is also this decision pertaining to the Formula: "The church shall be admonished that: when the pastors by subscription to the above-mentioned form promise to be ready to explain more fully their opinion concerning points of the faith at the request of the brethren, such is not to be understood as though they are thereto obligated [to do so] at everyone's pleasure, but only when they shall have given just reason for suspicion, concerning which the judgment remains with the ecclesiastical assembly." De Ridder, *Ecclesiastical Manual*, 189.

There was no consensus. The hang-up was whether or not provinces would still be free to use existing regulations. The next morning, Bogerman presented his own draft, which, after an amendment, was adopted as a revision of article 4. Among its changes was that synod added that "election of ministers may not take place without good correspondence with the Christian authorities in their respective places."[27] Synod also revised article 5 by adopting similar language about "approval by the magistrate" with respect to the calling of ministers already in the ministry.[28]

Thursday morning ended when synod, without any indication about where it originated, read a proposal concerning "friendly correspondence between the Christian magistrates and the ministers."[29] Synod adopted this proposal and inserted it into the Church Order at the end of the section on offices. It would become article 28. Although lengthy, it deserves quotation because it again illustrates the view of church-state relations at the time:

> Since it is the duty of the Christian authorities to promote the worship services in every way, to recommend them to their subjects by their example, and to extend a helping hand to ministers, elders and deacons in all existing need and to protect them by their good order, all ministers, elders, and deacons are duty bound diligently and sincerely to impress upon the whole congregation the obedience, love, and honor which they owe the magistrates. All who hold office in the church shall set a good example to the congregation in this, and by proper respect and correspondence seek to stir up and preserve the favor of the Authorities to the churches, to the end that each one on both sides, doing what he can in the fear

---

27 De Ridder, *Ecclesiastical Manual*, 180.
28 De Ridder, *Ecclesiastical Manual*, 180–81.
29 De Ridder, *Ecclesiastical Manual*, 182.

of the Lord, may avoid all suspicion and distrust and maintain proper unity for the welfare of the churches (session 161).[30]

Thursday afternoon, the six gravamina presented the day before were treated. Only the first resulted in a change to the Church Order. But it was lengthy and concerned observance of special holidays, use of hymns, and administration of baptism to adults and children. Treatment of it resulted in the addition of one article and revision of three other articles. Synod revised article 58, which required use of the baptism form for all baptisms, adult and infant. Synod added article 59, which required adults being baptized to promise to partake of the Lord's supper. Synod made a major revision to article 69. Before it had stipulated singing only the 150 Psalms, but as revised it allowed singing of the ten commandments, Lord's prayer, Apostles' Creed, and songs of Mary, Zacharias, and Simeon; and left to the judgment of each church whether or not to sing the hymn "O God, Who Art Our Father." All other hymns were to be kept out or discontinued. Lastly, synod made a minor revision to article 67 on special services.

The revision of article 67 by the Synod of Dordt was minor. A common misconception is that the synod made a major change to the article by requiring for the first time worship services on certain weekday holidays. But this is not the case. That change had already happened forty years earlier in 1578. Prior to that, the accepted position was that of the Provincial Synod of Dordt (1574), in article 53 of its Church Order.

> As to church holidays aside from the Sunday, it is decided that people shall be content with the Sunday only. The normal material about Christ's birth shall be dealt with in the church on the Sunday before Christmas, and the people

---

30 De Ridder, *Ecclesiastical Manual*, 182.

shall be exhorted not to consider Christmas as a holiday. In case Christmas falls on a Sunday, then one shall deal with the same material. It is also allowed to teach about the resurrection of Christ and the sending of the Holy Spirit on Easter and Pentecost. This is left to the freedom of the ministers.[31]

Four years later, the first national Synod of Dordt (1578) made a major change to this position in its article 23:

> It would be desirable that freedom to work six days as allowed by God be maintained by the church and only Sunday be kept holy. Nevertheless, since some other festive days are observed by authority of the government, such as Christmas with the day following, the second Easter day and the second Pentecost day and in some places New Year's Day and Ascension Day, the ministers shall show diligence to have sermons in which they shall especially teach the congregation concerning the birth and resurrection of Christ, the sending of the Holy Spirit and other articles of faith and how to change the unprofitable exercise. The same shall be done by the ministers in the cities where more holidays are observed by authority of the government. Meanwhile all churches shall work to the end that the ordinary use of all holidays except Christmas (since Easter and Pentecost are on Sunday) be abolished as much as possible and as early as possible.[32]

The reason the Synod of Dordt (1618–19) entered into this matter is mainly due to confusion over the wording of article 60, as adopted by the National Synod of The Hague (1586) about church holidays.

---

31 De Ridder, *Ecclesiastical Manual*, 69.
32 De Ridder, *Ecclesiastical Manual*, 95.

> The congregations shall observe in addition to Sunday two Christmas days, Easter Monday and two Pentecost days, but in places where more holidays are held by order of the government in commemoration of the benefits of Christ (as the circumcision of Christ and Ascension Day) the ministers shall put forth effort to change by preaching the idleness of the people into sacred and beneficial observance.[33]

Adding to the confusion was that later printed editions of the Church Order changed the article to read "Christmas day, Easter Monday, and two Pentecost days."[34] So the Synod of Dordt (1618–19) made a minor change that clarified the wording, and it would become article 67:

> The congregations shall observe, in addition to Sunday, also Christmas, Easter, and Pentecost, with the following day; and since in most cities and Provinces of the Netherlands, besides these there are also observed the day of Circumcision and Ascension of Christ, the ministers everywhere where this is still custom, shall put forth effort with the authorities that they may conform with the others.[35]

The last change to the Church Order was made the final morning of that week, Friday, May 17. Again in response to a gravamen, synod added article 9, which required that newcomers, priests, monks, and those who leave any sect not be admitted to the ministry except with great care and caution, and only after they have also been well tested for a period of time.

With this last addition, the Church Order of Dordt was

---

33 De Ridder, *Ecclesiastical Manual*, 151.
34 De Ridder, *Ecclesiastical Manual*, 151.
35 De Ridder, *Ecclesiastical Manual*, 172. The day after Pentecost is known as Whit Monday.

complete. Final tally of changes indicates that to the original seventy-nine articles of the Church Order of The Hague were added seven more articles: 8, 9, 28, 42, 48, 49, and 59. Seven articles were revised: 4, 5, 20, 44, 58, 67, and 69. In both cases, these are their new numbers due to the addition of articles to the Church Order.

Influence of the Belgic Confession

As mentioned earlier, another influence on the development of the Church Order that receives comparatively little attention is the Belgic Confession. This is strange because this Confession was written already in 1561, seven years before the Convention of Wesel and ten years before the first Synod at Emden—two assemblies that are usually cited as the first examples of Dutch Reformed church polity. But the Belgic Confession, especially in its articles 30–32, has the most legitimate claim to being the first official expression of Dutch Reformed church polity. If the Church Order's family tree is to be traced through Calvin's *Ecclesiastical Ordinances* (1541), the work of a'Lasco, Datheen, and Macron (1550s), and the church orders of the French (1559) and Scots (1560), it cannot go to Wesel (1568) and Emden (1571) without first running through Guido de Bres and his Confession (1561).

Given its early and honorable place in the Dutch churches, it is inconceivable that the Belgic Confession would not be recognized as basic by any synod formulating, developing, revising, or adopting a church order. And one would especially expect this to be the attitude of the Synod of Dordt since it showed considerable deference to this Confession on a number of occasions.

In its very first session (session 155) after the doctrinal matters were settled, and immediately after reading the Church Order with a view to revising it, the synod decided to compare each of the various editions of the Confession in French, Latin, and Dutch, in order to adopt a standard version in each language.[36]

---

36 De Ridder, *Ecclesiastical Manual*, 176.

The synod also resisted making any major changes to the Belgic Confession when it had ample opportunity to do so. Throughout, while reviewing the proposed versions of it in each language, "ways by which the editions ought to be improved are pointed out,"[37] but few changes were made. One example is the proposal to replace "and so many most holy works which [Christ] has done for us" in article 22 with the phrase "and obedience of Christ."[38] After a spirited debate, Synod declared unanimously: "That the sense expressed in the…Confession shall be completely retained, and that it is in no wise advisable that there be any change in the words…for which excellent reasons are presented by many. Nevertheless, at the request of some it is decided that in the same article there should be added to the words 'for us' for further clarification the words 'and in our place.'"[39]

The synod also showed its respect for the Belgic Confession when, in the newly adopted Formula of Subscription, it referred to the Canons as "the explanation of some points of the aforesaid doctrine,"[40] i.e., of the Belgic Confession. When it overtured the government, it summarized its work as having "thoroughly examined anew according to God's Word," as it had been mandated, "the doctrine…contained and explained in its Confession…[and] by unanimous vote…declared [it] to be found in agreement with the Word of God and with the Confessions of all other Reformed churches" (session 177).[41]

---

37 De Ridder, *Ecclesiastical Manual*, 190.
38 De Ridder, *Ecclesiastical Manual*, 190–91.
39 De Ridder, *Ecclesiastical Manual*, 190–91. The synodical minutes give a rare glimpse into the spirited yet united nature of this particular debate as it occurred over two days. On the first day the minutes conclude: "Since this change was opposed and time had expired, the matter was postponed until another day, and the brethren are admonished to answer in a fraternal spirit" (session 172). The second day begins with the minutes recording that the final decision is passed by unanimous vote (session 173).
40 De Ridder, *Ecclesiastical Manual*, 188.
41 De Ridder, *Ecclesiastical Manual*, 196.

The evidence of the foundational nature of the Belgic Confession for the development of the Church Order is numerous and compelling. And it is found within the Church Order itself. One example is the inclusion throughout the Church Order of the Belgic Confession's view, in article 36, of the established church. This was a principle that the Synod of Dordt even expanded on in its revisions. But it is especially the principles of church polity found in the Confession's articles 30–32 that provide the most significant and abundant contributions to the Church Order.

Article 30 of the Belgic Confession states that the "true Church must be governed by that spiritual policy which our Lord hath taught us in his Word."[42] The policy to which it refers is church polity. The true church is governed by good polity; the false church by evil polity. Good polity is not carnal, civil, or worldly, but spiritual policy—basically the same thing article 30 of the Church Order calls "ecclesiastical matters" and "manners."[43] The Confession, however, does not identify this spiritual policy with the Church Order as such, but rather with the three offices of minister, elder, and deacon—the offices together forming the council of the church—and the specific work assigned to each office by Christ. The stated benefit of this spiritual policy is that "everything will be carried on in the church with good order and decency" with one caveat—provided "faithful men are chosen according to the rule prescribed" in scripture.[44] The Confession then describes the benefit of "good order and decency," that "by these means the true religion may be preserved and the true doctrine everywhere propagated, likewise transgressors punished and restrained by spiritual means; also that the poor and distressed may be relieved and comforted."[45]

---

42 *Confessions and Church Order*, 64.
43 *Confessions and Church Order*, 389.
44 Belgic Confession 30, in *Confessions and Church Order*, 65.
45 Belgic Confession 30, in *Confessions and Church Order*, 65.

Article 30 of the Belgic Confession also establishes the principle of the autonomy of the local congregation as a self-governing church in its own right, apart now from any federation with other Reformed churches in a denomination. It does so when it specifically identifies the "spiritual polity" by which the church is governed with the three offices of minister, elder, and deacon, "who together…form *the council of the church,*" and says that "by these means…everything will be carried on *in the church* with good order and decency."[46] In other words, while teaching that there is one, universal body of Christ called the church, the Belgic Confession also insists that each congregation instituted under the spiritual polity of these three offices is itself a self-governing church regardless of any federative affiliation. Article 31 of the Confession confirms this principle when it states that ministers, elders, and deacons "ought to be chosen to their respective offices by a lawful election *by the church,*" which can in no way refer to a federation or the church universal.[47]

The Synod of Dordt maintained this confessional Reformed principle that the local congregation is a self-governing church and incorporated it into the Church Order in two particular ways. First, the original Dutch of the Church Order (and the Acts of the Synod) consistently uses the plural, *kerken* or churches, to refer to the federation, and singular, *kerk* or church, to refer to the individual congregation.[48] This consistency even holds true with regard to the title of the Church Order. Although the Dutch, as we do in English, commonly call it the *Church* Order, its official title is actually "The *Churches* Order Formulated in the National Synod of the Reformed *Churches*" (*Kerkenordenige Gestelt inde Nationalen*

---

[46] *Confessions and Church Order,* 65 (emphasis added).
[47] *Confessions and Church Order,* 65.
[48] The PRCA reflect this principle in their official title, The Protestant Reformed Churches of America.

Synode der Ghereformeerde Kercken).[49] And in article 86, the Church Order also refers to itself as "the lawful order of the *churches*" (*de wettelijcke Ordeninghe der Kercken*).[50] Second, the Church Order of Dordt maintains this confessional Reformed principle in its requirement in articles 4, 20, and 23 that the election to all three offices be carried out by the local congregation under the judgment and supervision of its council; and in its requirement in articles 64–72 that the responsibility for the discipline of all members, including officebearers, rests in the hands of the local consistory (the exception is that deposition also requires the judgment of a neighboring consistory, and ministerial suspension also requires the judgment of classis).[51]

Article 30 of the Belgic Confession may therefore be rightly considered the basis for the entire Church Order, as the explanation for its spiritual nature and contributing source of its division into four sections: the first of twenty-eight articles "Concerning the Offices," the second of twenty-four articles "Concerning Ecclesiastical Assemblies," the third of eighteen articles "Concerning Doctrine, Sacraments, and Ceremonies," and the fourth of sixteen articles "Concerning Censure and Ecclesiastical Admonitions."

Article 31 of the Belgic Confession further defines and explains certain aspects of this spiritual policy concerning the offices, especially

---

49 Salomon de Roy, *Kercken-ordeninge gestelt inden Nationalen Synode der Gereformeerde Kercken te samen beroepen ende gehouden by laste vande Hoogmo: Heeren Staten Generael van de Vereenighde Nederlanden Binnen Dordrecht inden jare 1619 ende 1619* [Churches-Order formulated in the National Synod of the Reformed Churches called together and held by order of the High and Mighty States General of the United Netherlands, at Dordrecht, in the years 1619 and 1619] (Utrecht: Drucker, 1620), accessed August 23, 2019, www.kerkrecht.nl/node/439.

50 De Roy, *Kerkorde opgesteld*, accessed August 23, 2019, www.kerkrecht.nl/node/525.

51 *Ecclesiastical Manual*, 141, 144–45, 151–53. The PRCA maintain this principle by rejecting the common practice in Reformed denominations whereby classes or synods themselves suspend and depose officebearers, as the CRC did in 1924 to the founding fathers of the PRCA and their consistories.

the minister. First, it expands on the election of officers mentioned in article 30, by adding that they must be chosen "by the church," or congregation, and "with calling upon the name of the Lord, and in that order which the Word of God teacheth."[52] The Church Order explains this election of officebearers in its articles 22 and 24.

Second, article 31 then elaborates on the principle of calling—no man may hold church office unless called by God. It does so when it exhorts "everyone [to] take heed not to intrude himself [into office] by indecent means, but is bound to wait till it shall please God to call him."[53] The Church Order requires the calling of officebearers in article 3; defines lawful calling of ministers in articles 4–5; and establishes further rules, obligations, and limitations of the calling in articles 6–15. The calling of elders and deacons is implied in their election under articles 22 and 24.

Last, the article establishes the principle of equality among the ministers based on their relationship to Christ: "As for ministers of God's Word, they have equally the same power and authority wheresoever they are, as they are all ministers of Christ, the only universal bishop, and the only head of the church."[54] Based on this same ground, the Church Order extends this equality to the other two offices in its article 17: "Equality shall be maintained among the ministers of the Word…which shall also be maintained among the elders and deacons."[55] It is also reasonable to assume this principle underlies article 36 of the Church Order, which requires equality also in jurisdictions: "The classis has the same authority over the consistory that the particular synod has over the classis, and the General Synod over the particular."[56]

---

52 *Confessions and Church Order*, 65.
53 *Confessions and Church Order*, 65.
54 Belgic Confession 31, in *Confessions and Church Order*, 65–66.
55 De Ridder, *Ecclesiastical Manual*, 164.
56 De Ridder, *Ecclesiastical Manual*, 167.

Article 32 of the Belgic Confession elaborates on various principles stated earlier in articles 30 and 31, while also establishing a significant number of new principles.

> In the meantime we believe, though it is useful and beneficial that those who are rulers of the church institute and establish certain ordinances among themselves for maintaining the body of the church, yet they ought studiously to take care that they do not depart from those things which Christ, our only master, hath instituted. And therefore, we reject all human inventions, and all laws which man would introduce into the worship of God, thereby to bind and compel the conscience in any manner whatever. Therefore we admit only of that which tends to nourish and preserve concord and unity, and to keep all men in obedience to God. For this purpose, excommunication or church discipline is requisite, with the several circumstances belonging to it, according to the Word of God.[57]

In only the first main clause, three principles of Reformed church polity are either established or explained further. First, the article establishes the authority of the church to make its own order through elected officials by common consent or majority vote: "It is useful and beneficial that those who are rulers of the church institute and establish certain ordinances among themselves." This principle is incorporated into several articles of the Church Order. Article 31 states that "that which is decided by majority vote shall be considered settled and binding unless it is proved to conflict with the Word of God."[58] Article 33 states that "only those [delegated] to the assemblies shall be entitled to vote."[59] And article 86 says: "These

---

57 *Confessions and Church Order*, 66–67.
58 De Ridder, *Ecclesiastical Ordinances*, 166.
59 De Ridder, *Ecclesiastical Ordinances*, 166.

articles concerning the lawful order of the churches have been so formulated and adopted by common consent...[and] no individual congregation, classis or [provincial] synod shall be permitted to [alter, add to or diminish them]."[60]

Second, the first clause of Belgic Confession article 32 explains further the practical necessity and purpose of church polity mentioned in article 30, that "this true church must be governed by that spiritual policy...[that] by these means everything will be carried on in the church with good order and decency."[61] Although it is "useful and beneficial" that church rulers establish polity "among themselves," the benefit is not for themselves, but more importantly "for maintaining the body of the church." This principle is the basis of the first and last articles of the Church Order. The first article virtually quotes the Belgic Confession: "To maintain good order in the church of Christ [*Om goede orde in de Gemeente Christi te onderhouden*]."[62] And the last article, article 86, uses the principle of article 32 of the Belgic Confession as the ground for changing the Church Order: "These articles concerning lawful order of the churches have been so formulated and adopted by common consent that, if the welfare of the churches demand otherwise, they may and ought to be altered, added to or diminished."[63] Reformed church polity is not the lawlessness of the Anabaptists, nor the unchangeable law of the Medes and Persians, nor hierarchical edicts of Roman Catholic Canon Law or the infallible pronouncements of popes. Much less does it support the notion that change is necessarily apostasy. Rather, for the sake of Christ's body, Reformed church polity confidently and pastorally declares that its own lawful order may and ought to be altered.

---

60 De Ridder, *Ecclesiastical Manual*, 175.
61 *Confessions and Church Order*, 64–65.
62 De Ridder, *Ecclesiastical Manual*, 161.
63 De Ridder, *Ecclesiastical Manual*, 175.

Third, when article 32 of the Belgic Confession speaks of "certain ordinances…for maintaining the body of Christ," it further explains what it means in article 30 of the Belgic Confession by "spiritual policy." This is what the Church Order will call "ecclesiastical matters…and manner."[64] The church does not have the right to make whatever ordinances it pleases, but only "certain" ordinances which are those "for maintaining the body of Christ." Therefore, in its assemblies, the church may not enter into whatever matters it pleases, but only certain matters. Those matters are ecclesiastical matters, not civil, political, or earthly matters. And since such ordinances must pertain to the care of Christ's body, the church may not treat them in the manner of earthly assemblies or institutions, but only in an "ecclesiastical manner" that is in harmony with Christ's own love for his body.

Moving on from the first clause, article 32 of the Belgic Confession next elaborates on the principle alluded to in its article 30, that "this true church must be governed by that spiritual policy which our Lord hath taught us in his Word."[65] The principle is that Christ is the sole sovereign and head of the church: "They [church rulers] ought studiously to take care that they do not depart from those things which Christ, our only master, hath instituted."[66] This principle places certain limits on church polity. The first is *sola scriptura*, for obviously "those things which Christ…instituted" are those things that he has instituted in scripture, or "according to his Word."

The Belgic Confession makes clear that this limit does not require that every article of a church order is explicitly a biblical principle or derived from one. Rather, church rulers have freedom to establish ordinances, as long as they meet two requirements: First, as noted in the first clause, they must be "useful and beneficial…for

---

64 De Ridder, *Ecclesiastical Manual*, 166.
65 *Confessions and Church Order*, 64.
66 *Confessions and Church Order*, 66.

maintaining the body of the church."[67] And second, they "ought studiously to take care that they do not depart from those things which Christ, our only master, hath instituted."[68]

In the Church Order there are many examples of such freedom in minor points of practice. One example is found in article 20, which provides for the support of seminary students out of the public treasury (later, church treasury).[69] Another can be found in article 27, which limits the terms of elders and deacons so that each year a proportionate number of officebearers retire.[70] Yet another is article 85: "In indifferent matters the foreign churches which have different customs from ours shall not be rejected."[71]

The second limitation placed on church polity on account of the headship of Christ is that it may not infringe on the authority and freedom of the individual to worship according to the dictates of conscience. Article 32 of the Belgic Confession puts it this way: "We reject all human inventions and all laws which man would introduce into the worship of God, thereby to bind and compel the conscience in any manner whatsoever."[72]

Notice only four things about this statement: First, it does not reject all church polity drafted by men as human inventions that ought to be rejected, but only that which would bind (prevent) or compel (force) the conscience to do something it regards as sinful. Second, it does not concern all matters of conscience, but only matters of conscience concerning worship. Third, it recognizes that when men make laws, including church rulers, there is an inherent danger (due to the depravity of man) that they infringe upon this right of conscience with regard to worship. Fourth, this inherent

---

67 Belgic Confession 32, in *Confessions and Church Order*, 66.
68 Belgic Confession 32, in *Confessions and Church Order*, 66.
69 De Ridder, *Ecclesiastical Manual*, 164.
70 De Ridder, *Ecclesiastical Manual*, 165.
71 De Ridder, *Ecclesiastical Manual*, 175.
72 *Confessions and Church Order*, 66.

danger implies that good church polity must include safeguards for the individual conscience.

Since this matter of conscience specifically concerns worship, it applies especially to a particular sequence of articles in the Church Order, articles 62–69, many of which would be revised in subsequent editions.[73] Article 62 of the Church Order of Dordt allowed churches to administer the Lord's supper in the manner judged most conducive to edification, but with some caveats. The PRCA edition remains essentially the same. Article 63 of the Church Order of Dordt specified that the Lord's supper must be administered once every two months and allowed for its administration also on Easter, Pentecost, and Christmas. The PRCA edition requires administration of the Lord's supper every two or three months, and removes the provision for its administration on special days. Article 64 of the Church Order of Dordt allowed churches to hold evening prayers if this practice is "deem[ed] to be most edifying."[74] The PRCA edition removes this provision from the Church Order and instead requires that the Lord's supper should be administered only under the supervision of elders in a public gathering of the church. Article 65 of the Church Order of Dordt forbids funeral sermons where they have not been introduced. The PRCA edition states that funerals are not ecclesiastical but family affairs and should be conducted accordingly. Article 66 of the Church Order of Dordt allowed ministers, in times of certain calamities, "to petition the government that by its authority and order public fasting and prayer days may be designated and set aside."[75] The PRCA edition removes the reference to fasting and

---

73 De Ridder, *Ecclesiastical Manual*, 171–72. Included are summaries of these articles as adopted by the Synod of Dordt, followed by the changes that have been made to the Church Order of the Protestant Reformed Churches (PRCA). The articles in the Church Order of the PRCA can be found in *Confessions and Church Order*, 398–400.
74 De Ridder, *Ecclesiastical Manual*, 171–72.
75 De Ridder, *Ecclesiastical Manual*, 172.

ministers petitioning the government and instead gives classes the authority to proclaim a day of prayer "in times of war, pestilence, national calamities, and other great afflictions, the pressure of which is felt throughout the churches."[76]

Article 67 of the Church Order of Dordt required churches, in addition to Sunday, to observe six holidays: Christmas, Easter, Pentecost, the day after Pentecost (Whit Monday), and days of Christ's circumcision and ascension. The PRCA edition requires the churches observe nine special days: Christmas, Good Friday, Easter, Pentecost, Ascension Day, the Day of Prayer, the National Thanksgiving Day, and Old and New Year's Day. Article 68 of the Church Order of Dordt required that the ministers on Sunday "ordinarily in the afternoon service, briefly explain the sum of Christian doctrine contained in the Catechism."[77] The PRCA edition elides the reference to the afternoon service. Article 69 of the Church Order of Dordt allowed for singing only the 150 psalms, ten commandments, Apostles' Creed, Lord's prayer, the songs of Mary, Zacharias, and Simeon, and left optional the singing of "O God, Who Art Our Father." The PRCA edition leaves out the optional hymn but includes three additional hymns: the morning and evening hymns and the hymn of prayer before the preaching of the sermon.

One could certainly argue that some of these articles violate article 32 of the Belgic Confession because they bind or compel the conscience in worship. Others could argue that some of them also allow too much freedom and hinder unity. The point here is only that we should assume the synod considered such arguments and concluded that it struck a balance, without infringing on individual conscience.

Furthermore, the synod made its decisions knowing that the Church Order also included three significant safeguards to the

---

76 De Ridder, *Ecclesiastical Manual,* 172.
77 De Ridder, *Ecclesiastical Manual,* 172.

individual conscience. First, synod maintained the individual's right to protest and appeal any decision of the churches in article 31. Second, in article 82, synod maintained the individual's right to their membership papers. This included the right to receive or transfer their membership papers elsewhere, upon request to the consistory. And third, in article 86, synod maintained the right of the churches in common to change any article of the Church Order, including those pertaining to worship. This has been done in a number of instances in the history of the PRCA and in the history of the sister churches of the PRCA. An example would be article 67 and what it permits as far as singing in the divine worship service.

Further, with regard yet to the principles of article 32 of the Belgic Confession, the article identifies what specifically the Church Order must maintain in the church of Christ and what it ought to forbid: "Therefore, we admit only of that which tends to nourish and preserve concord and unity, and to keep all men in obedience to God."[78] Here, church polity that maintains the church is identified as that which does two things, nourishes and preserves its members, and that with regard to three objectives: concord (or peace), unity, and obedience to God. If anyone wonders why nourishing and preserving doctrine is missing, then they should consider that this is implied in the rest of the Belgic Confession, which sets forth that doctrine in terms of "we believe," so that it is here simply assumed. And this is precisely what the polity of Dordt did in its first article, where it includes supervision of doctrine as basic to maintaining the church.

Lastly, article 32 of the Belgic Confession establishes Christian discipline as an indispensable means for maintaining peace, unity, and obedience to God: "For this purpose, excommunication or church discipline is requisite, with the several circumstances belonging to it, according to the Word of God."[79] This should not

---

[78] *Confessions and Church Order*, 66.
[79] *Confessions and Church Order*, 66–67.

be surprising, for the Confession identifies discipline as the third mark of a true church in article 29. Therefore, it should also not be surprising that the Church Order concludes with a lengthy section "Concerning Censure and Ecclesiastical Admonitions" (articles 71–86), which articulates the specifics and circumstances of Christian discipline, the discipline necessary for maintaining concord, unity, and obedience to God in the body of Christ.

Subsequent History of the Church Order

As far as the subsequent history of the Church Order is concerned, after the Synod of Dordt, the Dutch government, both at the national and provincial levels, blocked full implementation of the Church Order. Provincial governments frequently interfered in ecclesiastical matters and blocked discipline of members, including heretical ministers. The national government prevented the convening of a national synod for the next two hundred years. In 1795 Napoleon's army swept in, and the Union was dissolved and replaced with the Batavian Republic. In 1815 the first national synod since Dordt was called by King Willem I, but he bypassed lower assemblies to pack synod with delegates who would forge a new church polity that placed church assemblies under civil committees and emasculated the Formula of Subscription.

It appeared that all the good accomplished by Dordt, both doctrinal and church political, had been lost. But Christ is King. In 1834–35 over one hundred churches seceded under the leadership of Hendrik de Cock, in the reformation that was known as the Afschieding. At their first synod, they adopted the Church Order of Dordt. Elsewhere, in 1857, the Christian Reformed Church in North America (CRCNA) was formed, and it adopted the Church Order of Dordt. Likewise did the Reformed Church of South Africa in 1862. Back in the Netherlands, in 1886 a second main secession from the mainline Dutch Reformed church occurred under

Abraham Kuyper, the movement known as the Doleantie. It also adopted the polity of Dordt. In 1892, the Doleantie united with the Afschieding churches. And in 1905, these united churches (GKN) would revise the Church Order, especially as its concerned church-state relations.

In 1914 the Church Order was also revised by the CRCNA, which revisions were incorporated into the Church Order of the Protestant Reformed Churches in America and her sister churches. Again, the most notable revision was that all references to state authority over the church or state involvement in church affairs were removed or revised. As great as was the Church Order of Dordt, and without at all disparaging or minimizing the monumental and glorious work of that synod, these revisions of 1914 (and 1905) were necessary and right.

In spite of the fact that at the time of the Synod of Dordt, the Dutch churches enjoyed the support and approval of the civil government, the synod's toleration and even expansion of state authority and involvement in ecclesiastical matters was a mistake that needed to be corrected. This mistake proved to be costly. Witness only the subsequent history described earlier. Scripture and history testify to the absolute sovereignty of the church under its Lord to determine its own business. Although church polity must recognize and honor the authority that God gives to the state in civil and earthly matters, even over such earthly affairs as church property, money, and the physical lives of its members, it may not do so at the expense of its spiritual relationship to Christ. The Church Order must express the exclusive covenant God has established between Christ and his bride and between his heavenly body and its members by his Spirit. Christ's bride may never be married to or under the authority of another. Christ will not allow it. His body must remain united, holy, and distinct from the world.

Thus, in 1914, removed would be the insertion of Dordt into

article 4 that ministerial election "shall not take place without good correspondence with the Christian authorities" and its requirement for "approbation and approval of the authorities."[80] Gone would be similar language in article 5. Gone would be the right given magistrates in article 37 to sit in on consistory meetings "to listen and to deliberate."[81] Gone would be the requirement of article 50 to inform the government so that "with its knowledge…time and place [for a national synod] may be decided in the presence and with the advice of its deputies."[82] And article 28, which Dordt added, would also be replaced with a much more biblical expression of the church-state relationship:

> The consistory shall take care that the churches, for the possession of their property and the peace and order of their meetings, can claim the protection of the authorities; it should be well understood, however, that for the sake of peace and material possession they may never suffer the royal government of Christ over His church to be in the least infringed upon.[83]

We should be thankful for these changes and others too. We should be thankful for the right granted by the Church Order for the churches to make such changes among themselves. And let none of this prevent those who subscribe to this Church Order in its various forms from considering it to be the Church Order of Dordt. In spite of changes made over the last four hundred years and, in my opinion, especially due to its origins in the Belgic Confession, the Church Order remains the same in its essence, principles, and the vast majority of its articles.

---

80 De Ridder, *Ecclesiastical Manual*, 161.
81 De Ridder, *Ecclesiastical Manual*, 167.
82 De Ridder, *Ecclesiastical Manual*, 169.
83 *Confessions and Church Order*, 389.

It may rightly be claimed to be the polity of Dordt. And like the theology of Dordt, it is magnificent. Like the theology of Dordt, the polity of Dordt does not set forth the rule of men, by men, and for men, but it sets forth the spiritual rule of Christ, by Christ, through and for the body of Christ. And like the theology of Dordt, the polity of Dordt has not only stood the test of time but has flourished over time by the rule of Christ so that today in many other lands than the Netherlands, among many more people than the Dutch, and in many more churches than those that drafted it, this same Church Order of Dordt continues to accomplish its purpose—to nourish and preserve concord and unity, and to keep all men in obedience to God. *Om goede orde in de Gemeente Christi te onderhouden*—to maintain good order in the church of Christ!

Chapter 7

Illustrating and Recommending the Grace of Election: Dordt's Doctrine of Reprobation

Ronald L. Cammenga

Introduction

Reprobation—the reformer John Calvin referred to it as the "*decretum horriblile*," that is, the "horrible decree."[1] Calvin did not mean to denounce the doctrine of reprobation as a horrible doctrine. He was not of the opinion that reprobation was a loathsome teaching that ought to be rejected by every right-thinking person, as many theologians would say today. Surely not, for no one taught, defended, wrote, and preached reprobation as Calvin did. Rather, by "horrible," Calvin meant "awesome" and "awe-inspiring." No one ought to speak about reprobation lightly; reprobation is no joking matter. The subject of predestination, and the subject of reprobation in particular, demands seriousness. We are talking about people's souls. We are talking about their eternal destiny. We are talking about God's

---

1 John Calvin, *Institutes of the Christian Religion*, 2 vols., ed. John T. McNeill, trans. Ford Lewis Battles (Philadelphia, PA: Westminster Press, 1960), 3.23.7, 2:955.

sovereign decree. We are talking about the God who brings all things to pass according to the good pleasure of his eternal will.

From a certain point of view, it can be said that reprobation was the main point of controversy at the Synod of Dordt. More than any of the other doctrines that they disputed, the Remonstrants, or Arminians, contested the Reformed doctrine of reprobation. Over and over again, the spokesmen for the Arminians claimed that their main difference with the Counter-Remonstrants concerned the doctrine of reprobation. That was a lie, of course. It simply was not true that their only or even their chief objection was to what they regarded as an extreme doctrine of reprobation. In fact, they denied and twisted every one of the doctrines of sovereign grace—every one! For that reason, Arminianism is not a "less complete gospel." It is rather an attack on and rejection of the gospel altogether. That is what the Synod of Dordt said, and that is what the faithful Reformed church and church member must say today.

But the Arminians in their public writings, their teaching in the universities, and their preaching in the churches objected to an absolute decree of reprobation. One of the leaders of the Arminian party at the Synod of Dordt, Simon Episcopius, said before the synod:

> We are not so much troubled with election, but the shoe pinches us above all in respect to that doctrine of reprobation which says that God by an absolute and unconditional decree reprobated the majority of mankind to eternal destruction, for the glory of His severity and freedom. This vexes us. Therefore, we must refute it.[2]

The Synod of Dordt articulated and defended the biblical doctrine of *double* predestination, that is, both election and reprobation.

---

2 Donald W. Sinnema, "The Issue of Reprobation at the Synod of Dort (1618–19) in Light of the History of This Doctrine," 2 vols. (Ph.D. dissertation, Toronto School of Theology, 1985), 2:235.

The synod vindicated the doctrine of double predestination as that doctrine had been restored to the church through the Reformation of the sixteenth century. For this reason alone, it may be said that the Synod of Dordt safeguarded the Reformed tradition. But double predestination was not only the tradition that went back to the reformers; it went as far back as Augustine of Hippo—foe of Pelagius—and to the apostles of Christ before him.

Not only did the synod safeguard the Reformed tradition regarding the doctrine of sovereign predestination, but it also carefully set forth the biblical underpinnings of this doctrine—"the express testimony of sacred scripture."[3] Thus, Dordt assured that the church would be reminded not only of *what* she believed, but *why* she believed it. Dordt did not cling to tradition for tradition's sake. Rather, the fathers of Dordt were committed to preserve the Reformed tradition out of the conviction that the Reformed tradition was the truth of the word of God.

Significantly, the Synod of Dordt confessed reprobation *in the interest of* election. Dordt was convinced that reprobation stands in the service of election. They saw reprobation as "illustrat[ing] and recommend[ing] to us the eternal and unmerited grace of election."[4]

Dordt's Doctrine of Reprobation

Dordt's doctrine of reprobation is set forth especially in the fifteenth article of the first head of doctrine. It is worth noticing that it is not until article 15 that the subject of reprobation is treated in the first head or chapter of the Canons of Dordt. That is significant. That, all by itself, indicates that Dordt viewed election, the positive side of predestination, as the more important aspect of the doctrine of predestination. That is Dordt's starting point. Only after fourteen articles that are more or less devoted to election does the Canons

---

3 Canons of Dordt 1.15, in *Confessions and Church Order*, 158.
4 Canons of Dordt 1.15, in *Confessions and Church Order*, 158.

finally come to treat reprobation. This is an indication of Dordt's viewpoint. It did not treat reprobation apart from election. But it treated reprobation as it stands in relationship to election. Reprobation is viewed as subordinate to and exalting the free grace of God in election.

Article 15 of the first head of doctrine gives a full description of Dordt's doctrine of reprobation.

> What peculiarly tends to illustrate and recommend to us the eternal and unmerited grace of election is the express testimony of sacred Scripture that not all, but some only, are elected, while others are passed by in the eternal election of God; whom God, out of his sovereign, most just, irreprehensible, and unchangeable good pleasure, hath decreed to leave in the common misery into which they have willfully plunged themselves, and not to bestow upon them saving faith and the grace of conversion; but leaving them in his just judgment to follow their own ways, at last for the declaration of his justice, to condemn and punish them forever, not only on account of their unbelief, but also for all their other sins. And this is the decree of reprobation which by no means makes God the author of sin (the very thought of which is blasphemy), but declares him to be an awful, irreprehensible, and righteous judge and avenger thereof.[5]

Although article 15 of the first head is the fullest statement concerning reprobation in the Canons, there are many other references to reprobation throughout the Canons. It is significant that the original title of the first head of the Canons of Dordt was not "Of Divine Predestination," which is the title in our English translation. But the original title was "On Divine Election and Reprobation," with the

---

5 *Confessions and Church Order*, 158.

subtitle, "Divine Predestination." The title of this first chapter of the Canons indicated the synod's conviction concerning the reality of reprobation. Also, the rejection of errors section following the first head is introduced with these words: "The true doctrine concerning *Election* and *Rejection* having been explained, the Synod *rejects* the errors of those…"[6] "Rejection" is reprobation. The synod rejects the errors of all who attack and deny not only election, but also reprobation.

Prior to article 15, already in article 6 of the first head, the Canons refers to reprobation. This article begins by stating "that some receive the gift of faith from God and others do not receive it proceeds from God's eternal decree." The article goes on to teach that "herein is especially displayed the profound, merciful, and at the same time the righteous discrimination between men equally involved in ruin; or that decree of election and reprobation."[7] It is worth noticing that the article concludes by asserting that this doctrine is clearly "revealed in the Word of God, which, though men of perverse, impure, and unstable minds wrest to their own destruction, yet to holy and pious souls affords unspeakable consolation."[8]

Article 15 of the first head defines reprobation. Really, all the articles that follow to the end of the chapter, articles 16–18, are related to reprobation. Article 16 is addressed to those who may be struggling with various doubts and fears regarding reprobation—the great fear that *they* might be reprobate. "Those who do not yet experience a lively faith in Christ, an assured confidence of soul, peace of conscience…ought not to be alarmed at the mention of reprobation, nor to rank themselves among the reprobate."[9]

Article 17 makes no mention of reprobation. However, it arises out of the clear teaching of scripture and the testimony of experience

---

6 *Confessions and Church Order*, 159.
7 *Confessions and Church Order*, 156.
8 *Confessions and Church Order*, 156.
9 *Confessions and Church Order*, 158.

that election and reprobation run through the generations of believers. In that light, what can we say regarding children who die in infancy? At the same time, the article is Dordt's response to a calumny of the Arminians that God, as some sort of fiendish monster, tears little children from the breasts of their mothers in order to cast them headlong into hell. This same false accusation will be addressed again in the conclusion of the Canons. Article 17 teaches that covenantal parents "have no reason to doubt of the election and salvation of their children whom it pleaseth God to call out of this life in their infancy."[10]

Article 18 responds to those who murmur against the free grace of God shown in election and his just severity displayed in reprobation. The fathers quote the apostle Paul's response to this accusation as found in Romans 9:20, "Nay but, O man, who art thou that repliest against God?" The rhetorical question denies to puny man the right to question the justice of God. To the article, Dordt adds Jesus' words in Matthew 20:15, "Is it not lawful for me to do what I will with mine own?"

Besides the articles dealing with reprobation in the first head, there is a very clear reference to reprobation in Canons 3–4.7, which contrasts the "sovereign good pleasure and unmerited love of God" in election to "the severity and justice of God's judgments displayed to others, to whom this grace is not given."[11] Those to whom God does not give his grace are the reprobate.

In addition to the references to reprobation in the body of the Canons, there are several references to reprobation in the conclusion of the Canons. In the conclusion, the fathers of Dordt were especially concerned to deny various false accusations against and caricatures of reprobation. There are no less than four references to reprobation in the conclusion.

---

10 *Confessions and Church Order*, 159.
11 *Confessions and Church Order*, 167.

First, in the conclusion, the charge is rejected "that the doctrine of the Reformed churches concerning predestination…makes God the author of sin, unjust, tyrannical, hypocritical."[12] This was the charge that Arminians at the time of the Synod of Dordt and Arminians today level against the teaching of reprobation. Like the proverbial broken record, this was the song that the Arminians repeated over and over again.

Second, the conclusion also rejects the charge "that the same doctrine teaches that God, by a mere arbitrary act of his will, without the least respect or view to any sin has predestinated the greatest part of the world to eternal damnation, and has created them for this very purpose."[13] Though an act of God's sovereign will, reprobation is not an arbitrary act of God's will. Reprobation is not God randomly choosing this one and rejecting that one. God's good pleasure is not the arbitrariness of a high-stakes gambler.

Third, the conclusion rejects the allegation of the enemies of predestination "that in the same manner in which the election is the fountain and the cause of faith and good works, reprobation is the cause of unbelief and impiety."[14] Significantly, the fathers do not say in the conclusion that in no sense of the word is reprobation the cause of unbelief and impiety. Rather, "in the same manner" in which election is the cause of faith and good works is reprobation the cause of unbelief and impiety. Jesus' word in John 10:26 has already been referenced: "Ye believe not, *because* ye are not of my sheep" (emphasis added).

And last, the conclusion rejects the Arminian caricature

> that many children of the faithful are torn, guiltless, from their mothers' breasts and tyrannically plunged into hell, so

---

12 *Confessions and Church Order*, 179.
13 *Confessions and Church Order*, 179.
14 *Confessions and Church Order*, 179.

that neither baptism, nor the prayers of the church at their baptism, can at all profit them; and many other things of the same kind, which the Reformed churches not only do not acknowledge, but even detest with their whole soul.[15]

Reprobation the Target of Attack

It is historically accurate to say that the Arminians targeted reprobation in their assault on the doctrines of grace. That was true of the father of Arminianism, Jacob or James Arminius (1560–1609). He opposed the Reformed doctrine of reprobation in his public preaching and in his instruction of theological students. Arminius was first an ordained pastor, serving the church in Amsterdam, the Netherlands, for several years. Later he was appointed to the theological faculty of the University of Leiden.

Arminius was very subtle and did everything in his power to preserve his standing in the Dutch Reformed church. He did not come out boldly in opposition to reprobation. But in his preaching on Romans 9, he denied an absolute decree of predestination that determined the eternal destiny of every human being. He also taught that reprobation is conditional. God chooses those whom he foresees will choose him.[16] He taught reprobation—in a way. But he completely changed the meaning of the word. Reprobation is not an eternal and absolute decree of God, but is God's reaction to what he foresees will happen in time and in history. Arminius said about reprobation:

> This decree has its foundation in the foreknowledge of God, by which he knew from all eternity those individuals who *would*, through his preventing grace, *believe*, and, through

---

15 *Confessions and Church Order*, 179.
16 Carl Bangs, *Arminius: A Study in the Dutch Reformation* (Nashville, TN: Abingdon Press, 1971), 193–98.

his subsequent grace *would persevere*, according to the before described administration of those means which are suitable and proper for conversion and faith; and, by which foreknowledge, he likewise knew those who *would not believe and persevere*.[17]

Arminius taught what would become the fundamental feature of Arminianism—conditions. Arminianism is conditional from beginning to end. Election is conditional, based on foreseen faith. Reprobation is conditional, based on foreseen unbelief. God deals with human beings on the basis of conditions. Everything turns, then, not on the will of God, but on the will of the sinner.

Arminius' conditional predestination was adopted by the Remonstrants. This became plain in their official documents. One of those documents is the "Remonstrance of 1610," written shortly after Arminius' death. In the very first article, the Arminians expressed their view:

> That God by an eternal and immutable decree has in Jesus Christ his Son determined before the foundation of the world to save out of the fallen sinful human race those in Christ, for Christ's sake, and through Christ who by the grace of the Holy Spirit shall believe in this his Son Jesus Christ and persevere in this faith and obedience of faith to the end; and on the other hand to leave the incorrigible and unbelieving in sin and under wrath and condemn (them) as alienate from Christ.[18]

At the time of the Synod of Dordt, the Arminians made their views known in the "Opinions of the Remonstrants." Regarding the decree of predestination, they said:

---

17 Nichols and Bagnall, *The Writings of James Arminius*, 1:248.
18 As quoted in DeJong, *Crisis in the Reformed Churches*, 208.

God had not decided to elect anyone to eternal life, or to reject anyone from the same, prior to the decree to create him, without any consideration of preceding obedience or disobedience, according to His good pleasure, for the demonstration of the glory of His mercy and justice, or of His absolute power and dominion…

God has not decreed to leave the greatest part of men in the fall, excluded from every hope of salvation, apart from intervening actual sins.[19]

Clearly, the Arminians made God's decree of reprobation a conditional decree. God's rejection of men is based upon their prior rejection of him. If they reject God, God also rejects them. That is the Arminian conception of reprobation.

The Express Testimony of Sacred Scripture

Over against the Arminian distortion of scripture, the Counter-Remonstrants (Reformed) insisted that reprobation was an eternal and absolute decree of God on the basis of "the express testimony of sacred Scripture."[20] Both the Old Testament and the New Testament clearly teach sovereign reprobation. Reprobation is not a theological construct invented by theologians living in ivory towers. Rather, it is the teaching of the Bible. And since the Bible is the word of God, reprobation must be believed and confessed.

That reprobation is expressly the teaching of scripture does not take away from the fact that reprobation is the logical deduction from the Bible's teaching of election. The biblical word for election means "to choose out of." Election is not simply God's choosing of a people as his own special possession, but it is God's choosing of his people "out of" the rest of fallen humanity. That clearly implies

---

19 De Jong, *Crisis in the Reformed Churches*, 222–23.
20 Canons of Dordt 1.15, in *Confessions and Church Order*, 158.

that not all are chosen; there are some who are not chosen. They are those out of whom and in distinction from whom the elect are chosen.

Reprobation also follows from the truth that election is God's choice of *some particular* persons. Not every human being, but some only are elected by God. This is also true of the angels. In 1 Timothy 5:21, Paul speaks of the "elect angels." That some angels are elect angels implies that there are other angels who are not elect but are reprobate. There would be no sense in referring to some of the angels as "elect" angels, if all the angels were chosen by God. The same is true of human beings.

In connection with the express testimony of scripture with regard to reprobation, it is worth noting the approach of the Synod of Dordt and its Canons. In treating election, the Canons of Dordt follows what may be called the Romans pattern, not the Ephesians pattern. In the epistle to the Romans, Paul proceeds from time to eternity, from the effects of predestination to the cause in the decree of predestination. The Canons moves from the historical fact that not all men believe the preaching of the gospel to the reason for that difference in election and reprobation. In the epistle to the Ephesians, Paul proceeds from eternity to time, from the decree of predestination to the outworking of that decree in time. He moves from the eternal will of God and his choice of some men in Jesus Christ to the actual salvation of those human beings in time and history. This is not the approach of the Canons, as the first article of head one indicates. It begins with the historical fact that "all men have sinned in Adam, and are deserving of eternal death."[21]

What precisely is "the express testimony of sacred Scripture" with regard to reprobation? The Synod of Dordt appealed to four distinct types of testimony to reprobation in holy scripture. First,

---

21 *Confessions and Church Order*, 155.

there is the testimony from the Old Testament in God's choice of one nation and its people to be his peculiar people and to enjoy salvation. That one, tiny nation was Israel. No other people enjoyed God's favor and were the objects of his blessing in the Old Testament. He saved Israel alone. "This mystery of His will God discovered to but a small number under the Old Testament."[22] Concerning God's election of Israel in distinction from all the other nations, Moses says in Deuteronomy 7:7–8,

> 7. The Lord did not set his love upon you, nor choose you, because ye were more in number than any people; for ye were the fewest of all people:
>
> 8. But because the Lord loved you, and because he would keep the oath which he had sworn unto your fathers, hath the Lord brought you out with a mighty hand, and redeemed you out of the house of bondmen, from the hand of Pharaoh king of Egypt.

The whole of Old Testament history bears testimony to God's sovereign election and reprobation, his choice of Israel and rejection of all the other nations.

Second, there are those texts of scripture that explicitly teach reprobation. Many are referred to or quoted in the Canons of Dordt. Texts from the Old Testament that make clear reference to reprobation include:

> Proverbs 16:4: "The Lord hath made all things for himself: yea, even the wicked for the day of evil." There are certain people whom the Lord has made for the day of evil, the judgment day. They are "made" for this day; they do not simply come to this day, but by God they are made for this day.

---

22 Canons of Dordt 3–4.7, in *Confessions and Church Order*, 167.

Jeremiah 6:30: "Reprobate silver shall men call them, because the Lord hath rejected them." There are some men whom the Lord has rejected. The reference is to some in Judah, some from among those who were outwardly the people of God. As the founder rejects "reprobate silver," so does God reject some men, not bestowing upon them the blessings of salvation.

Besides the testimony to reprobation from the Old Testament, there are also numerous texts from the New Testament. They include:

John 10:26: "But ye believe not, because ye are not of my sheep, as I said unto you." Certain unbelieving Jews are not of Jesus' sheep, that is, are not of the number of the elect given to Jesus by his heavenly Father. Notice that Jesus does not say, "Ye are not of my sheep because ye believe not." But he says, "Ye believe not, because ye are not of my sheep." Not being of the number of Jesus' sheep, these people are reprobate.

Romans 9:11–13: "(For the children being not yet born, neither having done any good or evil, that the purpose of God according to election might stand, not of works, but of him that calleth;) it was said unto her, The elder shall serve the younger. As it is written, Jacob have I loved, but Esau have I hated." God's purpose of election distinguishes between people. According to that purpose of election, some are chosen by God unto salvation, while others are rejected by God unto condemnation. This election and rejection involve individuals, including Jacob, whom God loved and elected, and Esau, whom he hated and reprobated.

Romans 9:21–22: "Hath not the potter power over the clay, of the same lump to make one vessel unto honor, and another unto dishonor? What if God, willing to show his wrath, and to make his power known, endured with much longsuffering the vessels of wrath fitted to destruction." Out of the same lump of humanity, the divine Potter makes vessels unto honor and vessels unto dishonor. We might say that he makes out of the same lump of clay a beautiful vase and a garbage can. As the potter who owns the clay, he has the right to make out of the clay the vessels that he sees fit to make. So God makes vessels unto dishonor, vessels of wrath that are "fitted to destruction."

1 Thessalonians 5:9: "For God hath not appointed us to wrath, but to obtain salvation by our Lord Jesus Christ." That God has not appointed us to wrath implies that there are those whom he does appoint to wrath. We may be thankful that he has not appointed us to wrath. But the fact is that there are those whom he has appointed to wrath.

1 Peter 2:8: "And a stone of stumbling, and a rock of offence, even to them which stumble at the word, being disobedient: whereunto also they were appointed." There are some who stumble over the word, to whom Christ is an offence. But their stumbling and their disobedience—their unbelief—is something unto which they have been appointed. Clearly the one who has appointed them so to stumble and disobey is the sovereign God.

Jude 4: "For there are certain men crept in unawares, who were before of old ordained to this condemnation, ungodly men, turning the grace of our God into lasciviousness, and denying the only Lord God, and our Lord Jesus Christ." There are certain men who have been ordained to condemnation. God is the one who has so ordained them. That

God has ordained them to condemnation does not take away their responsibility. Although they have been ordained to condemnation, they are "ungodly men," who "turn the grace of God into lasciviousness [license]," and they actively "deny the only Lord God, and our Lord Jesus Christ."

In addition to the texts that expressly teach reprobation, there are also those texts of scripture to which the fathers of Dordt appealed that teach that all God's works in time have their source in eternity. That which takes place in time and in history is the outworking of what God had decreed in all eternity.

> Psalm 135:6: "Whatsoever the Lord pleased, that did he in heaven, and in earth, in the seas, and all deep places." What God does in heaven, in earth, and in the seas he has "pleased," that is, has determined and willed in all eternity. That which takes place in time—unbelief, hardening, rejection of the word of God, refusal to worship God aright, impenitence in sin—are all determined by God in eternity.

> Acts 15:18: "Known unto God are all his works from the beginning of the world." From the beginning of human history, all the works of God have been known from the very beginning. If all God's works in time were known prior to his actually accomplishing those works, known already at the very beginning of the world, God's work of judging and condemning some human beings must have been determined also from the very beginning. That is reprobation.

One last line of argumentation used by the fathers of Dordt to establish the teaching of reprobation was to appeal to those texts that teach the fruits and consequences of God's decree of reprobation. From those fruits and consequences, the Synod of Dordt reached back to the source and cause.

Romans 9:18: "Therefore hath he mercy on whom he will have mercy, and whom he will he hardeneth." God shows mercy on some human beings. Other human beings he hardens. That God not only shows mercy, but actively hardens in sin can only be the outworking of the decree of predestination, both election and reprobation.

Matthew 11:25–26: "At that time Jesus answered and said, I thank thee, O Father, Lord of heaven and earth, because thou hast hid these things from the wise and prudent, and hast revealed them unto babes. Even so, Father: for so it seemed good in thy sight." God does not only reveal the things of the gospel and of salvation to some men—babes. But he also actively hides the things of the kingdom of God from other men—the wise and the prudent of this world. God's hiding of the things of the kingdom from some men, so that they do not repent and are not saved, is the fruit of God's decree of reprobation. Not only does Jesus recognize this aspect of the will of God, but he thanks God for it.

1 Samuel 2:25: "Notwithstanding they hearkened not unto the voice of their father, because the Lord would slay them." This verse concerns the wicked sons of Eli, Hophni and Phinehas. They hearkened not to their father "because the Lord would slay them." Literally, we read that the Lord "delighted" to slay them. The idea, of course, is that the death and eternal destruction of the sons of Eli was according to the good pleasure of God. Their destruction pleased him because he had determined it in his decree of reprobation.

2 Thessalonians 2:11–12: "And for this cause God shall send them strong delusion, that they should believe a lie: that they all might be damned who believed not the truth, but

had pleasure in unrighteousness." According to the apostle Paul, God sends some people "strong delusion," according to which they "believe a lie." God does this "that," that is, "so that," these people might all be damned. They actively reject the truth in unbelief and they actively find pleasure in unrighteousness, but this does not take away from the fact that God sends the strong delusion, and God wills that they should be damned. That is reprobation.

Indeed, reprobation is the "express testimony of sacred Scripture." Only those who refuse to bow before scripture and who are intent on twisting the scriptures can possibly avoid this testimony. And only they do.

Outstanding Characteristics of Reprobation according to Dordt

Not only does the Canons of Dordt give an accurate definition of reprobation in Canons 1.15, but it also provides a very complete description of the outstanding characteristics of reprobation. In order to be thoroughly grounded in the truth of reprobation, it is worthwhile to take note of its characteristics, as those characteristics are referred to in head one, article 15.[23]

- Reprobation is a divine decree. Besides those whom God has elected, "others are passed by" whom God "hath *decreed* to leave in the common misery into which they have willfully plunged themselves." The article concludes with a sentence that begins, "And this is the *decree* of reprobation." Like election, reprobation is a decree of God—one aspect of the decree of predestination. It is a decision of the will of God, a determination that God has made within himself.

---

23 The following quotations are taken from Canons 1.15, in *Confessions and Church Order*, 158. In every instance, italics have been added for emphasis.

- Reprobation is an eternal decree of God. Reprobation is compared to "the *eternal* and unmerited grace of election" and speaks of those who "are passed by in the *eternal election* of God." Reprobation is not God's reaction to what takes place in time and in history, which would be the case if reprobation were conditional. On the contrary, in eternity God has not only chosen the elect, but rejected the reprobate.
- Reprobation is unto everlasting condemnation. Just as election is unto everlasting glory and bliss in heaven, so reprobation is unto the everlasting torments and judgment of hell. According to Canons 1.15, according to the decree of reprobation, God determines "to condemn and punish them [the reprobate] forever." With regard to the reprobate, God reveals himself "to be an awful, irreprehensible, and righteous judge and avenger." This is always, of course, in the way of their own unbelief and other sins. The reprobate go to hell in the way of their sins. But that does not take away from the fact that the reprobate are "before of old ordained to condemnation," to use the language of Jude 4.
- Reprobation is particular, or definite. Just as election concerns certain definite individuals, so does also reprobation. According to the Canons, others, that is, other people are passed by and reprobated by God. There are those whom he leaves in their sins and in the guilt of Adam. They are left in the guilt into which they have plunged themselves. According to his decree of reprobation, God determines "to condemn and punish *them* forever." Reprobation is not a vague and general decree that some will be excluded from the blessings of salvation and everlasting life, though no one in particular is

reprobated. Certain definite persons are reprobated by God. According to the book of Revelation, there are those "whose names are not written in the book of life" (Rev. 13:8; 17:8; 20:15).

- Reprobation is sovereign and unconditional. Reprobation is not at all dependent on anything in or done by those who are reprobated. Just as election is unconditional, so also is reprobation. Canons 1.15 speaks of those who are passed by "out of His [God's] sovereign…good pleasure." The reprobate do not deserve reprobation, any more than the elect deserve election. They deserve hell and the judgment of God, but their reprobation itself is altogether apart from anything in them but is due to God's sovereign will alone, the will of the divine Potter.
- Reprobation is grounded in the good pleasure of God alone. The only explanation for reprobation is that so it seemed good in the sight of God. Why did God reprobate? Why did he reprobate whom he reprobated? Why did he reprobate Esau and not Jacob? Why does he not reprobate *me*? To all of these questions that the child of God may ask, the answer is the good pleasure of God. For no other reason than that it seemed good unto him, he not only elected unto salvation, but reprobated unto condemnation.
- Reprobation is just. God's decree of reprobation is "most just." In God's "just judgment," they are left "to follow their own ways," until "at last for the declaration of His justice," God condemns and punishes them forever. The decree of reprobation declares God to be a "righteous [just] judge and avenger" of sin. Reprobation is just inasmuch as no man deserves anything from God. Reprobation is just inasmuch as God the creator has the

right to do with his creatures as he pleases. And reprobation is just inasmuch as God elects and saves out of "the common misery into which [men] have plunged themselves."
- Reprobation serves the glory of God. In the final analysis, this is the explanation for reprobation. God decreed reprobation and decreed who would be reprobate for the glory of his own name. Canons 1.15 speaks of the declaration of God's justice in reprobation. And it speaks of God's "declaring Himself to be an awful, irreprehensible, and righteous judge and avenger." In reprobation there is a declaration concerning God. It is the declaration that he is God and God alone. It is the declaration that he is sovereign, the absolutely sovereign God of heaven and earth. To him is and must be the glory in heaven and on earth.

These are the outstanding characteristics of reprobation, according to the Canons of Dordt and on the basis of "the express testimony of sacred Scripture." These characteristics are essential to reprobation. Apart from them—any one of them—reprobation would not be biblical or confessional reprobation.

Calvin's Teaching of Reprobation

The fathers of Dordt defended the doctrine of reprobation as it had come down to them from the Reformation. The delegates to the Synod of Dordt—the vast majority of them, at least—were convinced that the doctrine of reprobation that they confessed had been restored by the Protestant reformers before them. In particular, they acknowledged their debt to the great Genevan reformer John Calvin. What is shocking is that barely fifty years after Calvin's death, it was necessary for the church to be convulsed by a great controversy in order that through that controversy the heritage of the Reformation might be preserved. That is how quickly apostasy took place. That must be a warning to the church today to be vigilant. The doctrine of reprobation was a unique aspect of the Reformation heritage. The Synod of Dordt was used by God to preserve this doctrine and the still greater truth of which it was a part, the doctrine of sovereign predestination.

Clearly, Calvin taught the absolute sovereignty of God in salvation, including double predestination, both election and reprobation. He did so against several heretics who railed at him for his teaching. One of those heretics was Albert Pighius. To Pighius, he wrote:

> You dazzle the sight of the ignorant and the inexperienced by setting before their eyes as a shining cloud your doctrine that God will have all men to be saved. But if these words of the apostle [in Romans 9:22, "vessels of wrath fitted to destruction"] are not in perfect harmony with that election whereby God predestinated his own children unto eternal life, let me ask you this question: How is it that if God willed all men to be saved, he did not show unto all nations and all men the way of salvation?[24]

In his classic *Institutes of the Christian Religion*, Calvin wrote:

> We call predestination God's eternal decree, by which he determined with himself what he willed to become of each man. For all are not created in equal condition; rather, eternal life is foreordained for some, eternal damnation for others. Therefore, as any man has been created to one or the other of these ends, we speak of him as predestined to life or to death.[25]

---

24 Calvin, *Calvin's Calvinism*, 304.
25 Calvin, *Institutes*, 3.21.5, 2:926.

In another place in the *Institutes*, he wrote:

As Scripture, then, clearly shows, we say that God once established by his eternal and unchangeable plan those whom he long before determined once for all to receive into salvation, and those whom, on the other hand, he would devote to destruction.[26]

In his treatise entitled "God's Eternal Predestination and Secret Providence," Calvin insisted:

[W]hat I have ever invariably taught, and still teach to this day, is that whenever election is the subject of discussion, the great point to be maintained from first to last is that all the reprobate are justly left under eternal death because they died and were eternally condemned in Adam; also, that those perish justly who are by nature the children of wrath; finally, that therefore no one can have cause to complain of the too great severity of God, seeing that all men bear in themselves and in their individual persons the guilt and just desert of death eternal.[27]

At the beginning of this same treatise, Calvin had said,

Let those roar at us who will. We will ever brighten forth with all our power of language the doctrine that we hold concerning the free election of God, since it is only by it that the faithful can understand how great that goodness of God is that effectually called them to salvation...Now if we are not really ashamed of the gospel, we must of necessity acknowledge what is therein openly declared: God by his eternal goodwill (for which there was no other cause than

---

26 Calvin, *Institutes,* 3.21.7, 2:931.
27 Calvin, *Calvin's Calvinism,* 112.

his own purpose) appointed those whom he pleased unto salvation, rejecting all the rest...[who] continuing of their own will in unbelief, are left destitute of the light of faith in total darkness.[28]

And once more, in this same treatise, Calvin had this to say:

God, the maker of men, forms out of the same lump in his hands one vessel, or man, to honor and another to dishonor, according to his sovereign and absolute will [Rom. 9:21]. For he freely chooses some to life who are not yet born, leaving others to their own destruction, which destruction all men by nature equally deserve.[29]

God's Purpose in Reprobation

What can we say as to God's purpose in reprobation? Can we say anything as to the reason on account of which God determined that predestination should be *double* predestination, not only election, but also reprobation? Why did God choose to save some human beings, while passing by and reprobating others?

Hypothetically speaking, he could have willed and done differently. He is God, the sovereign God, and the divine Potter. Hypothetically speaking, he could have saved and willed to save every human being. He could have decreed to save every single man, woman, and child ever born into the world. At the same time, it would also have been possible that God saved and willed to save no one—not a single man, woman, or child. He did not owe salvation to anyone. No sinful, fallen human being had a right to salvation, and God was under obligation to save no one. The very first article of the first head of doctrine of the Canons of Dordt puts it this way: "God would have done no injustice by leaving them all [all men,

---

28 Calvin, *Calvin's Calvinism*, 20–21.
29 Calvin, *Calvin's Calvinism*, 64–65.

that is] to perish, delivering them [all] over to condemnation on account of their sin."[30] Why did God do neither; why did he choose to elect some unto salvation and reprobate others to condemnation? Why reprobation, in particular? Canons 1.15 gives a very important part of the answer to this puzzling question when it says that reprobation "peculiarly tends to illustrate and recommend to us the eternal and unmerited grace of election."[31]

Certainly one of the reasons on account of which God did not save every human being, but reprobated some, is that this underscores his absolute sovereignty. He is God! Because he is God, he does with his creatures as pleases him, and no one has the right to question him. As the apostle says in Romans 9:20, "Nay but, O man, who art thou that repliest against God?" That of the same lump of fallen humanity God fashions vessels of honor, like a beautiful vase or elegant sculpture, and vessels of dishonor, like an ashtray or a waste basket, is his prerogative. And that he does is a testimony to his right to do with what is his as he pleases. No one may question him or bring his actions under scrutiny. He is God, and as God, he is absolutely sovereign. The truth that he has determined to save some and reject others magnifies his sovereignty.

Additionally, in predestination both God's mercy is displayed in his election of some, and his holiness and justice in his reprobation of others. Inasmuch as predestination consists of both election and reprobation, both of these attributes of God shine forth, as otherwise they would not. If God had rejected and reprobated every human being, his mercy would not be magnified as it is when instead he wills to rescue some of the fallen race of Adam. On the other hand, if God had chosen and elected every human being, his righteousness and holiness would not be magnified as they are when instead he wills not to save all, but to reprobate some of the

---

30 *Confessions and Church Order*, 155.
31 *Confessions and Church Order*, 158.

posterity of Adam. Especially does reprobation serve to underscore the greatness of God's mercy in salvation. Canons 1.15 says that reprobation "recommend[s] to us the…unmerited grace of election."[32] The light always shines the brighter against the darkest of backgrounds. Against the dark background of reprobation, the brilliance of God's free grace in saving some, those whom he has chosen, shines the brighter.

Every believing child of God ought to make this personal. Reprobation ought to recommend to *me* the unmerited grace of *my* election. What mercy God has shown to *me*!

And that, in turn, ought to produce humility in the lives of elect believers. And is there any virtue of which we are more in need than the virtue of humility? An arrogant Christian, a proud believer—these are contradictions in terms. Impossible! Utterly impossible! The unmerited grace of God in election ought to inspire in us humility. It ought to inspire humility not just in our dealings with fellow Christians, but humility in our dealings also with the world of unbelievers. There, but for the grace of God, go we. Every elect child of God ought to say with the apostle Paul, "For who maketh thee to differ from another? And what hast thou that thou did not receive? now if thou didst receive it, why dost thou glory, as if thou hadst not received it?" (1 Cor. 4:7).

Many times over, the scriptures speak of the grace that has been *given* to us, as in 1 Corinthians 1:4: "I thank my God always on your behalf, for the grace of God which is given you by Jesus Christ." God's grace is given to us as a free and undeserved gift. Why has God seen fit to choose me and set his grace upon me, who am no better than any whom God has not chosen? Why has he seen fit to choose me, who am the least of all saints? I do not deserve this election and salvation. What I deserve is to be cast off and to perish everlastingly.

---

32 *Confessions and Church Order*, 158.

With that knowledge, every elect believer says with Paul, "But by the grace of God I am what I am" (1 Cor. 15:10).

For that reason too, the Reformed rejected the charge of the Arminians that this doctrine makes men careless and profane. That charge of the Arminians usually arises as a calumny, that is, a false and malicious charge against the Reformed doctrine of election and reprobation. That charge is answered in Canons 1.13:

> The sense and certainty of this election [and reprobation] afford to the children of God additional matter for daily humiliation before him, for adoring the depth of his mercies, for cleansing themselves, and rendering grateful returns of ardent love to him, who first manifested so great love towards them. The consideration of this doctrine of election [and reprobation] is so far from encouraging remissness in the observance of divine commands, or from sinking men in carnal security, that these, in the just judgment of God, are the usual effects of rash presumption, or of idle and wanton trifling with the grace of election, in those who refuse to walk in the ways of the elect.[33]

It is simply impossible that the grace of God in election should inspire a careless attitude on the part of the elect child of God, the attitude that if I'm elect, I'm elect, and if I'm reprobate, I'm reprobate, and there is nothing that I can do about it. I might as well, then, live as I please, for in either case, what God has decreed is going to come to pass. Absolutely not! The grace of God that elects unto salvation also works gratitude in the heart of the elect, a gratitude that manifests itself in holiness. For the elect child of God, there is no truth like the truth that God has been pleased to elect and save a sinner like me to inspire heartfelt gratitude and a life lived to the praise of God.

---

33 *Confessions and Church Order*, 157.

ILLUSTRATING AND RECOMMENDING THE GRACE OF ELECTION

The second calumny against the doctrine of sovereign reprobation defended by the Synod of Dordt was that if God reprobated men in an eternal and absolute decree, God is the author of their sins. This is a theological charge levelled against the Reformed doctrine of reprobation, not a practical charge. Every reprobate, wicked person knows that they are responsible for their sins, sins that arise out of their own evil heart and that are done for their own self-serving purposes. No reprobate, wicked person having committed a sin blames God for that sin. Every sinner feels that they have incurred God's wrath and stand exposed to his judgment.

The very article of the Canons in which the subject of reprobation is introduced addresses this false accusation: "And this is the decree of reprobation which by no means makes God the author of sin (the very thought of which is blasphemy), but declares Him to be an awful, irreprehensible,[34] and righteous judge and avenger thereof."[35] In an utterly mysterious way, God's sovereignty does not rule out man's responsibility. God sovereignly reprobates men to hell, in the way of their unbelief and other sins, and yet not God, but they themselves, remain responsible for their sins. The scriptures teach this clearly. One such passage is Luke 22:22, in which verse Jesus himself is speaking: "And truly the Son of man goeth, as it was determined: but woe unto that man by whom he is betrayed!" Jesus goes to the cross "as it was determined," of course, by God in his counsel. In his counsel, he reprobated Judas Iscariot and determined that he would be guilty of the most heinous of sins, the betrayal of the Lord Jesus Christ into the hands of his enemies. Nevertheless, although that evil—the greatest of evils!—was determined by God, Jesus adds, "But woe unto that man by whom he is betrayed!" God's

---

[34] That God is "irreprehensible" means that he is free from blame or reproach, in this case, free from any blame or legitimate reproach because he has reprobated some to hell.

[35] Canons of Dordt 1.15, in *Confessions and Church Order*, 158.

sovereignty is placed alongside of man's responsibility. There is absolutely no contradiction between them.

Thus, it is plain that election serves reprobation. Why has God reprobated? He has reprobated for the sake of and in the service of election. Not only has God decreed reprobation, but he has decreed reprobation in order to serve election. Election and reprobation are not two equally ultimate decrees. Not at all! Election is always first in the mind of God, and then reprobation in the service of election.

Reformed theologians of the past have often described reprobation as the husk inside of which is the kernel of election. In cereal grains, among other things, the husk serves the kernel by protecting it, providing for its nourishment, and maintaining its moisture. In much the same way a peel or skin functions in relation to the fruit around which it grows. But in the harvesting process, the husk is separated from the kernel of grain so that the kernel can be used as a food source, whether for animal or man. The husk is inedible, while the kernel is edible. The husk has no food value, but the kernel of grain is full of nutrients and vitamins. In eating an orange or kiwi fruit, the outer skin is peeled away and the fruit that is inside the peel or skin is what is eaten.

That reality in natural life highlights the relationship between election and reprobation. Reprobation serves election. As reprobate Pharaoh and Egypt served Israel's enrichment at the time of the exodus, as the reprobate element in Israel served throughout the Old Testament for the protection of the nation of Israel in which was found the elect remnant, and as reprobate Judas served *the* elect, our Lord Jesus Christ, and the righteousness he would accomplish by his death on the cross, so do the reprobate throughout history serve the elect. Until the great harvest! God has his eye on the coming harvest, and on the elect kernels of grain, just as the farmer has his eye on the useful kernels of grain when he harvests his crops. And as the farmer in the end burns the chaff or uses it for bedding, so does God burn up the reprobate husk after it has served his purpose. The apostle refers to that day when he describes the second coming of Christ: "In flaming fire taking vengeance on them that know not God, and that obey not the gospel of our Lord Jesus Christ" (2 Thess. 1:8).

Doubts and Fears

But what about the doubts and fears that arise from time to time in the heart of every child of God? What about the fear that I might not be an elect child of God? The fear that I might be reprobate? The fathers of Dordt knew something about these doubts and fears, both within themselves and in their pastoral work with the people of God. In the article that follows the one devoted to reprobation, they immediately address these doubts and fears.

> Those who do not yet experience a lively faith in Christ, an assured confidence of soul, peace of conscience, an earnest endeavor after filial obedience, and glorying in God through Christ, efficaciously wrought in them, and do nevertheless persist in the use of the means which God hath appointed for working these graces in us, ought not to be alarmed at the mention of reprobation, nor to rank themselves among the reprobate, but diligently to persevere in the use of means, and with ardent desires devoutly and humbly to wait for a season of richer grace. Much less cause have they to be terrified by the doctrine of reprobation who, though they seriously desire to be turned to God, to please him only, and to be delivered from the body of death, cannot yet reach that measure of holiness and faith to which they aspire; since a merciful God has promised that he will not quench the smoking flax nor break the bruised reed. But this doctrine is justly terrible to those who, regardless of God and of the Savior Jesus Christ, have wholly given themselves up to

the cares of the world and the pleasures of the flesh, so long as they are not seriously converted to God.[36]

Every child of God knows something of the struggle with doubts and fears concerning their election and salvation. We see our sins, the sins into which we fall again and again. And behind those sins we see our old Adam nature. How can I possibly be an elect child of God? Perhaps I am a reprobate? Maybe I am an Esau or a Judas? Those are the darkest hours in the Christian life.

But the faith that believes in Jesus Christ is also assurance of election and salvation. Assurance is of the essence of faith. God did not only eternally will our salvation, but he willed our assurance of salvation as well. God is pleased that in this life already believers enjoy the assurance of salvation and thus enjoy the only comfort for life and for death and live unto God in gratitude.[37] The whole Christian life is grounded in the assurance of our salvation. Apart from assurance, there cannot be gratitude. We are thankful for what we have been given, that which we know we have been given. The assurance of faith looks away from one's self and looks upon, trusts in, embraces, and clings to Jesus Christ. As soon as we are gifted with faith, the activity of faith—for such it is—manifests itself as taking refuge in and casting one's self upon Jesus Christ. The great work of the Holy Spirit in the life of the believer is to work and to strengthen this assurance.

For the development of our assurance, God has also decreed the use of certain means, chief of which is the preaching of the gospel, along with the use of the sacraments, as well as prayer, the reading of God's word, and meditation thereon. The Holy Spirit does not drop assurance from the heavens in a parachute, or give assurance through some spectacular, mysterious occurrence, which we can

---

36 Canons of Dordt 1.16, in *Confessions and Church Order*, 158–59.
37 Heidelberg Catechism Q&A 1, in *Confessions and Church Order*, 83–84.

later recount in detail. But rather, he works assurance through the use of the ordinary means of grace. The seriousness of despising and absenting one's self from the means of grace is that the child of God foolishly forfeits the assurance of his salvation and election. Under the grace of God, it is usually the case that the loss of the assurance of salvation is the very thing that God uses to bring his wayward child to repentance.

At the same time, the believer is confirmed in the assurance of his election—that he is not a reprobate—by observing in his life the infallible fruits of election. This is not glorying in men's works or denying that assurance is a gift of God, as some allege. Not at all! Rather, it is recognizing the work of the Holy Spirit in the lives of the saints by beholding the fruits of that work as they come to manifestation. Sometimes this is referred to as the "practical syllogism." As a syllogism, it is a matter of logic, in this case *spiritual* logic. It is the spiritual logic of reasoning from the fruits to the cause and source of those fruits in eternity.

The Canons of Dordt engages in such spiritual reasoning. In Canons 1.12, the synod engaged in this kind of reasoning:

> The elect in due time, though in various degrees and in different measures, attain the assurance of this their eternal and unchangeable election, not by inquisitively prying into the secret and deep things of God, but by observing in themselves, with a spiritual joy and holy pleasure, the infallible fruits of election pointed out in the Word of God—such as a true faith in Christ, filial fear, a godly sorrow for sin, a hungering and thirsting after righteousness, etc.[38]

Notice that this article affirms that the elect "attain the assurance of this their eternal and unchangeable election." They attain this

---

38 *Confessions and Church Order*, 157.

assurance of their eternal and unchangeable election, and therefore the assurance that they are not reprobate, "by observing in themselves...the infallible fruits of election pointed out in the Word of God." The fruits of election are used by God to confirm the faith and salvation that we already enjoy.

In Canons 1.16, the fathers of Dordt address in a pastoral way those who may be struggling with assurance, urging that they "experience a lively faith in Christ, an assured confidence of soul, peace of conscience, an earnest desire after filial obedience, and glorying in God through Christ" who "diligently...persevere in the use of means."[39] The means to which the article refers are especially the official means of grace in the church, the preaching of the word of God and the sacraments.

In the last head of the Canons of Dordt, the whole matter of the assurance of election and salvation comes up again. Once again, in head five, article 10, the synod addressed the matter of assurance directly:

> This assurance, however, is not produced by any peculiar revelation contrary to, or independent of the Word of God, but springs from faith in God's promises, which He has abundantly revealed in his Word for our comfort; from the testimony of the Holy Spirit, witnessing with our spirit, that we are children and heirs of God (Rom. 8:16); and lastly from a serious and holy desire to preserve a good conscience and to perform good works. And if the elect of God were deprived of this solid comfort, that they shall finally obtain the victory, and of this infallible pledge or earnest of eternal glory, they would be of all men the most miserable.[40]

---

39 *Confessions and Church Order*, 158.
40 *Confessions and Church Order*, 175.

"Solid comfort" is enjoyed by faith and through the testimony of the Holy Spirit, who witnesses with our spirits that we are God's children and heirs. The article references Romans 8:16, "The Spirit itself beareth witness with our spirit, that we are the children of God." But in his work on behalf of our assurance and comfort, the Holy Spirit works in and through "a serious and holy desire to preserve a good conscience and to perform good works." Once again, the Holy Spirit works assurance in the people of God through the testimony of the fruits of election and salvation.

The teaching of the Canons that the fruits of election are a testimony to the certainty of our election is in harmony with the teaching of holy scripture. In many places, the word of God teaches the assurance of election and salvation. One such passage is Romans 8:14–16:

> 14. For as many as are led by the Spirit of God, they are the sons [children] of God.
>
> 15. For ye have not received the spirit of bondage again to fear; but ye have received the Spirit of adoption, whereby we cry, Abba, Father.
>
> 16. The Spirit itself beareth witness with our spirit, that we are the children of God.

That the Spirit uses the fruits of election as a testimony to our election is plain from a passage like 1 Thessalonians 1:4–6:

> 4. Knowing, brethren beloved, your election of God.
>
> 5. For our gospel came not unto you in word only, but also in power, and in the Holy Ghost, and in much assurance; as ye know what manner of men we were among you for your sake.

6. And ye became followers of us, and of the Lord, having received the word in much affliction, with joy in the Holy Ghost.

We may know our "election of God." We may know our election, that is, be assured of it—"much assurance." How may we know our election by God, according to the apostle in this passage? The answer is, by observing in our lives three outstanding fruits of faith, says the apostle.

The fruit of our election is, first of all, that we, like the Thessalonians, believe the gospel. That is the very first fruit of election, by which we may know most assuredly our election of God. Assurance of salvation, like salvation itself, is by faith. Second, the fruit of election is that we strive to live a holy life. The apostle refers to this fruit of election when he says, "Ye became followers of us, and of the Lord" (v. 6). Discipleship of Christ, striving to live in obedience to his word and commandments—that is another infallible fruit of election. Included, obviously, is sorrow over our sin when we do not live as followers of the apostle and of the Lord. Do you experience that sorrow over sin? If you do, it is only because the Spirit of Christ is in you. That sorrow over sin is one of the infallible fruits of election. And third, it is an infallible fruit of election that we are willing to suffer for Christ's sake. The willingness to endure persecution because of our faith and because of our holy walk, as the Thessalonians were, is also a fruit of election. The Thessalonians "received the word with much affliction" (v. 6).

Among the fruits of election, this is one of the most preeminent. Are you willing to suffer reproach, ridicule, imprisonment, even death for the sake of the gospel? Are you willing to lay down your life, if it comes to that, for Christ's sake? Then know that you are an elect child of God! This is a fruit of election. Know, then, that you are an elect child of God; you are not a reprobate. No reprobate, wicked man is willing to endure the loss of all things for the sake of the gospel. That is true only of the elect.

In 2 Peter 1:10, the apostle urges those to whom he was writing, "Wherefore the rather, brethren, give diligence to make your calling and election sure: for if ye do these things, ye shall never fall." We are to "give diligence" with a view to making our calling and election sure, that is, certain and assured. "Give diligence" is an imperative, a command. By doing these things we make our calling and election sure. The apostle is referring to what he has just mentioned. Strikingly the same word is used in the context: "giving all diligence" (v. 5) is the same word that the apostle uses in verse 10, "give diligence to make your calling and election sure." How? By

> 5. Add[ing] to your faith virtue; and to virtue knowledge;
>
> 6. And to knowledge temperance; and to temperance patience; and to patience godliness;
>
> 7. And to godliness brotherly kindness; and to brotherly kindness charity.
>
> 8. For if these things be in you, and abound, they make you that ye shall neither be barren nor unfruitful in the knowledge of our Lord Jesus Christ. (vv. 5–8)

We give diligence to make our calling and election sure by living out of our faith. The fruits of faith are used by God to strengthen the assurance of our election.

The apostle John confirms the teaching of Peter. He writes in 1 John 2:3, "And hereby we do know that we know him, if we keep his commandments." Knowing that we know him is simply the certainty of God's election and salvation of us. Knowing that we know him is *personal* assurance of election and salvation. That certainty—knowing that we know him—is in the way of keeping God's commandments: "if we keep his commandments." Those who do not keep God's commandments, who go on impenitent in disobedience to the commandments, cannot enjoy the assurance of their salvation. They cannot know that they know him. God will not give the assurance of election and salvation to those who despise his good commandments.

A Doctrine Despised and Rejected

This is the glorious, robust predestination doctrine of the Canons of Dordt. But as in the days of the Synod of Dordt, so today it is a doctrine that is despised and rejected. Sadly, it is often despised and rejected by those who stand in the tradition of Dordt and who officially subscribe to the Canons of Dordt. In many Reformed churches and pulpits there is a deafening silence with regard to predestination, especially reprobation. Reformed ministers and theologians publicly deny double predestination. Karl Barth did, and so did G. C. Berkouwer. And both are applauded as among the greatest Reformed theologians of recent times. In the Christian Reformed Church, Harold Dekker, James Daane, and Harry Boer led the charge against the church's confession of double predestination. They called for revision of the creeds and the excising of reprobation from the church's official confessions. And then there is the heresy of the federal vision, which has infected a goodly number of Reformed and Presbyterian churches. This heresy robs Reformed churches of the treasures of Dordt—every one of the five precious jewels in the glorious crown of sovereign grace. And as in the days of the prophet Jeremiah, when the prophets prophesied lies, "My people love to have it so" (Jer. 5:31). The proponents of the federal vision, by their teaching of a conditional covenant and resistible grace, make of the Canons of Dordt a laughing stock.

Reformed theologians and Reformed churches of our day are

often embarrassed by Dordt's doctrine of reprobation—embarrassed by a sovereign God who reprobates. That which was a fundamental issue at the Synod of Dordt is glossed over at the conferences and in the books that advertise themselves as celebrating the anniversary of the great synod. Ostensibly they commemorate the Synod of Dordt, but with nary a word about reprobation. That is like commemorating the victory of the Allies in World War II and mentioning that the defeated enemy was Hitler's Germany, but without any mention of the atrocities perpetrated by the Nazis. How can there be a celebration of the glorious victory of World War II without describing the dark background that makes the victory of the Allies shine the more brightly?

Historically predestination is always stabbed through the side of reprobation. That was the case at Dordt, and that is also the case today. The opposition is against predestination, but men suppose that predestination is most vulnerable at the point of reprobation. It is seen as the weak link in the golden chain of salvation. But when men stab reprobation, in reality the life-blood of predestination spills onto the ground. The death of reprobation in the church is, in reality, the death of predestination. That is always the outcome. But in the end, it is not merely the death of predestination. It is the death of the church—the church that is faithful to the sovereign God and to his holy word.

There is an explanation for the widespread opposition to the doctrine of reprobation. The one great cause for this rejection of reprobation is the widespread embrace of the well-meant offer of the gospel. In Reformed and Presbyterian churches today, the well-meant offer of the gospel is accepted almost without question. That is the teaching that God loves all men, that God desires the salvation of all men, and that Christ died for all men. That teaching simply cannot be squared with double predestination, particularly reprobation. According to the teaching of reprobation, there are those whom God does not love and does not desire to save. That directly conflicts with the theology of the well-meant offer of the gospel. Not only has God determined that some men will not be saved, but he has decreed that they will be rejected and damned eternally in hell. There are those theologians and those churches that attempt to teach both reprobation and the well-meant gospel offer. But that attempt fails in the end. It must fail. And it fails invariably with the result that reprobation is victimized. In the interests of maintaining the well-meant offer of the gospel and a love of God for all men, reprobation is denied.

For this reason, it is crucially important that we oppose the false teaching of the well-meant gospel offer. If we are going to pass on the heritage of the truth preserved by the Synod of Dordt to the next generation, we must resist the attempt to give a place in the Reformed tradition, the Reformed seminary, the Reformed pulpit, or the Reformed congregation to the well-meant gospel offer. Herman Hoeksema was convinced of this and issued the call to the church to stand against this heresy for the sake of the truth of sovereign predestination. He issued that call in his treatise entitled "The Place of Reprobation in the Preaching of the Gospel":

> We must not surrender an inch of ground to the idea that God wills to save all, some of whom are nevertheless lost. God's counsel will stand, and he will remain sovereign—sovereign regarding eternal life, and at the same time sovereign regarding eternal perdition. Therefore, reprobation must be preached, for God must remain sovereign even over the kingdom of darkness. Reprobation must be preached to the congregation from the viewpoint of election. Believers must understand that salvation is not of him who wills, nor of him who runs, but of God who shows mercy. According to

God's good pleasure they have received a place in the consummation of all things. This means so much more to us when we understand that God could also sovereignly have reprobated us. There can be no question that reprobation should be preached if one wishes to divide the word of truth properly.[41]

May God keep us faithful to Dordt and to Dordt's confession of the absolute sovereignty of God in the salvation of sinners—all those sinners who by him have been chosen to everlasting life through belief of the truth.

There is no better conclusion to this chapter than the conclusion of the apostle Paul to his teaching of predestination in Romans 11:33–36:

> 33. O the depth of the riches both of the wisdom and knowledge of God! how unsearchable are his judgments, and his ways past finding out!
>
> 34. For who hath known the mind of the Lord? or who hath been his counsellor?
>
> 35. Or who hath first given to him, and it shall be recompensed unto him again?
>
> 36. For of him, and through him, and to him, are all things: to whom be glory forever. Amen.

---

41 Henry Danhof and Herman Hoeksema, "The Place of Reprobation in the Preaching of the Gospel," in *The Rock Whence We Are Hewn: God, Grace, and Covenant*, ed. David J. Engelsma (Jenison, MI: Reformed Free Publishing Association, 2015), 489–90. Originally, this was a public lecture by Hoeksema that was published in the Dutch language under the title, "*De Plaats der Verwerping in de Verkondiging des Evangelies.*"

Chapter 8

ASSURANCE: SOVEREIGN GRACE'S SPEECH TO THE HEART

Barrett Gritters

Introduction

It could be argued convincingly that assurance is the main theme of the Canons of Dordt. It could *even* be argued (really, who would want to disagree?) that the Canons, as to its address of the believer's heart to comfort and assure, stands shoulder to shoulder with the other Reformed creeds and is no less pastoral and comfort themed than the Heidelberg Catechism. But *especially* it can be argued that the comforting doctrine of assurance is one of the main themes, if not the main theme, that runs through this confession with a clarity and purpose that no one ought to miss. One who reads the Canons will not miss it. It is the purpose of this chapter to demonstrate that the Canons aims at the assurance of believers.

I speak of the doctrine of assurance even though assurance is not a separate head of doctrine in the Canons. Head one is predestination; head two is atonement; head three is depravity; head four is conversion and regeneration; head five is preservation and perseverance. There is no chapter entitled "Assurance." Nevertheless, the doctrine of assurance is given such a prominent place in the

Canons that one can at least argue that the *primary pastoral goal* of the great synod was to restore to the people of God true doctrine in order to give to them the assurance of salvation; and to remove from them the doubts and fears that the Arminian doctrine had spread like a bad infection in the Reformed churches of the Netherlands and beyond.

In the conclusion of the Canons, preachers are exhorted to *preach* the doctrines established by the synod to three chief ends. First, "to the glory of the divine name," because Arminian doctrine gave glory to man. Second, "to holiness of life," at least in part because the Arminians had charged the Reformed faith with promoting laxity in morals. And third, "to the consolation of afflicted souls," as the practical climax of the three purposes, because the Arminian doctrine robbed the people of God of their comfort and assurance.[1] Here we see the pastoral heart of the Canons. The Canons are not coldly scholastic, rigidly logical, or interested in doctrine merely for doctrine's sake. The fathers had in mind the consolation of afflicted souls.

Arminian Ruin of Assurance

Although I do not make it my main purpose in this chapter, one of the first things I must do is remind us that it was the Arminian doctrine that robbed the people of God of their assurance. If Arminianism is allowed to return, it will again rob God's people today of the precious assurance of their salvation. Let me briefly show that, following the order of the Canons themselves.

If faith is not a gift of God, sovereignly given to God's elect,[2] but instead a work of man, any assurance of salvation will be from a man mustering faith in himself.

If there is not one but two decrees of election, one unto faith and the other unto salvation, and the election unto faith is not a

---

1 Canons of Dordt conclusion, in *Confessions and Church Order*, 180.
2 Canons of Dordt 1.6, in *Confessions and Church Order*, 156.

guarantee of election unto salvation,[3] then the fact that one believes, even if faith *is* a gift of God and one is truly united to Christ, is no source of assurance.

If election is not sovereign but conditional, based on man;[4] or if election is changeable, even if it *is* confessed to be unconditional, sovereign, one decree, but yet changeable;[5] or if the death of Christ was for all men, and the purpose of God in the giving of his Son was not a particular purpose;[6] or if the depravity of man was not total but partial, leaving man with a free will,[7] and the regenerating work of God ineffectual[8] but waiting on the exercise of that free will;[9] or if man's preservation is uncertain (the Arminians claimed to be unsure about this) or is "in consequence of our own merits";[10] that is, if salvation in *any* sense of the word is determined by man, man's works, or man's will, there will be no consolation for wretched, sinful souls.

The Reformed Promotion of Assurance

But my main purpose is to show the positive truth of the Canons' doctrine that we are duty bound to protect: the glorious, soul-warming truth that the people of God can be absolutely certain of their salvation—from its foundation in eternity, to its culmination in glory.

To state the matter in a personal way, assurance has the believer confess, "I have personal certainty of God's eternal, unchangeable, unconditional love for me! That he loves me means that he has bound me to his Son by faith, has justified and does justify me, has

---

3   Canons of Dordt 1, error and rejection 2, in *Confessions and Church Order*, 160.
4   Canons of Dordt 1.9–10, in *Confessions and Church Order*, 157.
5   Canons of Dordt 1.11, in *Confessions and Church Order*, 157.
6   Canons of Dordt 2.8, in *Confessions and Church Order*, 163–64.
7   Canons of Dordt 3–4.1–4, in *Confessions and Church Order*, 166–67.
8   Canons of Dordt 3–4.11–12, in *Confessions and Church Order*, 168–69.
9   Canons of Dordt 3–4.10, in *Confessions and Church Order*, 168.
10 Canons of Dordt 5.8, in *Confessions and Church Order*, 174.

called and regenerated me, will preserve me in the days to come, and will glorify me in the end. Of this, I am sure!"

Assurance is not merely the certainty that God loves me now, that I have the life of Christ in me now, that I have forgiveness of sins now, but I have no confidence of these continuing in the future. That is precisely the Arminian doctrine that Dordt needed to demolish. True biblical assurance is assurance that the love of God for me will never end, the life I have of Christ in me now will never die, the promises God makes to me now will never be retracted, the Spirit that dwells in me now will never be withdrawn, and my membership in the church of Jesus Christ will never be revoked.[11]

To simplify matters, as well as to focus on the Canons, we may say that, at bottom, the believer's assurance is assurance of election. That is, rather than speaking separately of assurance of faith, assurance of salvation, assurance of justification, assurance of preservation, and so forth, we deal with assurance of our election. Let me demonstrate the propriety, even benefit, of this approach. And I remind us that the Canons emphasize election and its assurance.

If you would speak of assurance as assurance of faith, then assurance is assurance of election because faith "flows forth from" election[12] and is the "infallible fruit" of election.[13] Or, if you would speak of assurance as assurance of salvation, then assurance is assurance of election, because election is the root and cause of all our salvation, the decretal foundation of our salvation. Salvation is God's "good pleasure he works in his elect."[14] Or, if you would speak of assurance as assurance of preservation, then assurance is assurance of election because, according to Jesus in John 17, God preserves those who were given to him in election; of all of them he will lose none. The Canons is clearest

---

11 Canons of Dordt 5.8, in *Confessions and Church Order*, 174.
12 Canons of Dordt 1.6, in *Confessions and Church Order*, 156.
13 Canons of Dordt 1.9, in *Confessions and Church Order*, 157.
14 Canons of Dordt 3–4.11, in *Confessions and Church Order*, 168.

in its connecting preservation and election.[15] Or, if you would speak of assurance as assurance of forgiveness and justification, then assurance is assurance of election, because it was the Father's electing decree that our sins would be paid for by the death of his Son.[16] Again, if you would speak of assurance as assurance that we belong to Jesus Christ and therefore are true and living members of his body, the church, then assurance is assurance of election because (again) in election we were given to Jesus Christ to be his precious possession.[17]

If we are assured of our election, we may be sure of everything! And "the elect…obtain the assurance of…their…election."[18]

Reformed folk are predestinarians and proud of it. Without the biblical doctrine of predestination—sovereign, double, gracious, eternal predestination—we are with the rest of mankind most miserable; we will have no assurance and therefore no comfort.

Consider that the word of God speaks to the believer's heart, as the Canons itself explains it. Again, we will put it in terms of the believer's personal confession.

Because election is God's eternal setting of his love upon a people (Deut. 7:7–8) I may be sure that God loves me. Deuteronomy 7:7, 8 teaches me that election is the Lord setting his love upon me. He chose me. Ephesians 1:4 reminds me that in love God predestinated me!

The Canons explains election in the language of love. Canons 1.10 describes election in terms of Romans 9: "Jacob have I loved" (v. 13). Canons 1.13 shows that election is that God "first manifested so great love towards"[19] me.

---

15 Canons of Dordt 5.6, 8–10; 5, error and rejection 1, in *Confessions and Church Order*, 174–76.
16 Canons of Dordt 2.8; 2, error and rejection 7, in *Confessions and Church Order*, 163–64, 166.
17 Canons of Dordt 1.14; 5.9, in *Confessions and Church Order*, 158, 175.
18 Canons of Dordt 1.12, in *Confessions and Church Order*, 157.
19 Canons of Dordt 1.13, in *Confessions and Church Order*, 157.

And if I am sure that God chose me in love, I may be sure that I am not reprobate. God does not hate me! I may be sure that he did not pass me by in his eternal decree, did not decree to leave me in my misery into which I plunged myself, to bestow no faith upon me, to condemn and punish me forever (the language of Canons 1.15)!

Then, because election is God's eternal giving of us to his Son, I know that God gave me to Jesus Christ! I belong to him, body and soul.

Election is God's decree to give a people to Christ. In Canons 1.7 election is explained this way: "a certain number of persons to redemption in Christ."[20] In head one, error and rejection 6: "Christ does not lose those whom the father gave him."[21] In this, the fathers had their eye on scripture. "All that the father giveth me shall come to me" (John 6:37, 39; see also John 17:2, 6, 9, 11–12; 18:9).

I have been given to Jesus Christ!

Because the Heidelberg Catechism has us confess with confidence, "I…am not my own, but belong unto my faithful Savior Jesus Christ,"[22] we see why the Formula of Subscription describes the Canons as "the explanation of some points"[23] found in the Heidelberg Catechism and Belgic Confession.

I know that I am a member of the body of Christ, the church.

Election is not merely God's choice of certain persons to be saved but his choice to place them in the security of, and into organic connection with, the body of his Son Jesus Christ. My comfort is inseparably bound up in the knowledge that I am a member—permanent member—of the church. Election is a doctrine "peculiarly

---

20 Canons of Dordt 1.7, in *Confessions and Church Order*, 156.
21 Canons of Dordt 1, error and rejection 6, in *Confessions and Church Order*, 161.
22 Heidelberg Catechism A 1, in *Confessions and Church Order*, 83.
23 Formula of Subscription, in *Confessions and Church Order*, 326.

designed" for the church.[24] Assurance is certainty that I "will continue true and living member(s) of the church."[25] As the Heidelberg Catechism puts it, "I am, and forever shall remain, a living member thereof."[26]

And I am sure that God chose me unconditionally, sovereignly. Not because God foresaw faith in me or holiness, not because he knew in advance that I would distinguish myself from any others. But God chose me to make me holy, to give me faith, to change me from death to life. I am "by nature neither better nor more deserving than others."[27]

The believer may be certain and assured of God's eternal election of him.

The great synod did not commission preachers—and Reformed seminaries today must not instruct their students when they enter the ministry—to say that it is not possible to know one's election, that it is not good to be sure of the love of God, that it would be spiritually dangerous to be confident of it. But that is the view these days in some churches: either that election itself cannot be known or that, if it can be, it is not healthy to know it.

The great synod taught that the doctrine of election must be preached and assurance of election must be preached. The fathers rejected "the errors of those who teach…that there is in this life… no consciousness of…election to glory."[28] As it was preached in the Old Testament and the New, "so it is still to be published in due time and place in the Church of God, for which it was peculiarly designed…for enlivening and comforting his people."[29] "The

---

24 Canons of Dordt 1.14, in *Confessions and Church Order*, 158.
25 Canons of Dordt 5.9, in *Confessions and Church Order*, 175.
26 Heidelberg Catechism A 54, in *Confessions and Church Order*, 104.
27 Canons of Dordt 1.7, in *Confessions and Church Order*, 156.
28 Canons of Dordt 1, error and rejection 7, in *Confessions and Church Order*, 161–62.
29 Canons of Dordt 1.14, in *Confessions and Church Order*, 158.

sense and certainty of this election"[30] are not dangerous, damaging, counter to Christian conduct, but wonderful!

So says the scripture. It is important to notice that the fathers at Dordt appealed so frequently, and so directly, to scripture. They did not appeal to the church fathers, to Calvin, Luther, Gotteschalk, or Augustine, but to scripture. And scripture teaches that we may know our election of God! "Knowing, brethren beloved, your election of God" (1 Thess. 1:4). The apostle Paul knows their election, by which he teaches that they may have knowledge and confidence of their own election. The apostle Peter teaches that the child of God can, even must, be certain of his election. "Wherefore the rather, brethren, give diligence to make your calling and election sure" (2 Pet. 1:10). The exhortation to become certain of one's election clearly implies that a believer can be certain.

But even if Dordt did not appeal to the church fathers, the worthies of generations past also emphasized the importance of assurance being rooted in election. Calvin is representative. "There cannot, however, be a better assurance of salvation gathered than from the decree of God."[31] "Those men who at this day obscure, and seek, as far as they can, to extinguish the doctrine of election, are enemies to the human race; for they strive their utmost to subvert every assurance of salvation."[32]

Besides, how foolish to suppose that our good God elects, loves, redeems, adopts, justifies, preserves, and will soon glorify a people, but does not want these beloved children to know it. Why, assuring his beloved children of his love for them is his best work. Just as a

---

30 Canons of Dordt 1.13, in *Confessions and Church Order*, 157.
31 John Calvin, *Commentaries on the Epistles of Paul the Apostle to the Philippians, Colossians, and Thessalonians*, trans. John Pringle (repr., Grand Rapids, MI: William B. Eerdmans, 1957), 290.
32 John Calvin, *Commentaries on the Twelve Minor Prophets, vol. 5, Zechariah and Malachi*, trans. John Owen (Grand Rapids, MI: William B. Eerdmans, 1950), 84–85.

godly husband wants his wife to know that he loves her, and just as godly parents want their children to know—and not doubt—their love for them, so the Father in heaven wills his children to know and works that certainty in them.

What a horrible teaching is the Arminian teaching that it is not possible to be sure of God's love.[33] What a heartwarming, comforting religion is the Reformed faith that believes a Christian can and will come to know that God loves him.

Assurance and the Problem of Doubt

God's people do sometimes struggle with doubts. The fathers at Dordt taught this over against the Arminians who charged the reformers with presumption, with carelessness, with an unrealistic view of the Christian life, as though believers go to glory without any struggles, any worries, any doubts or fears. If, the Arminians charged, salvation is certain for the elect, and they may know themselves to be elect, and if they will be preserved no matter what, Christians will become careless and proud—carnally secure. Over against that charge, the reformers taught that although Christians may be certain of their salvation, there are times when believers struggle with the assurance of their election. Believers sometimes doubt. Ponder too, regarding a proper response to the Arminian, that doubting one's election is not the corrective for sinfully and carnally presuming salvation.

Be careful not to misunderstand the Reformed view. Believers do not always doubt. The Canons says "*sometimes*" and that believers are "not *always* influenced." Christians doubt "in *some* instances."[34] The impression must not be left that doubts are the normal state of the child of God. Nor is doubt good. In Canons head five, error and

---

33 Canons of Dordt 1, error and rejection 7, in *Confessions and Church Order*, 161–62.
34 Canons of Dordt 5.4–5, in *Confessions and Church Order*, 174 (emphasis added).

rejection 6, the Canons rejects the error of those who teach that it is "praiseworthy to doubt."[35]

Doubting, therefore, may never be fostered or encouraged.

Nevertheless, the people of God sometimes struggle with doubts. This is the reality of the Christian life. At times their faith is weak, which means (according to the definition of faith by the Heidelberg Catechism) that their assurance that the blessings of salvation are for them wavers.

This is not the case for the presumptuous. The presumptuous will never doubt, never struggle with the assurance of faith or salvation, election or preservation, because their faith is not lodged in their heart but in their brains. Those whose confidence is a haughty confidence will not wrestle to come to assurance in times of doubt, for haughtiness does not doubt.

But this is the case for believers. In his commentary on the Canons, Homer Hoeksema says, "Assurance often can be weak and wavering."[36] So emphatic was he that, in commenting on head five, article 11, he says, "[This article] excludes from the Reformed family those who maintain that...the saints in this life always enjoy the full assurance of faith and the certainty of perseverance." And, "Who does not know by experience that the Christian must struggle with various carnal doubts in this life?...Who has not experienced that the child of God is placed in grave temptations and is the object of grievous attacks?"[37]

If assurance of his people is God's great work and our most blessed possession, then the devil's correspondingly great interest will be to rob believers of this possession. If thieves break into your home, you may be sure they are not interested in your toaster or

---

35 Canons of Dordt 5, error and rejection 6, in *Confessions and Church Order*, 178.
36 Hoeksema, *Voice of Our Fathers*, 69.
37 Hoeksema, *Voice of Our Fathers*, 470–71.

the broom in your garage. They will aim for your gold and jewelry, your expensive and precious possessions. Likewise, the devil wants to rob God's people of what is most valuable to them. Hoeksema says, "The tempter comes and sows seeds of doubt."[38]

The explanation for doubt is not that one may have true faith without having assurance, for assurance is of the essence of faith, as the Heidelberg Catechism teaches in Lord's Day 7. Rather, doubts are explained by the devil assaulting our faith, by faith becoming weak at times, by faith wavering. Regenerated Christians believe; at times they struggle with their unbelief and thus doubt (see, for example, Mark 9:24; 14:30–31; 17:20).

With greater clarity than the Catechism and Confession, the Canons teaches that our faith needs to be strengthened in times of weakness. The Belgic Confession, for example, teaches in article 35 that the Lord's supper comforts "our poor comfortless souls."[39] What is clearly but quietly taught in these confessions, the Canons spells out with emphasis.

Canons 1.16 speaks of those who "do not experience a lively faith," that is, of those who do not have an "assured confidence of soul."[40] The same article teaches that some "cannot yet reach that measure of holiness and faith to which they aspire"[41] and therefore doubt and fear. Assurance of election is attained "in due time… in various degrees, and in different measures."[42] Assurance of preservation comes "according to the measure of their faith."[43] By sin, believers can "interrupt the exercise of faith, wound their conscience, lose the sense of God's favor."[44] Believers in this life must "struggle

---

38 Hoeksema, *Voice of Our Fathers*, 474.
39 Belgic Confession 35, in *Confessions and Church Order*, 72.
40 Canons of Dordt 1.16, in *Confessions and Church Order*, 158.
41 Canons of Dordt 1.16, in *Confessions and Church Order*, 158–59.
42 Canons of Dordt 1.12, in *Confessions and Church Order*, 157.
43 Canons of Dordt 5.9, in *Confessions and Church Order*, 175.
44 Canons of Dordt 5.5, in *Confessions and Church Order*, 174.

with various carnal doubts" and "are not always sensible of this full assurance of faith and certainty of persevering." They are tempted. Indeed, Father does not allow them to be tempted above that they are able, but at times they succumb to temptations to doubt, so that God by the Holy Spirit must "*again* inspire them with [the] comfortable assurance."[45] For a time, they lost their assurance.

The Canons recognizes the temptation also in the rejection of errors. For believers must place the consciousness of their election over against the fiery darts of the devil, asking: "Who shall lay any thing to the charge of God's elect?" (Rom. 8:33).[46]

We may be assured. We must be assured. But we *need* assurance because of the great struggle of faith.

How Believers Attain This Assurance of Their Election

First, it must be understood that God grants assurance. It is not the case that God elects me, redeems me, grants me faith, and preserves me, but asks me somehow to give myself the assurance of these things. Then we are right back into the Arminian camp, in which God does his part and leaves the crucial parts to man.

The same God who elects, redeems, justifies, and preserves also assures his people of this. By his Spirit and word, God convinces me of his love for me. By his Spirit and word, God assures me that not only to others but to me also are freely given the remission of sins, everlasting righteousness, and salvation. By his Spirit and word, God makes me to know that no one shall pluck me out of his hand, that is, that he does and will effectively preserve me. And God, by his Spirit and word, assures me that, when I die, I shall be glorified with him. God assures his people.

That which the Heidelberg Catechism teaches in Lord's Day 1—

---

45 Canons of Dordt 5.11, in *Confessions and Church Order*, 175 (emphasis added).
46 Canons of Dordt 1, error and rejection 7, in *Confessions and Church Order*, 161–62.

that God, "by His Holy Spirit...assures me of eternal life"[47]—is now confirmed and clarified in the Canons: "The Scripture moreover testifies, that believers in this life have to struggle with various carnal doubts...*but God* who is the Father of all consolation, does not suffer them to be tempted above that they are able, but will with the temptation also make a way to escape...and by the Holy Spirit [God!] again inspires them with the comfortable assurance of persevering."[48] "The spirit [of God] itself beareth witness with our spirit, that we are the children of God" (Rom. 8:16).

But how God grants this assurance is of greatest importance. First, God grants the gift of faith in Jesus Christ revealed in the gospel. Faith embraces Jesus Christ revealed in the gospel, consciously, eagerly, actively, hungrily. And faith, according to the Canons, is God gifted, not man worked.

God does not grant assurance, the Canons teaches, by a special revelation to a select few Christians. The Canons makes a special point of rejecting this teaching, not only in the rejection of errors,[49] but in the positive articles: "This assurance, however, is not produced by any peculiar revelation contrary to, or independent of the Word of God."[50]

This is the serious error of some today. It was the Roman Catholic error. The Decree of the Council of Trent (XII) declared, "No one, moreover...ought so far to presume as regards the secret mystery of divine predestination, as to determine for certain that he is assuredly in the number of the predestinate...for except by special revelation it cannot be known whom God hath chosen to everlasting life."[51] And the spiritual children of some Puritans deny

---

47 *Confessions and Church Order*, 83–84.
48 Canons of Dordt 5.11, in *Confessions and Church Order*, 175 (emphasis added).
49 Canons of Dordt 5, error and rejection 5, in *Confessions and Church Order*, 177.
50 Canons of Dordt 5.10, in *Confessions and Church Order*, 175.
51 Hoekema, *Saved by Grace*, 146.

the possibility of assurance except by a special, unique experience, reserved for a few.

If that were necessary, Paul would have said about his assurance, "I received my certainty by special revelation on the Damascus road; and if you want assurance, you need a similar experience." Or, "Where *I* am in the confidence of my election, *you* cannot come, because you are not an apostle who has seen Jesus directly as I did." Instead, Paul says, "Knowing, brethren beloved, *your* election of God" (1 Thess. 1:4, emphasis added). And, "Make *your* calling and election sure" (2 Pet. 1:10, emphasis added). Common members of the church of Jesus Christ can and may be sure.

Faith in Jesus Christ revealed in the gospel is the means. By the preaching of Christ crucified and our embrace of him by faith, we are assured. The means by which God works faith and its assurance is the preaching of the gospel. Without this preaching of Christ and him crucified there cannot be assurance.

The reformers all emphasized the importance of faith in God's word. So the Canons declared, "This assurance...springs from *faith* in God's promises, which he has most abundantly revealed in his Word for our comfort; from the testimony of the Holy Spirit [not independently of that Word, but from that Word] witnessing with our spirit, that we are children and heirs of God."[52]

Even when Canons 1.12 relates assurance to observing some things in ourselves, what we observe first is faith, the faith that lays hold on the Lord Jesus Christ, faith worked by the sovereign giver of faith, faith worked by the word.

How does Paul know the Thessalonians' election? Because the gospel he preached brought forth the fruit of faith in them. For salvation, we are always bound to the word of God. For our assurance of salvation too. Faith, as it embraces Jesus Christ, revealed in the word, is the means of assurance.

---

52 Canons of Dordt 5.10, in *Confessions and Church Order*, 175.

God is pleased to grant assurance as the believer lives out of that faith. The Canons would be sure that no one misunderstands. There is strong warning in the Canons. Do not suppose that you will have assurance except you actively live out of your faith. Here again, the Canons are giving explanation of some points of the other Reformed creeds, specifically the Heidelberg Catechism's statement that "every one may be assured in himself of his faith by the fruits thereof."[53]

The Canons teach that intimately connected to the reality that assurance comes to believers through faith is the teaching that faith always comes to expression in a godly life. Always.

The Spirit witnesses with our spirit in the way of a holy life and *only* in the way of a holy life. The child of God who lives godly and *only* the child of God who lives godly may be sure of his or her election. On the path of godly living and *only* on that path of godly living does the child of God have assurance.

The Practical Syllogism

This is what has been called, in Reformed theology, the practical syllogism.

A syllogism is a simple, three-step, logical argument, with a major premise, a minor premise, and a conclusion, like this: only birds have wings; that creature I see in my tree has wings; therefore, I may conclude that that creature in my tree is a bird. Or, a better illustration for our celebration of Dordt: only those who love Dordt would appear at a conference celebrating Dordt; you have appeared at a conference celebrating Dordt. Therefore, I may conclude that you must love Dordt! Of course, all understand that in the three steps, both steps one and two must be clearly and unarguably true, or the argument's conclusion cannot stand. For example, in the first illustration, step one is questionable, for also airplanes and crazy

---

53 Heidelberg Catechism A 86, in *Confessions and Church Order*, 120.

people who jump off high cliffs in flying suits have "wings." And in the second, someone might attend a Dordt conference as a reporter, or to sell books, and thus the conclusions in each may not be infallibly true.

The practical syllogism is such a simple, logical argument regarding assurance of salvation that deals with one's practice of Christianity—not his head knowledge, but his practice of godliness, his holiness. The logic runs something like this: all God's elect practice godliness, or live in holiness; I cannot deny that, by the grace of God in me, I live in holiness, even though it is a very small beginning; therefore, I may conclude with certainty that I am one of God's elect.

But caution is in order regarding the practical syllogism, lest one quickly get into a quagmire. The practical syllogism, as the Heidelberg Catechism and Canons present it, is secondary, not primary, in the matter of assurance. Primary is my embrace, by faith, of Jesus Christ presented to me in the gospel; I believe what God says, and by that faith the Holy Spirit witnesses with my spirit. Secondary is the matter of observing in ourselves the fruits of faith. Also, the practical syllogism must never be considered apart from faith, but as faith itself embracing the promise of God that he will sanctify his people.

There is a real danger of losing balance here by so emphasizing the syllogism that we minimize faith. There is also a real danger of losing our way completely if we imagine that the practical syllogism is unrelated to faith.

Emphasizing the practical syllogism would be an understandable mistake, however, because sinful presumption is always found in the church. Our day is not unlike the days post-Reformation, when among some there was an orthodoxy that was dead, formal, intellectual; and the faith of that orthodoxy appeared to be a false faith because it was not accompanied by a godly life. A carelessness existed that emphasized doctrine over against godliness, knowledge over piety. It was an attitude of reckless presumption: "I am a child of God and believe the promises of God are for me. I am sure God loves me and that when I die I will go to heaven." But there was no corresponding godliness.

When that occurs, there can be proper and (understandably) improper reactions. The proper reaction is that pastors and elders boldly warn that no one may be sure of his salvation who only hopes in the promises of God but does not live out that hope in purifying himself (as 1 John 3 says). Assurance is presumption if it is not accompanied by a godly life. To paraphrase Psalm 1: that man, and only that man, is blessed with assurance who, fearing God, restrains his feet from sin.

But some went beyond that warning and made two mistakes that must be avoided if we are to remain faithful heirs of Dordt. First, the practical syllogism became the primary means by which the believer sought assurance. Second, the godliness that was allegedly the evidence of faith was questioned as to its genuineness. Elaborate and unbiblical standards were drawn up to determine whether the fruits were genuine fruits. The result was to create doubts in the people rather than assurance. Proper response to presumption is not such reaction.

Nevertheless, the Reformed faith teaches the reality that a godly life is inseparable from the assurance of salvation. There is a necessary connection, say the Canons, between the godly life of the believer and his certainty of his election and preservation.

The connection is not that the godly life is the ground of our assurance of election. A godly life is no more ground for assurance than apples are the grounds for the existence of an apple tree. But godliness is an evidence of election just as apples are the evidence that the tree is indeed a living apple tree.

"The elect obtain the assurance of this, their…election…by observing in themselves…the infallible fruits of election pointed out in the Word of God—such as true faith in Christ [faith must be primary!], filial fear, a godly sorrow for sin, a hungering and thirsting after righteousness, etc."[54]

"This assurance…springs from [first!] faith in God's promises… from [by faith] the testimony of the Holy Spirit, witnessing with our spirit, that we are children and heirs of God, and lastly [the Canons do not omit this, even if it is last] from a serious and holy desire to preserve a good conscience and to perform good works."[55]

"The Holy Scriptures constantly deduce this assurance…from the marks proper to the children of God, and from the constant promises of God."[56]

The people of God "sometimes lose the sense of God's favor… until on their returning into the right way of serious repentance, the light of God's fatherly countenance again shines upon them."[57] Not because they return, but only when.

Of all of that, Homer Hoeksema says, "The way of assurance is the way of sanctification."[58] And again, "The way of life is the way of repentance, not the way of sin and impenitence, and only in the way of repentance can one have the sense of God's favor."[59] That is, the path on which a believer walks who will be assured is the path of a holy life. Herman Hoeksema, commenting on Romans 8:1, says:

> Walking after the Spirit is the necessary characteristic of them who are in Christ Jesus. Why? Because we cannot be in Christ in the legal sense without being in Him in the vital sense. We cannot be justified without being sanctified. Therefore, he who is in Christ also walks after the Spirit. Nor can we have

---

54 Canons of Dordt 1.12, in *Confessions and Church Order*, 157.
55 Canons of Dordt 5.10, in *Confessions and Church Order*, 175.
56 Canons of Dordt 5, error and rejection 5, in *Confessions and Church Order*, 177.
57 Canons of Dordt 5.5, in *Confessions and Church Order*, 174.
58 Hoeksema, *Voice of Our Fathers*, 474.
59 Hoeksema, *Voice of Our Fathers*, 432.

peace and say that we are in Christ unless we walk after the Spirit. The assurance of our being in Christ is in the way of sanctification. The way of our being blessed is that we walk in sanctification. And the fruit of this walk in sanctification is that we say, "There is no condemnation for me."[60]

Making Our Calling and Election Sure

Again, the Canons teaches this way of assurance based on the testimony of scripture. This is what Peter means in the very important passage regarding the assurance of our election. "Give diligence to make your calling and election sure: for if ye do these things, ye shall never fall" (2 Pet. 1:10).

About this passage, note first that Peter is not calling Christians to make sure that God calls them or elects them, as though before their activity they were not called or chosen, and after their activity God called and elected them. This would hinge calling and election on man. Rather, he exhorts the believer to make certain *in his own mind and heart* that he is elect.

Second, Peter emphasizes the believer's activity in attaining the assurance of his calling and election. The activity is a strenuous one: "give diligence." That is, believers are called to a difficult activity, in the way of which activity they are assured of their calling and election. God does not assure believers who are inactive. Christians must not imagine that they may wait for God's assuring testimony to their spirit while they do nothing, passively waiting for assurance. "Give *diligence*." The exhortation in verse 5 is even stronger, expressed in the English, "giving *all* diligence" (emphasis added).

Third, the activity aims at assurance of one's election by way of assurance of one's calling. One begins with assurance of God's

---

60 Herman Hoeksema, *Righteous By Faith Alone: A Devotional Commentary on Romans*, ed. David J. Engelsma (Grandville, MI: Reformed Free Publishing Association, 2002), 308.

efficacious call of a man: the powerful, efficacious address of him through the gospel that brings him into a saving union with God's Son. Then, and as a result of the certainty of his calling, a believer is certain of his election, because only those and all those whom God has predestinated does he also call (Rom. 8:30).

Fourth, Peter explains that this activity is the activity of doing "these things." The "these things" in verse 10 refers back to the exhortation he gave in the preceding verses 5–7: "add to your faith virtue; and to virtue, knowledge," and so forth. That is, if a believer expresses his faith, prays that his faith may be busy in all these virtues, he will be more and more confident of his calling that gave him that faith and therefore of the election that stands behind them both.

The text does not teach that one is sure because he does these things. The believer has assurance because of God and God's works. But it is only in the way of living thus that God is pleased to give assurance. This is the experience of every believer because every believer knows that he would never be able to do these things if he were not called into union with Christ as one of God's elect. Thus, the Holy Spirit testifies with his spirit as he is active with these activities, living out of his faith by which he embraces Jesus Christ and lives the life of Christ. The holy God so works. His holy Son so works. The Holy Spirit so works. Those who are his own are holy. God's ways are always ways of holiness.

When the Canons says that by sin man "interrupt[s] the exercise of faith,"[61] the fathers are emphasizing man's own responsibility in his troubles. With regard to the sovereign purposes of God, it would not be wrong to say that God himself interrupts the gift of faith exercising itself, or withholds the giving of the gift, when his children walk so contrary to faith; and he renews and restores the gift when and only when (but not *because*) his children return in the way of repentance.

---

61 Canons of Dordt 5.5, in *Confessions and Church Order*, 174.

The pastor-theologians whom God used to pen the Canons knew of what they spoke because they knew scripture and because they themselves lived—and struggled in the living of—the holy Christian life. They were no armchair theologians, ivory-tower professors, but wise pastors who saw the breadth of biblical revelation as it applied to the lives of the people in the pew.

Assurance is God's sovereign gift! He works it in his people by his own gift of faith, as and only as that faith exerts itself to add to it temperance, patience, godliness, brotherly kindness, and charity.[62]

Conclusion

The return of Arminianism to Reformed churches has spelled disaster in many respects, not the least of which is disaster with regard to the most precious comfort of the assurance of election.

---

62 Among Reformed believers, zealous to guard the truth of salvation by grace alone through faith alone without works, there may be a question whether there is any connection between holiness and assurance, between a godly life and assurance of salvation, between godliness and any blessing of salvation. The following statements of Protestant Reformed theologians are a few among many examples of the historic Protestant Reformed teaching on the matter. From Herman Hoeksema's *The Heidelberg Catechism for Junior Catechumens* (the synodically approved catechism curriculum of the PRCA; first printing, 1929; sixth printing, 1995): "Have you any other evidence that you belong to Him? Yes, for he also made me sincerely willing to live unto him" (Lesson 1:6). "How can we know that we are in the faith? By the working and fruit of faith in us, especially by a hearty sorrow after God and hunger and thirst after righteousness" (Lesson 8:6). "Do we derive any spiritual benefit from doing good works? Yes, for everyone may be assured of his faith by the fruits thereof" (Lesson 22:4). David J. Engelsma wrote: "Only in the way of a holy life can, and do, believers enjoy assurance that they are the children of God. The Spirit witnesses with the spirit of the believer as the believer obeys God's commandments, and *only* as he obeys God's commandments. The believer has assurance as he walks in holiness of life, and *only* as he walks in holiness of life…Holiness is a confirming evidence of salvation to the believer, as good works are evidence of justification" (*The Gift of Assurance* [South Holland, IL: Evangelism Committee of the Protestant Reformed Church, 2009]), 50.

A conditional election has no comfort. A changeable election gives no assurance. What terror to teach (allegedly to motivate men to zeal and godliness) that "Christ has in no place prayed that believers should infallibly continue in faith,"[63] or to imagine that "the faith of those who believe for a time does not differ from justifying and saving faith (true faith) except in duration."[64]

And what horrible slander to allege, "The certainty of perseverance and of salvation from its own character and nature is a cause of indolence and is injurious to godliness, good morals, prayers and other holy exercises."[65] Another translation (paraphrase) puts it: "is by its very nature…an opiate of the flesh."[66]

At the same time, seeking assurance of election through a faith that is not lived out in all its fullness, a faith that does not give diligence, that does not heed the exhortation to "work out your salvation," spells the same disaster and also brings the end to true comfort.

But what comfort the Reformed, biblical faith is. Whom God has chosen will forever be Christ's. They all may be sure of that. And this—assurance and certain security—explains the "grateful returns of ardent love to him, who first manifested so great love towards [us]."[67]

---

63 Canons of Dordt 5, error and rejection 9, in *Confessions and Church Order*, 178.
64 Canons of Dordt 5, error and rejection 7, in *Confessions and Church Order*, 178.
65 Canons of Dordt 5, error and rejection 6, in *Confessions and Church Order*, 178.
66 Jaroslav Pelikan and Valerie Hotchkiss, eds., *Creeds and Confessions of Faith in the Christian Tradition*, 3 vols. (New Haven, CT: Yale University Press, 2003), 2:597.
67 Canons of Dordt 1.13, in *Confessions and Church Order*, 157.

Appendix 1

THE SESSIONS OF THE SYNOD OF DORDT, 1618–1619

Douglas J. Kuiper

The following is a summary of each session of the Synod of Dordt. It was originally published in weekly installments in the blog at www.dordt400.org, in conjunction with the Protestant Reformed Theological Seminary's conference commemorating the four hundredth anniversary of the Synod of Dordt.

The Synod of Dordt met in 180 sessions from Tuesday, November 13, 1618, to Wednesday, May 29, 1619. Strikingly, four hundred years later, the dates and days correspond: November 13, 2018, falls on a Tuesday, and May 29, 2019, on a Wednesday.

This summary is not concerned to explain *why* the synod decided what it did, but simply to inform the reader what the synod accomplished at each session.

WEEK ONE: SESSIONS 1–5

Session 1: Tuesday, November 13, 1618, AM

The morning began with Balthasar Lydius preaching a sermon in Dutch, and Jeremias de Peurs preaching another in French. Probably these sermons were preached in two different churches to different audiences. Both men were delegates to the synod. As the minister of the church in Dordrecht, Lydius was able to sleep in his own bed during the months the synod met. De Peurs was minister of the French refugee (Walloon) church in Middelburg.

After the sermons the delegates went in procession to the building in which the synod met, the *Kloveniersdoelen*. This building was an armory used by the local militia. The States General deputies (representing the national government) welcomed the other delegations and showed them their assigned seats. Then Balthasar Lydius opened the synod with prayer, after which Martin Gregorius made opening remarks. Gregorius was the president of the state delegation that week; this presidency rotated weekly.

The eighteen States General deputies presented their credentials, which Balthasar Lydius read. Then they elected Daniel Heinsius as their secretary. He was to keep minutes of the meetings of the State General deputies and to create his own set of minutes of the synod.

Session 2: Wednesday, November 14, 1618, AM

The Dutch churches had ten provincial (regional) synods, which delegated thirty-seven ministers and nineteen elders to the Synod of Dordt. These fifty-six Dutch delegates presented their credentials. The Provincial Synod of Utrecht sent three delegates who were Remonstrants (Arminians) and three who were Contra-Remonstrants (orthodox). Stay tuned for more about the three Arminian delegates (session 23).

Synod elected John Bogerman as its president, chose Jacob Rolandus and Herman Faukelius as its assessors, or vice presidents, and appointed Sebastian Dammannus and Festus Hommius to be its scribes.

Four Dutch professors of theology were present and showed their credentials.

Session 3: Wednesday, November 14, 1618, PM

Synod read the letters that were attached to some of the credentials of the Dutch delegations. The Synod of Overijssel expressed its insistence that the Arminian matter should be judged on the basis only of scripture, the Belgic Confession, and the Heidelberg Catechism. With this the synod agreed.

The credentials of the three Remonstrant delegates from Utrecht indicated that these were authorized to address only the Arminian issue and could make no final decision without consulting their provincial synod. Synod questioned these delegates regarding their credentials, and they responded in writing the next day (session 4), to the synod's satisfaction. Again, more about this later.

Synod asked the seven foreign delegations (twenty-three men) who were already present to present their credentials. They responded that they had already presented them to the States General deputies.

Delegations from France and Brandenburg had been appointed but were unable to come. The delegation from Nassau-Wetteravia would arrive later, as would one member of the British delegation who represented the churches of Scotland and one other Dutch professor (see session 5).

Session 4: Thursday, November 15, 1618, AM

On November 11, 1617 (almost a whole year earlier!), the national government had adopted rules of order for the Synod of Dordt. Synod read those rules.

Synod then decided to order thirteen Remonstrants to appear before it within fourteen days (see session 21). All delegates were exhorted to prepare for the appearance of the Remonstrants by reading their writings.

Session 5: Friday, November 16, 1618, AM

Synod read and approved the letter of summons that would be sent to the Remonstrants. The States General deputies also prepared a letter to send them.

Noting that one professor of theology (Sybrand Lubbertus) had not yet arrived, synod instructed him to come. He appeared on November 23.

While waiting for the Remonstrants to appear, synod decided to treat other matters that the provincial synods had placed on its agenda.

WEEK TWO: SESSIONS 6–12

Session 6: Monday, November 19, 1618, AM

In 1618 at least two Dutch Bible translations existed—a translation of the Latin Vulgate and a translation of Luther's German Bible. In response to a question from one of the provincial synods, the Synod of Dordt agreed that a new translation would profit the churches. Synod began to discuss how to implement this. This translation would become the *Statenvertaling*, the "States Translation."

Session 7: Tuesday, November 20, 1618, AM

The delegates from Great Britain explained the method used in translating the King James Version: six different committees were assigned separate portions of scripture, after which the translation was carefully edited twice. The British delegation also mentioned the rules that governed the translators in their work.

Session 8: Tuesday, November 20, 1618, PM

Continuing its discussion regarding Bible translation, the synod decided that this translation: firstly, should not be a revision of the existing translations but a new translation directly from the Hebrew and Greek; secondy, should be a precise translation of the Hebrew and Greek, treating God's word carefully, and at the same time should express the scriptures in the vernacular Dutch; thirdly, should include a note on the side of the text when the Hebrew or

Greek was difficult to express in Dutch; and fourthly, should use a different font for words that were added to fill out the text, similar to the KJV's use of italics.

Session 9: Wednesday, November 21, 1618, AM

Should the apocryphal books also be translated? At this session, some argued against it: the apocryphal books were not inspired, they contradicted the inspired scriptures at some points, and neither the Jews nor the ancient Christian church included them. One of the Utrecht Remonstrant delegates retorted that the Heidelberg Catechism should be treated similarly. The Dutch Bibles of that day included the Catechism after the New Testament; this delegate argued that the new translation should not include the Catechism and that the Catechism should not be preached.

The Synod did not make a final decision at this session.

Session 10: Thursday, November 22, 1618, AM

Four hundred years later, the United States observed this day as its annual Thanksgiving Day. We give thanks to God not only for his earthly and material gifts, but also for the synod's work and the ways in which we benefit from that work in the twenty-first century.

After more discussion, the synod decided to include the apocryphal books in the Bible translation but said that these did not need to be as carefully translated as did the inspired books, that the Apocrypha should be placed after the New Testament, and that it should be introduced by a disclaimer that these are human writings.

Synod decided it would appoint three men to translate the Old Testament and three to translate the New. It also decided to ask the national government, through its delegation at the synod, to promote and fund the translating project.

Session 11: Friday, November 23, 1618, AM

The fifth Dutch professor delegated to the synod (Prof. Lubbertus) arrived. So did John Hales, chaplain to the English delegate Carlton, who would observe the synod and write letters regarding its proceedings.

Synod decided that the work of Bible translation should begin three months after the synod adjourned and that the translators should report every three months regarding their progress. In spite of this decision, the work of translation did not actually begin until 1626.

Session 12: Saturday, November 24, 1618, AM

Regarding Bible translation, synod decided: firstly, to use the Dutch *du* when translating the second person singular pronoun referring to God (this meant that the less formal Dutch pronoun would be used); secondly, to translate the word "Jehovah" in large letters (as the KJV does with Lord); thirdly, to use the Hebrew form, rather than the Dutch, in translating Old Testament proper names; fourthly, to use the current division of chapters and verses but note in the margin where the chapter divisions are poor; and fifthly, to add a table of chronologies and genealogies at the end of the translation but not to include any pictures.

Not yet finished with the matter of Bible translation, synod recessed for the Sabbath, as was its practice.

WEEK THREE: SESSIONS 13–18

Session 13: Monday, November 26, 1618, AM

Previously the synod had decided to appoint three men to translate the Old Testament and three to translate the New. At this session the synod named those men. It also appointed men from each province to oversee the translation work.

APPENDIX 1: *THE SESSIONS OF THE SYNOD OF DORDT, 1618–1619*

Recall that the Provincial Synod of Utrecht sent to Dordt three delegates who favored Arminianism and three who opposed it. Those who opposed it asked the synod not to appoint overseers from Utrecht for the work of Bible translation, but to permit the Utrecht Provincial Synod to appoint them later. Dordt agreed to this. Because the Utrecht churches had many Arminian ministers, the list of men available for the work of overseeing the translation would change significantly if the synod were later to condemn Arminianism and insist that the Arminian ministers be put out of office, which in fact it did do.

Session 14: Tuesday, November 27, 1618, AM

The previous national synod, that of 's Gravenhage in 1586, had required every minister to explain briefly the Heidelberg Catechism at the Sunday afternoon services. For various reasons, this practice had fallen on hard times. The Remonstrants opposed the practice. Some country churches had lively preaching only once a Sunday because they shared ministers. And many Dutch people preferred to spend their Sunday afternoons in work or recreation.

The Synod of Dordt reiterated this requirement, later embodying it in article 68 of its Church Order. Synod then asked the magistrates to forbid work and recreation on the Sabbath and insisted that the church visitors ask whether the churches were complying with the requirement regarding Catechism preaching. In the case of the country churches, synod permitted the Catechism to be taught every other week.

Hendrik van Hell, elder delegate from Zutphen, died on this day.

Session 15: Wednesday, November 28, 1618, AM

The synod deemed it necessary to provide more catechism instruction than was given on Sunday. The foreign delegations explained the methods of catechizing that their churches used.

Session 16: Thursday, November 29, 1618, AM

Dr. Joseph Hall, a delegate from Great Britain, preached on Ecclesiastes 7:16. He exhorted the delegates to be righteous in their actions. He encouraged the synod to maintain the Heidelberg Catechism and Belgic Confession and advised it to require the Remonstrants to submit an explanation of Romans 9, "short, clear, and explicit, without colouring or artifice."[1] He urged all to seek peace as brothers and members of the same body. His concluding wish was that error would be opposed, "that truth alone may see the light, alone may reign, and may bring safety to you, glory to the Church, and peace to the State."[2]

Session 17: Friday, November 30, 1618, AM

The synod resumed its discussion regarding catechizing. The Remonstrant delegates from Utrecht continued to object to preaching and teaching the Heidelberg Catechism (see session 9).

The synod emphasized the need for catechism instruction in three spheres: home, school, and churches. In the churches, the Heidelberg Catechism itself would be preached; in the schools, a summary of the Catechism; and in the homes, a short catechism containing an explanation of the Apostles' Creed, ten commandments, Lord's prayer, sacraments, and church discipline, to all of which would be added some short prayers and scripture passages.

A committee was appointed to draw up the catechisms for school and home. It reported at session 177.

Session 18: Saturday, December 1, 1618, AM

The synod met during the Dutch Golden Age. Dutch merchants sent their ships to the Dutch East Indies, stopping at other Dutch

---

1 "Sermon of Joseph Hall to the Synod," in *The British Delegation and the Synod of Dort (1618–1619)*, ed. Anthony Milton (Suffolk: The Boydell Press, 2005), 131.
2 "Sermon of Joseph Hall," in *British Delegation*, 133.

colonies along the way. Dutch Reformed Christians inhabited these colonies and took heathen children into their families, not as *adopted* children, but as *servants*. The delegates from North Holland asked whether these children might be baptized. The various delegations gave their advice, but the synod did not finish treating the matter.

Some reasons for the lack of Heidelberg Catechism preaching and teaching have already been given. Could another reason be that students for the ministry were not well trained? The delegates from Zeeland were of this opinion, and they gave suggestions how better to prepare students for the ministry. Synod decided that it would take up this matter the following Monday and each delegation should prepare written advice over the weekend.

After recessing, the delegates attended the burial of Elder Hendrik van Hell.

WEEK FOUR: SESSIONS 19–24

Session 19: Monday, December 3, 1618, AM

Should heathen slave children in the East Indies be baptized? Synod decided that only those children should be baptized who had come to years, who had been instructed in the faith and made profession of faith, and who desired baptism. It applied the same decision to heathen adopted children who had not been sufficiently taught to that point.

Synod then began hearing the judgments of the delegations regarding preparing students for the ministry.

Session 20: Tuesday, December 4, 1618, AM

President Bogerman broadened the issue regarding preparing students for the ministry by putting these questions to the synod: May these students preach? May they administer baptism? May they attend consistory and classis meetings? May they read the holy scriptures during the church worship services? Synod insisted that only ordained ministers may baptize. Regarding the other activities, synod said that while students *may* do them, synod was not ready to make a rule for all churches. It encouraged each church and classis to face these questions themselves, stressing the urgency of students gaining experience.

The Utrecht Remonstrants presented written objections to previous decisions (sessions 14, 17) regarding Heidelberg Catechism preaching and teaching and asked synod to enter their objections in its minutes. President Bogerman responded that synod's decision was made by majority vote (requiring submission to it), and that the States General had instructed that the minutes include only final decisions, not discussions or objections.

Session 21: Wednesday, December 5, 1618, AM

Being ill, one minister delegate from the Provincial Synod of Groningen-Ommelanden had never arrived. His alternate, Wigbold Homerus, appeared at this session, presented his credentials, and was seated.

The Remonstrants whom the synod had instructed to appear for examination (session 4) were to appear before synod on this day but were not present. The Remonstrant delegates from Utrecht assured synod that these would appear soon. Remember that the Arminians were called "Remonstrants" because the core teachings of Arminianism had been written in a document called "The Remonstrance," written in 1610.

Books had been published, some anonymously, that had caused unrest in the churches, presumably because they promoted Remonstrant teachings. Some churches asked the synod to provide a way to regulate book publishing. The foreign delegations informed synod how their churches had addressed the matter. Synod decided that this was not an ecclesiastical matter but one that belonged to the civil government.

APPENDIX 1: *THE SESSIONS OF THE SYNOD OF DORDT, 1618–1619*

Session 22: Thursday, December 6, 1618, AM

Having just arrived in Dordrecht, the Remonstrants who were summoned asked permission not to appear before synod until Saturday or Monday. This would give them time to find lodging and put their books and writings in order. Synod decided that they should briefly appear at this session, since they had not appeared the previous day as required.

On this date the States General published a notice that no one was permitted to write, print, distribute, or sell a book that spoke ill of the civil authorities and that no book might be published without being approved by a government agency.

The Remonstrants appeared and were shown their table in the middle of the room. Their spokesman, Simon Episcopius, explained their delay and explained why they desired not to appear before the synod for several more days. But if synod desired, he said, they were ready to begin their "conference" immediately. Synod agreed to let them come the next day but reminded them that they were not at a "conference" for mutual discussion but were at a synod to be examined and judged.

Session 23: Friday, December 7, 1618, AM

Ready to turn its full attention to the Remonstrant controversy, synod confronted a problem: three delegates from Utrecht were Remonstrant (session 2). Could they judge impartially, or should they give up their seat at synod and join the Remonstrants in the middle of the room? When President Bogerman put this question to the delegates, they asked for time to consider the matter.

Episcopius then read from prepared notes for an hour and a half. Afterward, Episcopius was rebuked for speaking at length when the synod had not yet asked the Remonstrants any questions.

On this day the delegates took an oath, required of them by the States General, to judge the Arminian issue on the basis of God's word alone. Synod would not permit the Utrecht Remonstrant delegates to take the oath until they decided whether to sit with the synod or with the Remonstrants.

Session 24: Saturday, December 8, 1618, AM

The Utrecht Remonstrants expressed their desire to remain seated as delegates to the synod, noting that the instructions on their credentials did not mandate them to take a certain position. After reading their credentials again, the synod permitted them to remain under five conditions. Synod would hear their response to these conditions the following Monday.

WEEK FIVE: SESSIONS 25–33

Session 25: Monday, December 10, 1618, AM

The previous week, synod had permitted the three Remonstrant delegates from Utrecht to remain as delegates on five conditions. These delegates agreed to three of the five, including taking the synodical oath, but had reservations about the first two, including stating that they were able to judge the fallacy of the Remonstrant position. After further discussion, two of them agreed to join the Remonstrants seated in the middle of the room. The third was ready to take the synodical oath, but synod asked him not to return as a delegate.

Recall that Episcopius had made a long speech the previous Friday. After he had finished, when President Bogerman asked him for a copy to enter into synod's record, he said he did not have a presentable copy. Synod became aware that he had given a copy to some foreign delegates. President Bogerman rebuked Episcopius for his deception.

Synod then asked the Remonstrants to present their opinions regarding the Five Articles of the Remonstrants and their objections to the Belgic Confession and Heidelberg Catechism. They responded by presenting a paper that set forth twelve conditions that a synod must meet for it to be considered a proper synod.

Session 26: Monday, December 10, 1618, PM

Synod rejected the idea that these twelve conditions defined a proper synod and exhorted the Remonstrants to submit to the synod. The Remonstrants retorted by calling the synod schismatic.

Session 27: Tuesday, December 11, 1618, AM

Again synod asked the Remonstrants to present their opinions and objections. This time the Remonstrants expressed two grievances: first, the synod was prejudiced against them, and second, President Bogerman and the States General deputies were treating them unfairly. They compared themselves to Athanasius, who left the council that Constantine called because Athanasius knew that the council was biased against him. They also pointed out that the Reformed would not attend the Council of Trent for the same reason. The Remonstrants said they would not have come to the synod at all, were it not for the presence and authority of the national government, which they said they honored.

The ecclesiastical and state delegates all sided with Bogerman on the charge against Episcopius that he had been deceitful (session 25).

Session 28: Tuesday, December 11, 1618, PM

Synod expressed that if anything, President Bogerman had been too soft in his words to the Remonstrants. Synod declared that the Remonstrants could not say that they honored the national government, while at the same time despising the synod that the national government had called. Synod assigned each delegation to prepare written advice how further to respond to the Remonstrants.

Session 29: Wednesday, December 12, 1618, AM

The judgments of the foreign delegates regarding the protest that the Remonstrants had made the previous day were read. For the duration of the synod, the judgments of the foreign delegates were always presented in the same order: first the English delegates, then those from the Palatinate (Heidelberg), followed by the delegates from Hesse, from Switzerland, from Nassau-Wetteravia, from Geneva, from Bremen, and last, from Emden.

The States General deputies reprimanded Episcopius for his speech and conduct.

Session 30: Wednesday, December 12, 1618, PM

When Synod asked the Remonstrants if they were ready to proceed to business, Episcopius asked permission to read a prepared writing. He was given permission only after the States General deputies reviewed his writing to be sure it did not contain new allegations against the synod.

Episcopius recounted the injury done to his reputation and explained his failure to provide synod with a copy of his speech. He had written notes, he said, but they were not complete; and he did not provide them because he knew the synod was against him, and he expected the synod to use his speech against him. He had given the States General delegation a copy at their request, but without comparing it to the original. Synod responded that it did not need to hear his explanation; it knew the truth of the matter well enough.

Now would the Remonstrants get down to business? They said that they would. The States General delegation reminded them to speak to the point and not to speak without permission.

Encouraged that progress could be made, synod asked if the Remonstrants would provide their written opinions regarding predestination (the first of the Five Articles). They responded that they had prepared to discuss the matter, not to provide a written statement. They had never understood that synod desired a written statement from them; they had come to attend a "conference." The

States General delegation read aloud the letters summoning them to appear before synod, showing that these letters had clearly informed them that they were to give their explanation of the Five Articles, after which synod would judge the matter. The Remonstrants reiterated that a verbal discussion would be the better route. Synod instructed them to provide their written opinions regarding divine predestination at the morning session the following day.

And had they written out their objections to some teachings of the Belgic Confession and Heidelberg Catechism? No. They had objections, but the objections were not written out.

Session 31: Thursday, December 13, 1618, AM

Episcopius read aloud the opinion of the Remonstrants concerning the first article and predestination.[3] Each Remonstrant was asked if he agreed with Episcopius' comments, and each said that he did.

Session 32: Friday, December 14, 1618, AM

Synod required the Remonstrants to provide their written opinions regarding articles two through five by the following Monday. Synod also instructed the Remonstrants to express their opinions positively, because they had previously stated what they did *not* believe rather than what they *did* believe.

Session 33: Saturday, December 15, 1618, AM

Abraham Schultetus, professor from Heidelberg, preached a sermon on Psalm 122, in which he exhorted the synod to peace. Gerard Brandt notes that earlier in the synod, Schultetus had desired a way to reconcile the Remonstrants and orthodox, but that after finding such impossible, he stood firmly with the orthodox.

---

3 "Opinions of the Remonstrants," in Hoeksema, *Voice of Our Fathers*, 628–34.

WEEK SIX: SESSIONS 34–38

Session 34: Monday, December 17, 1618, AM

The delegates from Nassau-Wetteravia arrived, showed their credentials, and took the synodical oath.

The Remonstrants delivered in writing their opinions of the second, third, fourth, and fifth articles of the Five Articles of the Remonstrants, 1610.

Synod had previously told them to express their opinions positively (saying what they *did* believe) rather than negatively (saying what they did *not* believe). Because synod was to judge their opinions and writings, a forthright declaration of what they believed was necessary. At this session, the Remonstrants brought fifteen reasons why they expressed their opinions negatively. Hoping to put synod on the defensive, they also gave seven reasons why synod should express its judgment on reprobation, not only on election. One was that the writings of some Reformed men included "terrible and blasphemous claims regarding reprobation"[4] that detracted from God's glory and from godliness.

Synod required them to deliver their objections to statements in the Heidelberg Catechism and Belgic Confession by the following day and in writing. When they said that this was expected of them too soon, synod gave them four days.

Session 35: Tuesday, December 18, 1618, AM

Some members of the church in Kampen came to Dordt and sought permission to address the synod. They were told that they could do so on the following day.

A synod of the Protestant Reformed Churches in America reads its script minutes at the end of each day. The Synod of Dordt did not do so, partly because the scribes had to write into the record all

---

4 *Acta of Handelingen*, 135.

the supplements, including the judgments of the various delegations and the writings that the Remonstrants submitted. This took considerable time. At this session the minutes of some of the preceding sessions were read.

Session 36: Wednesday, December 19, 1618, AM

The men from Kampen alleged that four Remonstrant ministers in Kampen were preaching new doctrines. The delegates from the Provincial Synod of Overijssel said that the provincial synod was not finished treating the case. However, the Synod of Dordt agreed at least to investigate the matter and ordered some of the ministers to appear.

Synod planned to recess from December 22–26, 1618, in order to observe the Christmas holiday. All delegates were exhorted to remain in the city so that the sessions could resume promptly. The elders from Friesland informed the synod that they needed to return home "for important causes."[5] They were permitted to leave but urged to hurry back.

Session 37: Thursday, December 20, 1618, AM

The member of the British delegation who represented the Church of Scotland, Dr. Balcanquhall, arrived, was admitted to the synod, and took the oath.

The Remonstrants were reminded to bring their objections to statements in the Catechism and Confession. Synod also did its part to clear up a misunderstanding on the part of the Remonstrants. They had been submitting lengthy documents to synod, thinking they were free to give their opinions at length. Synod pointed out that they would serve synod better by submitting briefer documents, and that synod had required them to give only their *opinions* on the

---

5 *Acta of Handelingen*, 139. This English translation from the Dutch is the editor's.

Five Points, not an expansion of them. Even today, one who brings a matter to a broader assembly or is judged by that assembly helps the assembly, and usually his own cause, by being brief and to the point.

President Bogerman suggested that the synod draw up a historical account of the rise and progress of the ecclesiastical dissensions. Synod would later agree to this.[6]

President Bogerman also suggested that each Dutch delegation write out statements from Arminian writings to which the synod ought to respond, so that the synodical scribes could formulate a list of them to distribute to all the delegates.

Session 38: Friday, December 21, 1618, AM

The public galleries were full, and anticipation was high. The news around town was that the Remonstrants would present their reservations about some teachings of the Belgic Confession and Heidelberg Catechism. The Remonstrants said that they were not able to finish preparing their evaluation of the Catechism, but they would read their reservations to doctrines contained in the Confession. Synod instructed them not to read the document but simply to hand it in.

After reviewing the document, the States General delegation admonished the Remonstrants for not providing their reservations to the Catechism within the required time and required them to provide these by Thursday, December 27. They also admonished them for presenting their objections to the Confession as a body, rather than each doing so individually. Because the Remonstrants kept appealing to the wording of the summons letters to justify their actions, the States General delegation told them to stop their "animal-like sophistries."[7]

The Remonstrants expressed surprise at being accused of

---

6 See "Historical Foreword," in Hoeksema, *Voice of Our Fathers*, 567–624.
7 The Dutch is *"diergelijke sophisterijen." Acta of Handelingen*, 141.

disobedience when they had simply done their duty and had done it as best they could under the time constraints given them.

Synod then recessed for the Christmas holiday, resuming its sessions the next Thursday.

WEEK SEVEN: SESSIONS 39–43

Session 39: Thursday, December 27, 1618, AM

The Remonstrants provided in writing their reservations to some teachings of the Heidelberg Catechism. The delegates from the Palatinate, the region in which the Heidelberg Catechism was written, asked if they could be the first to see these objections of the Remonstrants and present their response to synod. This they were permitted to do.

President Bogerman then reminded the Remonstrants that synod was asking them only to defend their view, not to propose their opinions. Also, synod was waiting for them to provide their positive views on the doctrine of election (see session 34). The Remonstrants continued to insist that their doctrine of election was orthodox and that the primary issue the synod had to treat was the statements of some Contra-Remonstrant men regarding reprobation. Synod was of a different mind: it intended to treat the matter of election before that of reprobation, convinced that the Remonstrants were not orthodox regarding election. So synod was waiting for them to present their view of the Five Articles of the Remonstrants, and particularly of the first article.

The Remonstrants hinted that they might leave the synod and the city of Dordrecht if they could not express themselves as freely as they desired. The States General delegation admonished the Remonstrants and threatened them with civil penalties if they did not submit to the synod, and several times in the ensuing days forbad them to leave the city without permission.

Session 40: Friday, December 28, 1618, AM

The Remonstrants sent a letter explaining why they could not comply with synod's order to treat the doctrine of election first. The States General delegation ordered the Remonstrants to appear and, when they did, again admonished them to obey. Bogerman also admonished them again for continuing to view themselves as part of a conference of equals rather than as those summoned to a synod, which would judge them. When each Remonstrant was asked if a certain writing expressed his own sentiments, each refused to answer.

Session 41: Friday, December 28, 1618, PM

In a session closed to observers, synod read the letter from the Remonstrants and discussed how to proceed. The synod was of a mind that it had treated them no differently than it had told them they would be treated. Yet it decided to bear with them longer and even to give them a little more freedom than it had previously. Each delegation was to prepare advice regarding how to proceed in dealing with the Remonstrants.

Session 42: Saturday, December 29, 1618, AM

Synod informed the Remonstrants of its response to their recent letter: it maintained its judgment that they must present positively their views on election before presenting their views on reprobation. The Remonstrants asked for time to consider the matter and were given until that evening. Synod underscored that the Remonstrants had not been cooperating with it, and it read the judgments of the various foreign delegates regarding how to proceed with the Remonstrants.

Session 43: Saturday, December 29, 1618, PM

The Remonstrants presented their written response to the synod's decision. Their response was evasive; they did not answer synod's questions forthrightly. The Remonstrants said that they were ready to give their opinions regarding election, and that in stating their opinions they would refute the position of the orthodox (the Contra-Remonstrants).

Synod responded that the Remonstrants had not answered its questions and were continuing to be unsubmissive. At this session a consensus began to form that synod would have to dismiss the Remonstrants so that it could judge the matter entirely from their writings.

The States General delegation prepared to send a committee to The Hague that weekend, so that on Monday it could update the government regarding what the synod had accomplished so far and regarding the conduct of the Remonstrants. Informing the Remonstrants of this, the States General delegation forbad the Remonstrants to leave Dordrecht.

WEEK EIGHT: SESSIONS 44–48

Session 44: Monday, December 31, 1618, AM

Johannes Polyander, professor of theology from Leiden, preached on Isaiah 52:7. Meanwhile, the committee that was sent to The Hague to report to the national government fulfilled its mandate. The synod did not meet on New Year's Day 1619, but on that day the States General resolved to inform synod that if the Remonstrants would not cooperate, their views should be judged from their writings.

Session 45: Wednesday, January 2, 1619, AM

Synod received a letter from the magistrates of Bommel, in Gelderland, requesting that synod permit the Remonstrant minister from that city to return to preach and administer the Lord's supper. When synod realized that there were other ministers in Bommel, and that the church there was not deprived of the lively preaching of the word, synod declined this request.

President Bogerman reminded the delegations to read the writings of the Remonstrants and prepare their objections to those writings.

In the afternoon, not as part of the official meeting, a committee wrote out the Remonstrants' objections to some teachings of the Belgic Confession and Heidelberg Catechism, so that the synodical delegates could read them.

Session 46: Thursday, January 3, 1619, AM

The Remonstrants were called in to hear the report of the committee that visited the Hague. The States General required the Remonstrants to cooperate with the synod and threatened them with penalties if they would not.

After the report was read, President Bogerman asked them several questions: Did the five articles of 1610 express their doctrinal convictions? Did they believe that the entire decree regarding predestination was that God would save those who persevered in faith—that he decreed nothing more than that? And did they believe that God elected believers as a category, rather than electing specific individuals to whom he would give faith?

Episcopius refused to answer, except to refer to the written statement that the Remonstrants had presented to synod the previous Saturday. Each Remonstrant individually followed his lead. To give a further response, they said, would be to violate truth and their conscience. Finally synod read that paper and asked them what they meant by certain words and statements. After giving evasive answers, they were dismissed.

Two of the Remonstrants, Isaac Frederic and Henricus Leo, had not appeared at this session. Leo was the minister from Bommel whose magistrates had asked synod to permit him to return (session 45).

Session 47: Friday, January 4, 1619, AM

Synod summoned only Henricus Leo and asked him the same questions that it had asked the others the previous day. He answered more extensively than the others had, but also asserted his conviction that synod had prejudged him.

That evening, not at an official session, some of the "graver and discreeter"[8] members of synod held a private conference to discuss how best to proceed with questioning the Remonstrants. These then agreed that the Remonstrants should be asked questions, but if they refused to answer synod should take the answer from their writings.

Balthasar Lydius, minister of the church at Dordrecht, informed synod that the Lord's supper would be administered in his church the next Lord's day, and that all delegates were welcome to partake. He asked only that they give prior notice to his consistory.

Session 48: Saturday, January 5, 1619, AM

President Bogerman informed synod of some questions that he desired to ask the Remonstrants in order to draw out from them their convictions regarding predestination. The Provincial Synod of Gelderland had provided some past history of its dealings with the Remonstrants, and the clerks of the foreign delegations were asked to copy these for their delegations.

WEEK NINE: SESSIONS 49–56

Session 49: Monday, January 7, 1619, AM

Two Remonstrant ministers from Hoorn, in the province of North Holland, had been suspended from office, and they appeared at synod to appeal their suspension. Synod informed them that it would treat their case later (session 174).

---

8   Hales, *Golden Remains*, 70.

President Bogerman continued to dictate to the delegates the questions that he desired to ask the Remonstrants regarding their view of predestination.

Session 50: Monday, January 7, 1619, PM

The minutes of some of the previous sessions were read so that corrections could be made if necessary.

The delegates from the Provincial Synods of Gelderland, South Holland, North Holland, Utrecht, and Overijssel were asked to draw up a report of how their provincial synods had dealt with the Remonstrants.

The Remonstrants had already handed in their reservations regarding the Belgic Confession and Heidelberg Catechism. Someone proposed having them also present in writing their reservations to the liturgical forms and the Church Order. This idea was not pursued further.

Session 51: Tuesday, January 8, 1619, AM

President Bogerman had collected various statements regarding predestination from Remonstrant writings. He presented these to synod, asking the delegates to review them, to suggest additions or corrections, and to prepare to discuss them.

The synod did not meet on January 9, at the request of the professors.

Session 52: Thursday, January 10, 1619, AM

The delegates concurred that Bogerman's summary of the Remonstrant view of predestination faithfully expressed the Remonstrants' opinions. Synod discussed whether to express the same points differently and more briefly, but reached no final decision.

APPENDIX 1: *THE SESSIONS OF THE SYNOD OF DORDT, 1618–1619*

Session 53: Thursday, January 10, 1619, PM

Synod decided that before it would respond to the teachings of the Remonstrants regarding predestination, it would write down summaries of their opinions regarding the other four points of doctrine.

The president wondered whether to call in the Remonstrants to hear their response to his formulation of their view. Not all were eager to proceed this way, because the Remonstrants had not cooperated earlier when asked to present their opinions. However, the body agreed to call them in the next day and to require them frankly to answer the synod's questions.

Session 54: Friday, January 11, 1619, AM

One of the Remonstrants, Isaac Fredericus, had not been at the synod since the turn of the year. Especially for his sake, but also for that of all the Remonstrants, the States General delegation reminded them of the decision of the national government on January 1. They also reminded the Remonstrants how they were to conduct themselves while they were being examined. When President Bogerman began putting the synod's questions to them, they responded evasively and said that their intention was merely to refute error by scripture and reason. When President Bogerman and the president of the States General delegation required them to come to the point, they retorted that the synod was their enemy.

Session 55: Friday, January 11, 1619, PM

Synod discussed the non-answer that the Remonstrants had given it at the morning session. It decided no longer to ask the Remonstrants questions, but to judge their opinions from their writings, and it informed the Remonstrants of this. The Remonstrants were instructed to hand in their explanations regarding predestination by the following Monday.

Session 56: Saturday, January 12, 1619, AM

On December 19 (session 36), the synod had ordered two Remonstrant ministers from Kampen to appear to answer allegations that they were preaching new doctrines. Two other Remonstrant ministers from Kampen were already at synod, because they were among the thirteen men that synod had summoned on November 15. At session 56, the synod read two letters from the magistrates in Kampen. In the first, the magistrates assured the synod that they had been promoting the Contra-Remonstrant position. In the second they asked that synod either permit the two ministers still in Kampen to remain in Kampen or permit the two already at synod to return. Synod did neither but maintained its summons of the two ministers still in Kampen.

WEEK TEN: SESSIONS 57–63

Session 57: Monday, January 14, 1619, AM

The States General delegation had met with the Remonstrants the previous Saturday to urge them to cooperate. The Remonstrants responded that they were willing to work with the synod, provided it understood that they would refute the Contra-Remonstrant position, as they had previously told synod (sessions 43, 54).

Hearing this, the foreign delegations informed synod that in their judgment the Remonstrants were continuing "in the same stubbornness, willfulness and disobedience."[9] Yet, demonstrating patient forbearance, synod summoned the Remonstrants once again to ask whether they were ready to answer synod's questions forthrightly. Their response was written out and lengthy, indicating that it was premeditated. In sum, the answer was, "No."

---

9   The Dutch reads: "*hardnekkigheid, moedwilligheid en ongehoorzaamheid.*" *Acta of Handelingen*, 201.

APPENDIX 1: *THE SESSIONS OF THE SYNOD OF DORDT, 1618–1619*

When Bogerman heard this, he delivered the fiery speech for which he will always be remembered. In it he reiterated that the Remonstrants had tested the synod's patience by their lies and evasive answers. He assured them that the churches would be informed of their obstinacy and that spiritual weapons would be used against them. And he ended: "*Exite!*" (Be gone!)

Synod was in session two full months before reaching this turning point. It would meet for another four and a half months.

Session 58: Monday, January 14, 1619, PM

This session was closed, as were several following sessions. Synod decided to copy the Remonstrants' explanation of the article on predestination that they had submitted to synod that morning. Synod also discussed what order to follow in investigating the Remonstrant teachings.

Session 59: Tuesday, January 15, 1619, AM

The decisions of some of the past sessions were read and approved. The table, benches, and chairs in the middle of the room, which had been used by the Remonstrants, were removed.

Session 60: Tuesday, January 15, 1619, PM

Synod continued to discuss what order to follow in investigating the Remonstrant teachings. The advice of the various delegations was heard, and synod decided that a consensus would be drawn up and read to the synod for its approval.

Session 61: Wednesday, January 16, 1619, AM

President Bogerman proposed an explanation of the second point of the Remonstrants.

Synod heard the consensus regarding how to proceed. It would treat the Remonstrant views article by article. The "Remonstrance of 1610" treated predestination, the extent of Christ's atonement, the extent of man's depravity, the nature and work of God's grace, and the matter of preservation in salvation. The "Opinions of the Remonstrants," which they submitted to synod, followed the same order.[10] In this order the doctrines would be treated in the Canons of Dordt. Each delegation was to write out its opinions regarding each point of the Five Articles.

Session 62: Thursday, January 17, 1619, AM

Joseph Hall, a delegate from Great Britain, returned home because of illness. Thomas Goad appeared in his place and took the synodical oath.

The five Dutch professors of theology began, each taking a turn, to address the synod regarding predestination. In the service of defending the orthodox view of predestination over against the Remonstrant view, Sibrandus Lubbertus, professor at Franeker, explained John 3:36, John 6:40, Hebrews 11:6, and 1 Corinthians 1:12.

On January 12 (session 56), synod had denied the request of the church at Kampen that synod rescind its summons of two of its Remonstrant ministers. The church sent a letter pleading its cause, contending that it could not do without four ministers at the same time. President Bogerman and some other members of synod agreed to discuss the matter with the Kampen delegates later.

Session 63: Friday, January 18, 1619, PM

Franciscus Gomarus (professor at Groningen) explained Ephesians 1:4–6 as teaching that those who are elected will persevere in faith, rather than that those who persevere in faith will be elected. Discussion followed.

---

10 See Hoeksema, *Voice of Our Fathers*, 103–109.

APPENDIX 1: *THE SESSIONS OF THE SYNOD OF DORDT, 1618–1619*

That evening Johannes Biesterveld died. He had been a professor of theology from the University in Siegen and was a member of the Nassau-Wetteravian delegation. This means that he was from the area of Westphalia, Germany; Siegen is about thirty miles east of Cologne. He would be buried after the session of synod the following Monday. His replacement, Georg Fabricius, would not arrive until March 11.

WEEK ELEVEN: SESSIONS 64–67

Session 64: Monday, January 21, 1619, AM

The States General delegation had reported to the national government in The Hague regarding Bogerman's dismissal of the Remonstrants on January 14. On January 18, the national government issued a resolution, which synod now read. The national government had received clear evidence that the Remonstrants despised its authority and did not intend to obey it. The national government approved synod's decision to examine the Remonstrants by subjecting their writings to the light of God's word. It also repeated that the Remonstrants were not to leave the city of Dordrecht.

The previous week, two of the five Dutch professors of theology had given their judgments regarding the Remonstrant view of predestination and had explained certain texts. At this and following sessions, the other three Dutch professors did so.

Antonius Thysius, professor from Harderwijk, gave his judgment regarding whether God's determination to save believers is the entire decree of predestination and whether faith is a condition to election or the fruit of election. The official record tells us only who spoke and what topic he addressed; it gives no further details about what he said. However, Brandt says, "These explanations were almost always diametrically opposed to the opinions of the

Remonstrants."[11] The synod, and particularly the Dutch delegates, were orthodox men.

Synod attended Johannes Biesterveld's funeral.

Session 65: Tuesday, January 22, 1619, AM

The delegates all agreed that Christ is the foundation of election (Ephesians 1:4). But *how* is he this? On this point the delegates had differing views.

Gerard Brandt explains the two positions. Some, including Gomarus, said that God first decreed to choose some to everlasting life, then chose Christ as the way to accomplish this salvation: "God the Father alone was the Cause of Election, and Christ only the Executor of it."[12] Others, including Martinius of Bremen, considered that Christ was not only the executor, but "in some sense the Author and Procuror of it."[13]

Synod took time to discuss this question. The record indicates that the discussion was heated.

The synod did not meet in session on Wednesday, January 23. Brandt indicates that the foreign delegates met with Martinius regarding statements he had made the previous day.

Session 66: Thursday, January 24, 1619, PM

Professor Polyander, from Leiden, explained Philippians 4:3, Revelation 21:27, Luke 10:20, Romans 8:29, and 2 Timothy 2:19. After he was finished, Professor Walaeus, from Middelburg, explained Acts 13:48, Romans 9:11, and Romans 11:5.

Session 67: Friday, January 25, 1619, PM

Having heard from its five Dutch professors, synod began to hear from the foreign delegates, beginning with the British delegates.

---

11 Brandt, *History of the Reformation*, 3:206.
12 Brandt, *History of the Reformation*, 3:204.
13 Brandt, *History of the Reformation*, 3:208.

John Davenant set forth his understanding of predestination, which accorded with the orthodox view. Then he explained and refuted some of the distinctions that the Remonstrants made regarding predestination, such as these: Is it one decree, or more? Limited, or unlimited? Revocable and changeable, or irrevocable and unchangeable?

Next, Samuel Ward, another British delegate, spoke. He responded to the view of the Arminians that God's only decree of election was to save believers, which view denied that God eternally appointed specific individuals to salvation. After he spoke, Professor Goclenius from Marburg, a delegate from Hesse, addressed the synod. Concluding the session, Martinius again brought up his view of Christ as the foundation of election, desiring the synod to answer the matter definitively. Gomarus, we are told, kept silent.

WEEK TWELVE: SESSIONS 68–72

Session 68: Monday, January 28, 1619, PM

Abraham Scultetus, professor of theology at Heidelberg University, emphasized the necessity and possibility of the child of God being assured of his election and distinguished this true certainty from the Remonstrant idea of certainty.

Session 69: Tuesday, January 29, 1619, PM

Heinrich Altingius, another Heidelberg professor, turned the discussion from election to reprobation. He emphasized that God is not the author of sin, that sin is rooted in and proceeds from the depravity of our nature, and that the hardening and blinding of sinners is an aspect of God's work of judging sinners.

Session 70: Wednesday, January 30, 1619, PM

For the past two weeks synod had been hearing the judgments of various delegates regarding the first point of the Remonstrants (election and reprobation). Considering synod's pace to be tedious, some delegates wondered aloud if synod could do its work more quickly. Synod discussed the matter and decided to proceed as it had originally intended: it would not quicken its pace but would examine each of the five points carefully before formulating its conclusions.

Session 71: Thursday, January 31, 1619, AM

President Bogerman presented the synod with a proposed response to the second point of the Remonstrants, regarding the extent of Christ's atoning work.

The synod made an index of the writings of the Remonstrants regarding universal grace, so that the delegates could more easily find evidence of the Remonstrant position.

Session 72: Friday, February 1, 1619, PM

Walter Balcanquhall, a member of the British delegation who represented the Scottish churches, explained that God's intent in sending Christ to the death of the cross was not to save every human. He showed that the Remonstrant distinction "between the Acquisition of Redemption and the Appropriation or Application of it was groundless."[14] The Remonstrants had argued that God sent Christ to make salvation possible for each and every human, but that salvation was applied only to some. Balcanquhall demonstrated that salvation was applied to the same group of people for whom Christ obtained it. After he was finished, George Cruciger, professor of theology at Marburg University, spoke to the same point. No details of his speech are given; we presume he agreed with the orthodox view.

Several of the more recent sessions were evening sessions at which professors spoke about doctrinal points. These evening sessions began at either 4:00 or 6:00 p.m. At that time of day, at that

---

14 Brandt, *History of the Reformation*, 3:215.

time of year, in that place (Dordrecht, the Netherlands, latitude 51.8°N), it was dark. Hales says that the observers were not allowed to use candles,[15] and Brandt relates that Cruciger read his address by candlelight.[16] One wonders whether the delegates and visitors all stayed awake. Would we stay awake, sitting in church to hear a lecture or sermon, with such dim lighting?

WEEK THIRTEEN: SESSIONS 73–77

Session 73: Monday, February 4, 1619, AM

The delegates discussed writing three documents, but the Acts of Synod tell us nothing more about their nature. Other sources (Hale, Brandt, and Sinnema) tell us that one was to be a brief explanation of the orthodox position regarding the five disputed points, and another was to be a brief refutation of the Remonstrant errors. Both were intended to inform the lay people. Not every delegate agreed that these writings should be composed; some thought the synod should finish treating the Remonstrant error and render its official judgment before writing such documents. But synod decided to proceed with composing them. Despite this decision, these two writings were never composed.[17]

Synod also agreed to produce a summary of the synod's dealings with the Remonstrants, which document would be known as the "Acta Contracta." Synod hoped this document could be finished quickly, but it was not completed until 1620.

And synod appointed a committee to draft an answer to the objections of the Remonstrants to teachings of the Belgic Confession and Heidelberg Catechism.

---

15 Hales, *Golden Remains*, 90.
16 Brandt, *History of the Reformation*, 3:215.
17 Donald Sinnema, "The Canons of Dordt: From Judgment on Arminianism to Confessional Standard," in Goudriaan, *Revisiting the Synod of Dordt*, 319.

Session 74: Tuesday, February 5, 1619, PM

The delegates discussed the Remonstrant view on the second point, regarding the nature, effectiveness, and extent of Christ's atonement. The Remonstrant view was that Christ died to make salvation possible for every human. Three international delegates, John Davenant and Samuel Ward from Great Britain and Matthias Martinius from Bremen, publicly expressed their judgment that the Remonstrants were correct regarding the extent of the atonement. The other British delegates disagreed with these three. As the British discussed the matter, they realized that they were interpreting differently the phrase in article 31 of their confession, the Thirty-Nine Articles of the Church of England, which says that Christ died for all the sins of the whole world. This led them to ask President Bogerman to ignore their internal disagreement and to seek advice from their ecclesiastical superior, the Archbishop of Canterbury (see session 110).

Session 75: Wednesday, February 6, 1619, PM

Paul Steinius, delegate from Hesse, spoke regarding the irresistible character of God's grace. This indicates that the synod was beginning to consider the third and fourth points of the Remonstrants.

After Steinius was finished, the delegates continued to discuss the second point.

Session 76: Thursday, February 7, 1619, AM

Outside of the official session of synod, the Remonstrants on this day delivered a book of over two hundred pages to the deputies from the national government. In it they defended their position regarding conditional election and reprobation, they explained Romans 9 in defense of their view, they opposed the orthodox teaching regarding election, and they presented their view regarding the second point of doctrine, the nature and extent of Christ's atonement. In the preface, they thanked the synod for permitting them to defend their opinions according to their conscience; noted that had synod allowed them to do this earlier, synod might have already finished its discussions; asked for copies of any speeches given in opposition to their writing; noted that they had obeyed the command to remain in Dordrecht, but now asked permission to leave; and noted that they did not present their opinions regarding points three through five, but would do so within several more weeks.

The deputies from the States General reprimanded the Remonstrants for: passing censure on the synod; not bringing the entire document within the appointed time; opposing the doctrines of the orthodox; and being long-winded in their response.

In its official meeting, synod continued and concluded its discussion on the second point, regarding the extent of Christ's atonement. It also was informed that the Remonstrants had brought their opinions regarding the first two points of doctrine. Synod decided to treat this matter the following Monday.

Session 77: Friday, February 8, 1619, PM

At this session President Bogerman proposed a summary of the opinions of the Remonstrants regarding the third and fourth points of doctrine.

WEEK FOURTEEN: SESSIONS 78–81

Session 78: Monday, February 11, 1619, PM[18]

Synod discussed what effect the light of nature and the preaching of the gospel have on the unregenerate and how God works conversion

---

[18] I follow the order of the Acts of Synod in relating what synod did in sessions 78 and 79. Gerard Brandt switches the order, presenting for session 78 what the Acts presents for session 79, and for session 79 what the Acts presents for session 78. Brandt was following the lead of Walter Balcanquhall, a British delegate who kept his own record of the synod's proceedings. That the Acts has the order wrong is possible: the clerks were not recording every word at synod but were summarizing the sessions. Yet the Acts is the official record, and in several other instances Balcanquhall also seems to be a day off from the Acts. See also the note accompanying session 132.

in humans in such a way that God may justly require us to believe and obey.

Session 79: Tuesday, February 12, 1619, AM

Sebastian Beck, professor at Basel University, Switzerland, responded to the Remonstrant position that God's grace is resistible.

Synod discussed what to do with the 204-page document that the Remonstrants had given the States General delegates. Synod agreed that a committee should carefully examine it and inform synod if it contained anything new.

Tuesday, February 12, 1619, PM

This afternoon was set aside for a committee meeting. The committee, consisting of one person from every delegation, was mandated to discuss how to proceed with the matter of the Remonstrant ministers from Kampen. Synod had earlier required these to appear. When the church in Kampen had asked synod to change its mind, synod had maintained its summons (sessions 36, 56, 62). Those summoned had not appeared but had sent others in their place with letters of explanation.

Session 80: Wednesday, February 13, 1619, PM

Synod focused on the Remonstrant teaching regarding the freedom of the human will and the grace necessary for conversion. Do humans play a role in our initial conversion? Does our will cooperate with God's grace?

We know that synod expressed its final judgment on these matters in the Canons. This might lead us to think that synod arrived at its conclusion easily. However, such was not the case. Balcanquhall and Brandt relate that some members of synod, although agreeing that the Arminian teaching was wrong, disagreed on how best to state the truth. Even today at broader assemblies it can take time to express well the consensus of the majority.

Session 81: Friday, February 15, 1619, PM

Before the official session, the Remonstrants sent the States General deputies a sixty-page document containing their explanation of the third, fourth, and fifth articles. Their explanation, however, did not include their defense of these articles, as it ought to have. The States General deputies ordered them to supply this lack with haste. On the next day, the Remonstrants asked for ten extra days to finish this matter.

Sessions 14 and 63 recorded the death of a delegate during the meetings of synod. A third delegate, Meinert Idzerda, elder from Friesland, had died during the Christmas break. At this session, six weeks later, his replacement, Taecke Aysma, appeared with his credentials. After taking the synodical oath, he was seated.

Johann Alstedius, professor at Herborn, spoke in opposition to the third and fourth articles of the Remonstrants and in defense of irresistible grace. He called the Remonstrants Pelagians for their view of humans and of grace and defended his position from Matthew 11:12.

President Bogerman informed the synod that the Remonstrants had handed in their opinions regarding the last three articles and that their documents would be read the following Monday.

Synod read the letters from the ministers of Kampen who did not appear at synod, in which letters they gave their reasons. Many agreed that these men had flaunted synod's authority and deserved to be suspended from their office. However, synod would give them one more chance to appear within fourteen days.

Many people were coming to Dordrecht to observe the synod. They were disappointed that so many of the recent sessions had been private. Synod agreed that from this point forward, when it held private sessions, visitors could come into the public galleries, observe the synod's delegates take their seats, and stay through devotions. After that the visitors would have to leave while the synod did its work.

WEEK FIFTEEN: SESSIONS 82–90

Session 82: Monday, February 18, 1619, AM

The Remonstrants had submitted their written explanation regarding the five points of doctrine (sessions 76, 81). Synod read aloud the part from this document that regarded the first two points of doctrine.

Session 83: Monday, February 18, 1619, PM

The two ministers from Kampen whom synod had summoned had sent letters explaining why they had not appeared (session 81). The States General delegation declared them to be worthy of suspension from office. Most delegates agreed. The delegates from Bremen disagreed, preferring that synod treat these ministers more gently.

Session 84: Tuesday, February 19, 1619, AM

Synod read the portion of the Remonstrant document that regarded the third and fourth points of doctrine.

Session 85: Tuesday, February 19, 1619, PM

Synod informed the church of Kampen of its decision that the two ministers should be suspended (session 83).

Synod continued its discussion of the third and fourth points of doctrine. The discussion and disagreement regarding the relation of man's will to God's grace (session 80) was renewed and was intense. The Bremen delegate Martinius had quoted from a renowned Heidelberg theologian (David Pareus) in support of statements he had made, and other foreign delegates attempted to show that Martinius had misunderstood Pareus.

After this, the Dutch professors Gomarus and Thysius spoke regarding the third and fourth articles.

APPENDIX 1: *THE SESSIONS OF THE SYNOD OF DORDT, 1618–1619*

Session 86: Wednesday, February 20, 1619, AM

Synod read the part of the Remonstrant document that regarded the fifth point of doctrine.

Session 87: Wednesday, February 20, 1619, PM

Wolfgang Mayer, a Swiss theologian, spoke to the fifth point of doctrine. Every time he addressed the synod, he took off his cap and called it the "holy synod."[19]

Session 88: Thursday, February 21, 1619, AM

Synod read the Remonstrants' defense of their position regarding the first article.

Session 89: Friday, February 22, 1619, AM

Synod read the statements from the Remonstrants regarding reprobation.

Session 90: Friday, February 22, 1619, PM

The Remonstrants disagreed with the doctrine of the preservation of the saints and alleged that this doctrine implies that the child of God need not live a godly life. The five Dutch professors responded to this argument, showing that the preservation of saints does not diminish the need to pray or to guard against sin.

WEEK SIXTEEN: SESSIONS 91–97

Session 91: Monday, February 25, 1619, AM

Synod continued to discuss the third and fourth articles of the Remonstrants. It faced the questions whether unregenerate man can understand the scriptures by himself and whether unregenerate man has the power to do good and avoid evil.

---

19 Engelsma, *Always Reforming*, 36.

President Bogerman gave synod a catalogue of Remonstrant writings regarding the fifth point of doctrine.

On this day the Remonstrants presented the States General delegation with an eighty-page defense of their second article. The States General delegation again rebuked them for supplying a partial response, rather than a complete one. Episcopius said that the length and incompleteness of their documents to synod was "not of choice, but of necessity,"[20] and that they needed three or four more weeks to finish the task.

The States General delegation was informed that two Remonstrant ministers from Utrecht, who were present at synod, had been deposed from the ministry, and that the family of one of them had been ordered to move out of the house by Easter (March 31). This minister asked permission to leave the synod in order to attend to his family's needs. The States General delegation told the men that it would consider the matter.

Session 92: Tuesday, February 26, 1619, AM

Synod read the Remonstrant explanation of the extent of Christ's death. The Remonstrants were explicit that Christ died for every human being, not only for the elect.

Session 93: Wednesday, February 27, 1619, AM

Synod continued reading the document of the Remonstrants.

Session 94: Wednesday, February 27, 1619, PM

Theodore Tronchinus, professor at the Genevan Academy, explained and defended the doctrine of the perseverance of true believers. Since January 17, the Dutch and foreign professors had taken turns orally explaining and defending the orthodox view over against the

---

20 Brandt, *History of the Reformation*, 3:234.

five points. With Tronchinus's speech, this aspect of synod's work was now finished, with one exception (session 106).

Session 95: Thursday, February 28, 1619, AM
Synod read more of the Remonstrants' defense of the second article.

Session 96: Thursday, February 28, 1619, PM
Synod discussed the doctrine of perseverance.

Session 97: Friday, March 1, 1619, AM
Synod continued the discussion of the previous session.

WEEK SEVENTEEN: SESSIONS 98–106

Session 98: Monday, March 4, 1619, AM
Synod continued its discussion of the doctrine of the preservation of the saints that it had begun the previous week.

The magistrates of Kampen informed synod by letter that, acquiescing to synod, they suspended the two ministers whom synod had summoned but who had not appeared (sessions 83, 85). The ministers had given several reasons for not coming to synod, one being that the church in Kampen needed them. The magistrates informed synod that ministers from the church in Zwolle would help the church in Kampen for the time being.

Synod also received a letter from Dr. David Pareus, theologian from Heidelberg, who had been invited to the synod but who could not come because of old age (he was seventy years old). In this letter he expressed his judgment against the teachings of the Remonstrants in their five articles. Synod read the cover letter at this session.

Session 99: Tuesday, March 5, 1619, AM
Synod read the judgment of Dr. Pareus regarding the first two articles of the Remonstrants.

Session 100: Tuesday, March 5, 1619, PM

Martinius (professor from Bremen) addressed synod regarding the person and natures of Jesus Christ, particularly emphasizing that Christ was both the eternal Son of God and truly human. The Remonstrants were in error not only regarding the five points of doctrine, but regarding other doctrines as well. Martinius' speech was a defense of orthodox Christology over against the Remonstrants. Particularly he opposed Conrad Vorstius, who succeeded Arminius as professor of theology in Leiden in 1610, and whom the synod would later condemn for teaching false doctrine. Although sound in his theology on this point, Martinius excused the Remonstrants for some of their statements.

Session 101: Wednesday, March 6, 1619, AM

Synod read the judgment of Dr. Pareus regarding the last three articles of the Remonstrants and decided to thank him for sending his judgment to the synod.

Session 102: Wednesday, March 6, 1619, PM

All the delegations had handed in their judgments regarding the five articles. Synod discussed whether to read these on the floor of synod in open or closed session. The English delegation favored open session. Although the English generally opposed the Remonstrants, the English also opposed some expressions by the orthodox regarding reprobation, and they desired their comments to be publicly heard. However, synod decided to read all the judgments in closed session.

Synod read the judgments of the English and Heidelberg delegations regarding the Remonstrant teaching of election and reprobation. Both of these delegations agreed that the Remonstrant position was wrong. However, the Heidelberg delegation also expressed its judgment that ministers should treat the doctrine of reprobation "cautiously, seldom, and sparingly in their pulpits."[21]

Session 103: Thursday, March 7, 1619, AM

Synod read the judgments of the delegations from Hesse, Switzerland, and Wetteravia regarding the first point.

Session 104: Thursday, March 7, 1619, PM

Synod read the judgments of the delegations from Geneva, Bremen, and Emden regarding the first article. Most delegations either did not touch on the matter of the salvation of infants dying in infancy or said that parents of such infants have no reason to doubt their salvation (as synod later expressed in Canons 1.17). The delegates from Bremen put the matter more strongly. They said that every baptized child who died in infancy was, without question, saved.

Session 105: Friday, March 8, 1619, AM

Synod finished reading the judgment of the delegation from Emden, then read the judgment of the Dutch professors. The great point of dispute in the judgment of the professors was whether God, when he predestined some to eternal life, viewed the human race as fallen (infralapsarianism) or not yet fallen, using the fall as a means to carry out his decree of election and reprobation (supralapsarianism). Professors Polyander, Thysius, Waleus, and Lubbertus took the infralapsarian viewpoint, while Gomarus took the supralapsarian position.

Session 106: Friday, March 8, 1619, PM

Deodatus, professor in Geneva, had twice been scheduled to address the synod regarding the preservation of the saints but could not because of illness. He now explained that many who appeared for

---

21 Brandt, *History of the Reformation*, 3:252.

a time to be believers were in fact reprobate and manifested this by unbelief and ungodliness later in life. At the same time, though the elect do fall into grievous sins, God grants them repentance and brings them to heaven.

Average temperatures in Dordrecht in March indicate that the average low temperature is just above freezing, while the high is almost 10°C, or 50°F. The winter of 1618–19 was colder than usual; the severest cold was felt in late February and early March 1619. How were the Remonstrants to complete writing their defense when it was so cold? The Remonstrants informed the States General delegation "that by reason of the long and sharp frost, they could not get their papers ready against the appointed time; they therefore prayed their Lordships to admit of their excuses, and promised to complete the whole before the end of the next week."[22]

Merely another excuse? It would be easy to conclude that it was. However, we who have central heating in our homes cannot appreciate how the cold can hamper one's work.

WEEK EIGHTEEN: SESSIONS 107–117

Session 107: Monday, March 11, 1619, AM

On January 18 (session 63) Johannes Biesterveld, a member of the Nassau-Wetteravian delegation, had died. His replacement, Georg Fabricius, arrived at the present session, presented his credentials, took the synodical oath, and was seated.

The previous Friday synod had begun reading the judgment of the Dutch professors regarding the first article of the Remonstrants. Synod continued that now. The professors agreed that the Remonstrant position was wrong but disagreed whether God's decree of election was supralapsarian or infralapsarian (see session 105 for a fuller explanation).

---

22 Brandt, *History of the Reformation*, 3:253.

APPENDIX 1: *THE SESSIONS OF THE SYNOD OF DORDT, 1618–1619*

Session 108: Monday, March 11, 1619, PM

At numerous sessions (36, 56, 62, 81, 83, 85, 98), synod had discussed the matter of the four Remonstrant ministers from Kampen whom it had summoned. Two had never appeared and had been suspended from the ministry. Synod required the other two to submit a written defense of the charges against them, but they had not met the deadline synod had given them. Synod decided that if these did not provide their answer within two weeks, it would declare them also to be suspended from the ministry.

Synod continued to read the judgments of the various deputies regarding the first article of the Remonstrants (election and reprobation). At this session, synod read the judgments of the deputies from Gelderland, South Holland, North Holland, and Zeeland. All stated that they disagreed with Gomarus' supralapsarian position, but the delegates of South Holland also stated that they did not see the need to resolve the matter.

Session 109: Tuesday, March 12, 1619, AM

Synod read the judgments of the deputies from Utrecht, Friesland, Overijssel, and Groningen.

Session 110: Tuesday, March 12, 1619, PM

Synod read the last of the judgments regarding the first article of the Remonstrants, those of the deputies from Drenthe and from the Walloon churches.

Synod then turned to the judgments of the various delegations regarding the second article of the Remonstrants, which pertained to the extent and effectiveness of Christ's work. Synod read the judgments of the delegations from Great Britain, the Palatinate, Hesse, and Switzerland. The last three delegations stated that when scripture says Christ died for all, it means he died for the elect, not for every individual. The elect, they added, his death effectively saved.

The delegates from Great Britain did not touch on this point. These delegates had realized earlier (session 74) that they were not agreed among themselves on the interpretation of their own creed, the Thirty-Nine Articles. This realization led them to ask advice from the Archbishop of Canterbury. He responded that the British delegates should not speak more specifically than did the Thirty-Nine Articles.

Session 111: Wednesday, March 13, 1619, AM

Synod read the judgments of the delegations from Wetteravia, Geneva, Emden, and Bremen regarding the second article. The first three of these delegations agreed that Christ died only for the elect. The delegates from Bremen disagreed among themselves. Heinrich Isselburg was of the mind that Christ died for the elect throughout the world and effectually saved them. Matthew Martinius held the opposite view, that Christ died for all and every human. The third took a middle ground but in the end opposed Martinius' position that Christ died for every human.

Session 112: Wednesday, March 13, 1619, PM

Professor Isselburg addressed synod regarding Christ's atoning work. He opposed the error of Socinianism, which synod understood Conrad Vorstius to be defending (see sessions 100, 152). Isselburg emphasized the necessity of satisfaction and that Christ fully satisfied for the sins of God's elect. Brandt relates a quotable: according to Isselburg, "In Christ were one person, two natures, three offices, and four capital benefits, he [Christ] being to us wisdom, righteousness, sanctification, and perfect redemption," and all this can be considered "the four wheels, upon which the chariot of salvation moved."[23]

---

23 Brandt, *History of the Reformation*, 3:256.

APPENDIX 1: *THE SESSIONS OF THE SYNOD OF DORDT, 1618–1619*

Session 113: Thursday, March 14, 1619, AM

Synod read the judgment of the five Dutch professors. These all agreed that Christ died only for all the elect and that for them his death was both sufficient and effective. Synod then read the judgments of the delegates from the Provincial Synods of Gelderland, South Holland, and North Holland.

Session 114: Thursday, March 14, 1619, PM

Synod read the judgments of the delegates from Zeeland, Utrecht, Friesland, Overijssel, and Gronigen regarding the second article. On the matter of the extent of Christ's atonement, these all agreed with the majority consensus that would be later expressed in Canons 2.8.

Session 115: Friday, March 15, 1619, AM

Synod concluded reading the judgments of the delegations regarding the second article; the last two judgments that it read were those of the delegates of Drenthe and the Walloon churches.

In their third article, the Remonstrants taught that fallen man could do nothing good in himself and needed to be regenerated. In their fourth article, they taught that humans can resist God's grace. Synod, recognizing that the real error of the Remonstrants regarding fallen man manifested itself in the fourth article, decided to treat the two articles together. At this session, synod heard the judgments of the delegations from Great Britain and the Palatinate regarding these two articles.

Session 116: Friday, March 15, 1619, PM

Synod read the judgments of the delegates from Hesse, Switzerland, Wetteravia, Geneva, and Bremen and began reading the judgment of the delegates from Emden.

Session 117: Saturday, March 16, 1619, AM

Synod concluded reading the judgment of the Emden theologians, which was rather lengthy. It also read the judgments of the Dutch professors and the deputies from Gelderland.

WEEK NINETEEN: SESSIONS 118–127

Session 118: Monday, March 18, 1619, AM

The Synod of Dordt had been in session for four full months. Due to sickness and other circumstances, the delegates from Brandenburg had never arrived (see session 3). At session 118, synod received a letter from the Marquis of Brandenberg explaining the absence of his delegates. Convinced that synod's response to the Remonstrants would conform to the Reformed confessions, the marquis asked synod to send him its final judgment so that the clergy in his realm might sign it. The Acts of Synod do not indicate how synod responded to this letter.

Synod continued to read the judgments of the various delegations regarding the third and fourth articles of the Remonstrants. At this session synod read the judgments of the delegates from South Holland, North Holland, Zeeland, and Utrecht.

Session 119: Monday, March 18, 1619, PM

Synod concluded reading the judgments regarding the third and fourth articles. The judgments of the delegations from Friesland, Overijssel, Groningen, Drenthe, and the Walloon churches were read.

Session 120: Tuesday, March 19, 1619, AM

Synod read the judgments of the delegations from Great Britain and from the Palatinate regarding the fifth article of the Remonstrant teachings. This article regarded the preservation of the saints.

APPENDIX 1: *THE SESSIONS OF THE SYNOD OF DORDT, 1618–1619*

On this day the Remonstrants presented the States General delegation with the Remonstrants' defense of the fourth and fifth articles. In their conclusion they expressed why they rejected the orthodox (Contra-Remonstrant) position: "Being instructed by the Holy Scriptures, we firmly believe that they are repugnant to the honour of God, destructive to piety, and a scandal to the Christian religion."[24]

Session 121: Tuesday, March 19, 1619, PM

Synod read the judgments of the delegates from Switzerland, Hesse, Wetteravia, Geneva, and Bremen regarding the fifth article. All of these opposed the Remonstrant position.

Session 122: Wednesday, March 20, 1619, AM

Synod read the judgments of the Emden delegates, the Dutch professors, and the delegations from Gelderland and South Holland.

Session 123: Wednesday, March 20, 1619, PM

In a session open to visitors, Professor Crocius from Bremen addressed synod regarding the question whether God, in justifying humans, accepts our activity of faith as a substitute for the righteousness that God requires of us in his law. The Arminians and Socinians taught that God did indeed do so; the orthodox denied this. Crocius defended the orthodox position.

Session 124: Thursday, March 21, 1619, AM

Synod read the judgments from the delegations of North Holland, Zeeland, Utrecht, and Friesland regarding the Remonstrants' fifth article.

Session 125: Thursday, March 21, 1619, PM

Synod read the judgments of the delegations from Overijssel, Groningen, Drenthe, and the Walloon churches. This concluded the reading of the judgments of the various delegations.

---

24 Brandt, *History of the Reformation*, 3:258.

The nineteen delegations (eight international, the Dutch professors, and ten Dutch provincial) had each submitted their written judgment regarding the five articles of the Remonstrants. In total, synod had read seventy-six reports responding to the teachings of the Remonstrants.

President Bogerman noted with thanks to God that the delegations were united in their doctrinal convictions. This unanimity would make the next step, formulating a final response to the Remonstrants, easier. The States General was hoping that synod would finish this work by the end of the month, that is, within ten more days.

Bogerman informed synod that he had begun to formulate a proposed response. The next day each delegation was to send someone to copy Bogerman's proposal as he read it. That person would then return to his delegation so that the delegations could discuss the proposal in committee and could suggest any changes to Bogerman or his assessors (assistants).

Session 126: Friday, March 22, 1619, AM

President Bogerman read his proposed response to the first article of the Remonstrants, while representatives of the various delegations wrote it out. He also expressed his desire that the Canons have a preface, a section explaining the true doctrine and rejecting the Remonstrant error, and a conclusion.

Session 127: Friday, March 22, 1619, PM

The president read his proposed response to the second article of the Remonstrants.

Four hundred years ago the clerks of the synod and the scribes of the various delegations had no electronic word processors, no manual typewriters, no copy machines, and no carbon paper. They wrote many pages by hand. This in itself must have taken weeks. We can be thankful for the technology available today and the greater ease with which we can do our work.

WEEK TWENTY: SESSION 128

Session 128: Monday, March 25, 1619, AM

The previous week President Bogerman had dictated his proposed draft of the first two heads of the Canons to a representative of each delegation. These representatives copied Bogerman's proposal and brought it to their respective delegation so that each delegation could discuss it.

By proposing a draft of the Canons, some thought Bogerman was taking too much authority to himself. The States General deputies advised synod to appoint a committee of several delegates to work with the president and his two assistants in drafting the Canons. Agreeing with this proposal, synod formed a committee of nine. It included Bogerman and the two vice-presidents (Rolandus and Faukelius), three foreign delegates (Bishop Carleton from Great Britain, Jean Diodati from Geneva, and Abraham Scultetus from Heidelberg), and three Dutch delegates (Johannes Polyander, Antonius Walaeus, and Jacob Trigland).

This committee worked at least eight hours a day for over three weeks. While the committee met, synod recessed; its next session would be held on April 16.

On March 26, 1619, the Remonstrants informed the States General by letter that they thought the synod had wronged them and asked permission to return home. The States General denied their request. On the same day, the two Remonstrant ministers from Kampen submitted their written answer to the charges that synod had leveled against them (see session 108).

March 31, 1619, was Easter Sunday. On that day the Remonstrants at Dordt gathered in a private house for a worship service that included the baptism of an infant. Some consider this date to mark the beginning of a Remonstrant church that was separate from the state Reformed church.

WEEKS TWENTY THROUGH TWENTY-THREE: THE DRAFTING COMMITTEE[25]

The committee that drafted the Canons worked from March 26 through April 15, 1619. Using President Bogerman's proposed drafts of heads one and two as its starting point (see sessions 125–128), the committee completed its first draft of head one by Thursday, March 28. On that day, while the committee continued working, one of synod's secretaries dictated the draft to a representative of each delegation. The first draft of head two was similarly copied out on March 29. The draft of heads three and four was completed on April 4, and the draft of head five on April 5.

Each delegation considered these drafts and sent their responses to the drafting committee. On the basis of these responses, the committee drew up its second draft, containing almost two hundred changes to the first draft. The committee completely redrafted the second head in light of concerns expressed by the British and Bremen delegations. On April 8–10, these amendments were dictated to a representative of each delegation. On Friday, April 12, the delegations gave their comments in the morning, and the drafting committee responded to them in the afternoon.

On Monday, April 15, the third draft was dictated, containing over one hundred changes to the second. That afternoon all the delegates except the British signed this version of the Canons. The British would not sign before seeing a neat, finished copy.

---

[25] The material regarding the work of the drafting committee is gleaned from one main source: Donald Sinnema, "The Drafting of the Canons of Dordt: A Preliminary Survey of Early Drafts and Related Documents," in Goudriaan, *Revisiting the Synod of Dordt*, 291–311.

Although this third draft was signed, it was not the final draft. A few editorial changes still needed to be made, and two articles in the rejection of errors of head two needed to be changed. The committee would eventually entirely delete these articles and would revise the second article in the second head's rejection of errors.

When the synod reconvened on April 16, it began reading and discussing the Canons. On Friday, April 19, the committee made the final changes to the Canons and drafted the conclusion to the Canons.

Ever since, the Canons of Dordt have stood the test of time in Reformed churches throughout the world. Four hundred years later they are still subscribed to, taught, and loved. One reason for this is the carefulness with which they were drafted. Another is that the Canons explicitly set forth the teachings of scripture regarding the doctrines of sovereign grace. These teachings have not changed, and God's sovereign grace is as wonderful and lovely today as it ever was!

WEEK TWENTY-THREE: SESSIONS 129–133

Session 129: Tuesday, April 16, 1619, AM

Synod had not met as a body since March 25, when it appointed a committee to draft the Canons. At its 129th session the delegates heard the first head, including its rejection of errors, read aloud. Every delegate agreed that the doctrine contained in it conformed to scripture and the Reformed confessions. Then the second head was read. It soon became apparent that some delegates desired to discuss this at greater length.

Session 130: Thursday, April 18, 1619, AM

Synod discussed the second head at length. Some delegates commented on article 8 of the positive section and articles 2 and 6 in the rejection of errors. Synod approved the substance of the second head but agreed to make some further revisions. Because of these further revisions, the entire sixth article of the rejection of errors that was in the version that the delegates were discussing is not found in the final version of the Canons (see session 135).

Session 131: Thursday, April 18, 1619, PM

The delegates heard the third and fourth heads read. All agreed that the doctrine and its articulation were proper; only minor editorial changes were necessary. When synod heard the fifth head, all agreed to it.

The delegates from Great Britain thought it good to add a section opposing some slanderous expressions of the Remonstrants and Roman Catholics. President Bogerman suggested that in addition, a preface and conclusion should be written.

Session 132: Friday, April 19, 1619, AM[26]

The proposed conclusion to the Canons, including statements opposing the slanders of the Remonstrants and Roman Catholics against orthodox Reformed teaching, was read. The delegates from Great Britain, Hesse, and Bremen asked the synod to expand this section so that it would repudiate even more slanderous statements, as well as some harsh statements made by orthodox men. The drafting committee reworked its draft.

Session 133: Friday, April 19, 1619, PM

The second draft of the conclusion and its rejection of slanderous statements was read. Although the section regarding slanderous

---

26 The Acts of Synod say that this and the following session were held on Friday. The letters of Walter Balcanquhall, a British delegate, put the date for both sessions as Saturday the 20th. Donald Sinnema, who has done specialized work on the synod, takes the view that the dates of the Acts are incorrect and says that the drafting committee met on the 19th to draft the conclusion to the Canons.

statements was enlarged from the first draft, none of the additions included those that the British, Hessian, and Bremen delegates had desired. The reason for not including these was that the expressions and statements that these delegations desired to be expressly rejected had not been used by any Dutch theologians, but by English, French, and German theologians. The British again asked that more expressions be repudiated; however, the majority of the synod was content with the statements as proposed. The synod then recessed, allowing the delegation from the States General to review this part of the Canons over the weekend.

WEEK TWENTY-FOUR: SESSIONS 134–143

Session 134: Monday, April 22, 1619, AM

The previous week synod had been discussing the proposed conclusion to the Canons. At this session the States General delegation approved this conclusion and urged synod to finish its work quickly. Synod then adopted the proposed conclusion. The British delegates reminded synod that they desired this conclusion to include more, but for the sake of peace and expediency they would not insist on it.

In the afternoon the drafting committee met to rework articles two and six in the rejection of errors section of the second head.

Session 135: Tuesday, April 23, 1619, AM

The first head was again read, and all the delegations, both foreign and native, signed it. The changes that the drafting committee made to the second head were read. This included the removal of the entire sixth article that had been discussed earlier.

Session 136: Tuesday, April 23, 1619, PM

The second head as revised, the last three heads, and the section of the conclusion in which the synod rejected the blasphemous statements of others were read and signed.

Session 137: Wednesday, April 24, 1619, AM

The drafting committee had asked someone to draft a proposed judgment that the synod could pronounce on the Remonstrants. This draft was read. It called for the Remonstrants to be removed from their offices in the churches and universities. Most of the foreign delegations would not speak to the matter; they had been called to synod to discuss *doctrines* and thought it proper that only the Dutch should deal with *persons*. The Dutch delegates discussed whether this was a judgment they could pass, in light of the fact that the States General had authority over the ministers' offices. In the end synod agreed to pass such a judgment but decided to revise its wording.

Session 138: Wednesday, April 24, 1619, PM

The revision of the proposed judgment regarding the Remonstrants was read, and synod adopted it. The States General delegation informed the synod that it would report this adoption to the national government for its approval.

Session 139: Thursday, April 25, 1619, AM

Synod received the material relating to the case of John Maccovius. Maccovius, a strong defender of supralapsarianism, had been accused of heresy. The Classis of Franeker declared him guilty. He appealed to the Synod of Friesland, which forwarded the matter to the Synod of Dordt.

The introduction to the Canons was also read aloud. Most considered it too long and asked that it be revised.

APPENDIX 1: *THE SESSIONS OF THE SYNOD OF DORDT, 1618–1619*

Session 140: Thursday, April 25, 1619, PM

A revision of the proposed introduction to the Canons was read.[27] Some delegates desired that the phrase regarding the antichrist, referring to the Romish papacy, be further revised. Synod adopted the revised introduction.

Synod had finished its treatment of the Remonstrant errors. Some of the States General deputies were sent to The Hague to inform the national government what synod had done.

Session 141: Friday, April 26, 1619, AM

Synod began reading the material pertaining to the case of John Maccovius, including the fifty charges that had been made against him.

Session 142: Friday, April 26, 1619, PM

Synod continued reading the material of the Maccovius case, including his response to the charges.

Session 143: Saturday, April 27, 1619, AM

Synod appointed a committee of three Dutch delegates and three foreign delegates to bring recommendations regarding the Maccovius case.

The French king had prevented the French delegation from coming to the synod. Pierre du Moulin, a Reformed minister from Paris who had been one of the French delegates, sent synod his own judgment regarding the five points. Synod received and read Du Moulin's paper at this session. This paper revealed that he was emphatically opposed to the Remonstrant theology.

---

27 A new translation of this introduction is found in Godfrey, *Saving the Reformation*, 27–30.

WEEK TWENTY-FIVE: SESSIONS 144–152

Session 144: Monday, April 29, 1619, AM

Synod continued reading the treatise from Pierre du Moulin and decided to thank him for sending it.

The States General deputies who had gone to The Hague (session 140) reported that the national government was pleased with the synod's response to the Arminians and with the Canons. The government also desired synod to examine the Belgic Confession, to revise it if necessary, and to finish its work with haste. Synod was getting expensive!

Session 145: Tuesday, April 30, 1619, AM

The British delegation reported that it found no teaching of the Belgic Confession to be in conflict with scripture. The synod had decided that the British should not speak to the articles in the Belgic Confession regarding church government because the British and Dutch Reformed used two different systems of church government: the Dutch used the presbyterian system, while the British used the episcopal.

Synod attended the funeral of fellow delegate Lambert Canterus, an elder from Utrecht, who had died on April 24. After the funeral, it heard the report of the committee to which the Maccovius case was assigned. Synod did not adopt its recommendations but recommitted the matter (session 152).

Session 146: Tuesday, April 30, 1619, PM

The foreign and Dutch delegations all declared the doctrines in the Belgic Confession to be in harmony with scripture. The foreign delegates encouraged the Dutch to be faithful to this confession and to teach it to the coming generations.

APPENDIX 1: *THE SESSIONS OF THE SYNOD OF DORDT, 1618–1619*

Session 147: Wednesday, May 1, 1619, AM

The States General deputies informed synod that the national government desired synod to examine the Heidelberg Catechism as well. The Catechism was read aloud, and every delegation was told to prepare its judgment regarding it.

Session 148: Wednesday, May 1, 1619, PM

All the delegations expressed their judgment that the teaching of the Heidelberg Catechism was faithful to scripture and needed no improvement, and that the Catechism was suitable for instruction of children and adults.

Session 149: Thursday, May 2, 1619, AM

To this point synod had said nothing about the teachings of Conrad Vorstius, although two delegates had referred to his teachings in earlier speeches (sessions 100, 112). Vorstius was a Remonstrant, but his errors went beyond the Remonstrant errors that synod had condemned in the Canons: Vorstius held to heretical views regarding the Trinity, some of God's attributes, God's works of creation and providence, the union of Christ's two natures in his person, the sufficiency of Christ's atonement, and justification by faith alone. The States General informed synod that the national government desired synod to examine Vorstius's writings and pass judgment regarding them. Synod decided not to require Vorstius to appear before it but did read a letter that he had sent to synod.

Session 150: Friday, May 3, 1619, AM

Each of the delegations read its judgment regarding Vorstius. All agreed that his teachings were false and that he should be disciplined.

Session 151: Saturday, May 4, 1619, AM

Synod read aloud the first draft of a judgment against Vorstius. Various suggestions for changes were made.

Session 152: Saturday, May 4, 1619, PM

Synod approved its condemnation of Vorstius. It declared him unworthy to hold the office of minister and asked the States General to depose him.

Synod met late into the evening to finish the Maccovius case. It declared Maccovius to be not guilty of heresy, but to have been unwise in his use of certain expressions and terms. It exhorted him to adhere more closely to the language of scripture.

The following week, synod would wrap up its business that required the presence of the foreign delegates. The Dutch delegates would continue meeting until the end of May to treat other matters.

WEEK TWENTY-SIX: SESSIONS 153–154

Session 153: Monday, May 6, 1619, AM

After having opening devotions in the *Kloveniersdoelen* (the building in which the synod had been meeting), the delegates went in a stately procession to the *Grote Kerk* (Great Church), to which many people and dignitaries had also come.

President Bogerman opened with prayer, after which the synodical clerks read the Canons. The church was so large, and the effort required of the speakers to be heard was so great, that their voices tired, and they had to take turns reading. A collection of thanksgiving was taken for the cause of benevolence. Then the scribes read the judgment against the Remonstrants as well as the written testimony of the States General deputies indicating that they approved the work of the synod.

After Bogerman informed the audience that the synod had approved the doctrine contained in the Belgic Confession and Heidelberg Catechism, he closed with a long prayer.

Session 154: Thursday, May 9, 1619, AM

After the opening prayer, the States General deputy Martin Gregorius prayed, thanked the delegates for their work, and made other announcements on behalf of the national government. President Bogerman then expressed thanks to God and to the foreign delegates who had come to assist the Dutch churches. After he dismissed the foreign delegates from service, all the delegates gathered for a feast.

This was Ascension Day, 1619. It was fitting that on the day on which the churches commemorated Christ's ascension into heaven, the entire synod gathered to give thanks to God for guiding them in responding to the Remonstrant heresies.

WEEK TWENTY-SEVEN: SESSIONS 155–166

Session 155: Monday, May 13, 1619, AM

The foreign delegates had left, but the Dutch delegates remained in session to treat matters that pertained to the Dutch churches in particular. On this date, unrelated to the work of the synod but relevant to the political context of its work, the national government beheaded Johan van Oldenbarnevelt.

The States General deputies informed synod that it should review the Church Order adopted by the National Synod of 's Gravenhage in 1586. Synod read this Church Order.

Synod also decided to compare the Latin, French, and Dutch translations of the Belgic Confession. Various men had translated this Confession at different times, with the result that one translation sometimes used different words than others to express the meaning of the original. Anyone who translates from one language to another can understand how this would happen. Seeing the benefit of an authoritative Latin, French, and Dutch edition of the Confession, synod appointed four men to prepare such an edition (session 171).

Session 156: Monday, May 13, 1619, PM

Synod approved the substance of the articles of the 1586 Church Order. That Church Order, however, did not contain every article, or address every matter, found in the Church Order that the synod would finally adopt. Beginning with session 158, synod would approve additions to the Church Order, resulting finally in the Church Order of Dordt.

Synod began to discuss the "right of patrons." Remember that the national government supported the clergy and had its say in the government of the church. In keeping with this, it had been the practice to permit certain nobles or other influential people to nominate clergymen to fill church vacancies. If we had this practice today, consistories of vacant churches would permit certain members of the church, probably some of the wealthier or more influential, to nominate a name for the next minister.

Synod discussed whether this practice should be abolished. The States General deputies informed synod that abolishing the practice was not an option, but that the synod could devise a way to correct any potential abuses.

Session 157: Tuesday, May 14, 1619, AM

Synod recommended to the States General that the national government approve the following regulations regarding the right of patrons:

- Before proposing a minister's name, one must prove he had the right of patronage.
- The patron must make his nomination within three months after a vacancy begins.

- The patron's right was limited to the proposing of a minister's name. The patron did not have the right to dismiss a minister from office.
- The patron must support the minister financially but was not permitted to treat the minister as if he were the patron's employee.
- The patron might propose only men who were sound in doctrine and would serve the congregation well.
- If the church accepted the patron's proposal, the nominee must still be examined by the classis.
- The church had the right to reject the proposed name. If the church and patron disagreed regarding a nomination, the classis or synod must settle the matter or the name must be dropped.

Session 158: Tuesday, May 14, 1619, PM

Synod discussed six overtures, all relating to church political matters. One regarded appointing church visitors, a second regarded synodical deputies (which we also know as delegates *ad examina*), and a third regarded how the various provincial synods could correspond with each other to keep each other informed of their decisions. Synod also discussed overtures regarding admitting the insane to the ministry, regarding whether more than one minister per church may have a vote at classis, and regarding drawing up the Formula of Subscription.

Session 159: Wednesday, May 15, 1619, AM

Synod adopted its response to the six overtures that it had discussed at the previous session. Its answers to the first five overtures became incorporated in articles 44, 49, 48, 8, and 42 of the Church Order of Dordt, respectively. However, regarding the matter of how many ministers of any given church may vote at a classis meeting, synod originally permitted any minister the right to vote, whereas our Church Order now permits any minister the right of *advisory* vote.

Synod decided to prepare the Formula of Subscription, by signing which ministers could give testimony of their doctrinal soundness. Six more overtures regarding church political matters were then read so that the delegates could consider them.

Session 160: Wednesday, May 15, 1619, PM

Synod discussed a proposed form for calling ministers. Desiring that some points be added to the proposed form, it recommitted the matter.

Session 161: Thursday, May 16, 1619, AM

Synod adopted a revision of the form for calling ministers. What synod adopted is found in articles 4 and 5 of Dordt's Church Order.

Synod also adopted a resolution regarding the relationship of the civil authorities to the church. Synod stated that civil authorities were duty bound to promote the worship service and to protect church officers. It then required church officers to impress on the congregations the calling to love, honor, and obey the magistrates.

Session 162: Thursday, May 16, 1619, PM

In response to the overtures that were read at session 159, synod made decisions regarding the observance of ecclesiastical holidays (Church Order article 67), which songs could be sung in the worship services (article 69), and the use of the baptism forms and the procedure to follow in adult baptism (articles 58–59). Other decisions that are not specifically reflected in the Church Order were:

- A person who had been baptized by a Romish priest or Anabaptist need not be rebaptized.
- Marriages of those who had not yet been baptized might not be solemnized in the churches.

- Synod would ask the States General to decide how to correspond with the foreign churches, especially the French, regarding the decisions of synod.
- Synod would also request the States General to prepare a marriage ordinance that could be uniformly observed in the nation.
- Synod would exhort the churches to administer discipline in accordance with the articles of the Church Order. Synod's point here was to remind churches not of the necessity of discipline, but of the proper manner of discipline.

Seven more overtures were read that would be treated in upcoming sessions. Synod also appointed a committee to draw up the Formula of Subscription and questions to be asked of adults at adult baptism (see session 175).

Session 163: Friday, May 17, 1619, AM

Synod made several more significant decisions in responses to the overtures it had read at the previous session. First, it decided that baptism may be administered to the sick outside of the worship service only in instances of great need, with the consistory's approval, and in the consistory's presence. Regarding admitting to the ministry those who are newcomers or had been priests, monks, or members of a sect, synod said this may happen only with great caution and after a time of testing; this was incorporated into article 9 of the Church Order.

Third, it asked the States General to adopt some resolutions pertaining to the founding of universities and prestigious schools. These included that the curators should be learned Reformed men who serve terms; that the appointment of professors of theology should be approved by the provincial synods; that only those should be appointed as professors whose godliness and piety was assured, who had never been lawfully suspected of unsoundness of doctrine, and who were proficient in Hebrew, Greek, theology, and other areas of learning. Also it asked the States General to prepare some guidelines for the lower schools, so that the fundamentals of grammar, logic, and rhetoric would be uniformly taught.

Synod declared it unfitting that marriages of excommunicated persons or those unknown to Reformed churches should be publicly solemnized and blessed in the churches.

Synod asked the States General to address the increasing abuse and desecration of the Sabbath.

Session 164: Friday, May 17, 1619, PM

Synod adopted the six principles regarding Sabbath keeping. These emphasized that the fourth commandment has both a ceremonial element that is no longer in force (resting the *seventh* day) and a moral element that remains (setting aside a day for worship and rest from earthly labor).

Synod adopted the Formula of Subscription as the Protestant Reformed Churches and some other Reformed denominations use it yet today. A similar document was drawn up for school teachers to sign.

Session 165: Saturday, May 18, 1619, AM

Synod read the Dutch translation of the first head of the Canons.

Session 166: Saturday, May 18, 1619, PM

Synod continued reading the Dutch translation of the first head of the Canons.

APPENDIX 1: *THE SESSIONS OF THE SYNOD OF DORDT, 1618–1619*

WEEK TWENTY-EIGHT: SESSIONS 167–175

Session 167: Monday, May 20, 1619, PM

Synod read the Dutch translation of the second head of the Canons.

Session 168: Tuesday, May 21, 1619, PM

Synod read the Dutch translation of the third, fourth, and fifth heads.

The Provincial Synod of Utrecht was scheduled to meet soon. That synod had many Remonstrant ministers who were now disqualified from serving, and it would have to face the question of what to do with the Remonstrant ministers. At the request of the provincial synod, the Synod of Dordt appointed six minister delegates to help the Synod of Utrecht.

Session 169: Wednesday, May 22, 1619, AM

Synod had already declared worthy of suspension the two Remonstrant ministers from Kampen whom synod had required to appear before it but who had never appeared (articles 83, 85). In their absence, and on the basis of documents that had been submitted to synod, the synod declared the ministers worthy of deposition. It asked the magistrates of Kampen to implement this decision and advised the churches there to find and install orthodox ministers as soon as possible.

Session 170: Wednesday, May 22, 1619, PM

Synod read the Dutch translation of the introduction and conclusion to the Canons. It appointed two men to make some revisions to the Dutch translation of the Canons.

Session 171: Thursday, May 23, 1619, AM

Synod read the revised editions of the Belgic Confession (see session 155), which editions appeared in both the Dutch and French languages. Suggestions for improvement were given.

Session 172: Thursday, May 23, 1619, PM

Synod concluded the work it had begun the previous session. Synod considered a proposed change to article 22 of the Belgic Confession, to replace the words "many holy works which He had done for us" with the word "obedience," referring to the obedience of Christ.

Session 173: Friday, May 24, 1619, AM

Synod decided not to make the change that it had considered at the previous session. It did decide, however, to add one phrase to article 22 of the Belgic Confession: "and in our place." Some other changes, editorial in nature, were made by common consent. Synod approved this revised (*edited*, but not substantially changed) version of the Belgic Confession in both the Dutch and French languages and declared this edition to be the standard.

Session 174: Friday, May 24, 1619, PM

Synod read the minutes of some previous sessions. Synod also recognized that more overtures were waiting to be treated and that it did not have time to treat them. It decided to postpone their treatment to the next national synod. Because the next national synod was not held until 1816, it is unlikely that the next national synod actually treated these matters.

Synod appointed a committee to treat an appeal from three ministers of Hoorn against the decision of the Synod of North Holland (session 49).

APPENDIX 1: *THE SESSIONS OF THE SYNOD OF DORDT, 1618–1619*

Session 175: Saturday, May 25, 1619, AM

Two of the ministers from Hoorn withdrew their appeal. The third maintained his appeal. The committee to treat the matter met in an adjoining room.

Synod adopted the Formula of Subscription for theological professors and for visitors of the sick. It also adopted the Form for Adult Baptism (see session 162).

WEEK TWENTY-EIGHT: SESSIONS 176–180

Session 176: Monday, May 27, 1619, AM

Synod heard the advice of the committee regarding the appeal of the Remonstrant minister from Hoorn (session 175). It decided that the Synod of North Holland had judged him properly. At the same time, it decided to exhort the provincial synod to labor to get him to sign the Belgic Confession, Heidelberg Catechism, and Canons of Dordt; and if he would sign these, to restore him to office.

Session 177: Monday, May 27, 1619, PM

Synod read the judgment that it had made at the previous session to the delegates from North Holland and to the appellant.

The committee appointed to draw up two shorter catechisms (session 17) presented its drafts. Synod read and approved the shorter one. It decided not to read the longer one but to permit its use.

Synod appointed a committee to thank the States General for calling and supporting the synod and to ask it to approve and enforce the decrees of the synod. A letter was drawn up in which the States General was informed of specific decisions, particularly in the *Post-Acta* sessions (sessions 155–180, at which the foreign delegates were not present), and asked to ratify them.

Session 178: Tuesday, May 28, 1619, AM

One of the synod's clerks had been tasked to abbreviate the Acts of Synod before the synod adjourned. Time was running out; the task could not be completed before the synod adjourned. So synod appointed one member from each of its Dutch delegations, including one professor, to meet at some point after synod adjourned to review and approve the condensed Acts. Later in the session it also assigned this committee the task of reviewing the Dutch liturgical forms (an English translation of which is found in the back of the 1912 Psalter) with a view to adding them to the public editions of the Acts.

Synod made several decisions regarding the calling of the next national synod. This synod was to be called in three years; however, the United Provinces never called another national synod. The next national synod was held in 1816, after the Dutch Republic had become the United Kingdom of the Netherlands. Synod appointed Classis Dordrecht to arrange for the convening of the next national synod. It decided to ask the States General to invite the Dutch churches in Great Britain and Germany to the next national synod. And it appointed four men to bring these requests to the States General and to report to the next national synod.

Synod decided to close its meetings with a public worship service of thanksgiving at the *Grote Kerk*, led by Rev. Balthasar Lydius, the minister of the church at Dordrecht.

The president and two vice-presidents were delegated to thank the magistrates of Dordrecht for their courtesy and help in hosting the synod.

Session 179: Tuesday, May 28, 1619, PM

Synod read and approved the minutes of the sessions from May 22 to May 28.

APPENDIX 1: *THE SESSIONS OF THE SYNOD OF DORDT, 1618–1619*

Session 180: Wednesday, May 29, 1619, AM

Synod met at the *Kloveniersdoelen* for prayer, then proceeded to the great church in Dordrecht. There Balthasar Lydius preached on Isaiah 12:1–3. Lydius thanked God for his favor shown to the churches in the Netherlands and his blessing on the synod's work, and he asked God to bless the decisions of the synod for the good of the churches. The delegates then returned to the *Kloveniersdoelen*, while the president and vice-presidents went to the city hall to thank the city magistrates. When all were gathered together again, one of the States General deputies thanked the synod for its labors, and the officers of synod returned thanks to the States General for their support. After other closing formalities, the synod adjourned

Appendix 2

BALTHASAR LYDIUS' PRAYER AT THE CONVENING OF THE SYNOD OF DORDT

Translated and edited by
Prof. Douglas J. Kuiper and Dr. H. David Schuringa

Balthasar Lydius was a Reformed minister in Dordrecht from 1602 to 1629 and was delegated by the particular Synod of South Holland to attend the national Synod of Dordt.[1] As the local pastor, two honors fell to him on November 13, 1618: that of preaching a Dutch sermon in the morning before the synod opened, and that of opening the first session of the synod with prayer. He prayed in Latin, in which language all of the business of the synod was conducted until the foreign delegates were dismissed. Two partial English translations of the prayer have been available for centuries, one of which is based on the memory of some in the audience.[2]

---

1 Fred van Lieburg, "The Participants at the Synod of Dordt," in *Acta et Documenta Synodi Nationalis Dordrechtanae, Vol. 1: Acta of the Synod of Dordt*, ed. Donald Sinnema, Christian Moser, and Herman J. Selderhuis (Gottingen, Germany: Vandenhoeck & Ruprecht, 2015), XCII.

2 Gerard Brandt, *The History of the Reformation in and about the Low-Countries* (London: T. Wood, for John Nicks, 1722), 3:8. Also, "From the Prayer of Balthazar Lydius," in Samuel Hopkins, *General Liturgy and Book of Common Prayer* (New York, NY: A. S. Barnes and Co., 1883), 44–45.

What follows is a new and complete translation, based on the Dutch translation of the prayer in the *Acts of the Synod of Dordt*.[3]

The prayer is ornate. It breathes the language of scripture. Its long sentences include many subordinate phrases and clauses. As is the Dutch custom, in these long sentences the subject is near the beginning and the verb at the end. This translation divides the long sentences into shorter ones so that the English reader today can better understand the prayer. Bible citations and allusions are footnoted.

English Translation of the Prayer of Balthasar Lydius, at the Opening Session of the Synod of Dordt

Almighty, eternal God, Fountain of all wisdom, goodness, and mercy, compassionate Father in Christ! We pray that thou wilt open our lips so that our mouth may declare thy praise.[4]

We are unworthy of all thy mercies which thou hast bountifully bestowed upon the work and workmanship of thy hands.[5] Not only hast thou created us according to thy image,[6] but also, when we through sin had become by nature the children of wrath,[7] thou didst recreate us according to thy image.[8] Since we already are indebted to thee because thou hast created us, how much more do we owe because thou hast also freely redeemed us?

It is great and marvelous that man was made in thy image. How much greater it is that he who thought it not robbery to be equal with God made himself of no reputation, took upon him the form of a servant, and was made in our likeness,[9] who of God was

---

3 *Acta of Handelingen*, 2–4.
4 Ps. 51:15.
5 Eph. 2:10.
6 Gen. 1:27.
7 Eph. 2:3.
8 Col. 3:10.
9 Phil. 2:6–7.

made unto us wisdom, and righteousness, and sanctification, and redemption![10]

Also with these benefits thou wast not satisfied. We were a people dwelling in the darkness and shadow of death,[11] without hope of salvation, cast off in the unworthiness of our souls, for whom an unknown treasure would be of no use. But thou hast enlightened us by the revelation of the Sun of righteousness[12] and truth! Without this, we would have perished everlastingly in these errors, not knowing what way we must walk.

The enemy of mankind sowed tares among the wheat while men slept.[13] This darkness gradually gained the upper hand. Yet through the light of the Reformation thou hast delivered us from a greater darkness than that of Egypt. In these places thou hast planted thy vine,[14] whose shadow has covered the mountains and whose branches are the cedars of God.[15]

The enemy of the human race, that great red dragon,[16] begrudged us this blessed state. He spewed water from his mouth like a torrent to sweep us away as with a flood.[17] He raised high the stakes, provoking horrible wars against thy turtledove.[18] Thy enemies were out to devour thy congregation in these provinces. But thou hast delivered our soul from the snare of the fowler,[19] so that even in the Netherlands men of shield and spear[20] were left

---

10 1 Cor. 1:30.
11 Isa. 9:2.
12 Mal. 4:2.
13 Matt. 13:25.
14 Ps. 80:8.
15 Ps. 80:10.
16 Rev. 12:3. By the "great red dragon," Lydius refers to Satan, working through the Roman Catholic Church and the Spanish Empire.
17 Rev. 12:16.
18 Ps. 74:19.
19 Ps. 91:3; 124:7.
20 1 Sam. 17:47.

speechless. Thou hast ordained new weapons and hast become a wall of fire round about the cities.[21] Thou thyself hast taken possession of the gates of the enemy,[22] that her gates be lifted up, that the King of glory might enter in.[23]

Going forth with our forces, thou didst instruct the hands of the illustrious Prince of Orange to do battle.[24] Taking him by the hand, thou hast broken the bars of the gates of the enemy and hast granted peace to our lands. Thou hast made us fat with the finest of the wheat[25] and crowned us with thy lovingkindness.[26] Thy footsteps dripped with fatness.[27] The chief of thy temporal benefits toward us is this, that when the affairs were the weightiest and the storms were the highest, thou, our exalted Lord, hast given the rulers a pliable heart to direct thy people (over which thou hast appointed them) with wisdom, and especially to judge between good and evil.[28] Thou hast inspired them with sound counsel. Thou hast wonderfully blessed and made them as anointed children of honor, who would stand with the governor of the whole land.

For these benefits, thou hast expected lovely grapes from thy vine, but, behold, it has brought forth wild grapes![29] Thou hast exalted thy people, and they have despised thee! Therefore, thou

---

21 Zech. 2:5.
22 Gen. 22:17; 24:60.
23 Ps. 24:9.
24 Ps. 144:1. Lydius refers to Prince Maurice, who, in July 1617, openly sided with the Counter-Remonstrant cause against Oldenbarnevelt. Oldenbarnevelt was virtually the prime minister of the Netherlands (although that was not his official title) and had favored the Arminians.
25 Ps. 81:16; 147:14.
26 Ps. 103:4.
27 Ps. 65:11.
28 1 Kings 3:9.
29 Isa. 5:2. Following his review of the Reformation and victory following the brutal wars with Spain, Lydius now transitions to the Remonstrant controversy at hand.

hast not withheld from us what we deserved.[30] Thou art become as a visitor in the land, as a stranger who remains therein only overnight; as a man of valor who is defeated, and as a strong man who cannot help. Thou hast confounded our lips! The end of the foreign war has almost become the beginning of the internal one.[31] In peacetime the bitterness of thy bride has become exceedingly bitter.[32]

Thou hast laid the ax to the tree root, in order to cut down the unfruitful fig tree.[33] Thy inheritance has become like a wounded lion and has roared against thee. Many shepherds have destroyed thy vineyard, trodden thy portion under foot, and made thy pleasant portion a wilderness, desolate and empty.[34] Nowhere have the comings and goings been peaceful,[35] but exceedingly troubled by rumors of war.[36] This, because we did not heed thy warnings, O Lord! One people would rise up against the other, one city against another,[37] for thou hast afflicted them with every misery.[38]

But in thy wrath thou hast been mindful of thy mercies.[39] Thou hast inclined the hearts of the rulers of our fatherland, consuming them with zeal for thy house[40] so that they have earnestly sought that which serves the peace of Jerusalem.[41]

To this end have they summoned this national synod in order

---

30 Lam. 3:42.
31 In 1609, the Netherlands and Spain had declared a truce in the Eighty Years War, which truce lasted twelve years. During this truce, the Arminian controversy was at its height, and the country came close to civil war.
32 Cf. Jer. 2:32.
33 Matt. 3:10.
34 Jer. 12:10.
35 Deut. 28:6.
36 Matt. 24:6.
37 Matt. 24:7.
38 Ps. 119:75.
39 Hab. 3:2.
40 Ps. 69:9; John 2:17.
41 Ps. 122:6.

to inquire at the mouth of the Lord[42] regarding the quarrels that have been stirred up, and in order that thy law would be a light[43] to disperse the fog of errors. Nevertheless, as everything depends on thy blessing, O Lord, we pray that thou wilt preside at this national synod with thy Holy Spirit, with the Spirit of truth and of peace. We pray this according to thy promise, "Where two or three are gathered in my name, there I will be in the midst of them."[44]

The holy scripture must be interpreted by that same Spirit by which it was inspired and cannot be understood except by pure minds. Therefore, we pray that thou wilt first cleanse our intentions, then illumine us so that we may indeed understand thy holy word and handle it diligently. Grant, O God, that through the scripture we may mislead no one, nor be misled, but that in it we may seek and find the truth. Having discovered the truth, may we defend it with steadfast faith.

Sanctify us in thy truth.[45] Grant that we might exalt thee with one mouth. Permit no divisions among us, but rather grant that we be perfectly joined together in the same mind and in the same judgment.[46] Let us not be desirous of vain glory, provoking one another, envying one another.[47] Rather, let us endeavor to keep the unity of the Spirit in the bond of peace.[48]

Cause us always to remember that to an extent strife is much better for us who are united with God than peace that separates us from God. Cause us to remember that truth and peace are two

---

42 Lev. 24:12.
43 Prov. 6:23.
44 Matt. 18:20.
45 John 17:17.
46 1 Cor. 1:10.
47 Gal. 5:26.
48 Eph. 4:3.

APPENDIX 2: *BALTHASAR LYDIUS' PRAYER*

friends and twin sisters, so that peace shall not come to us if we do not cherish truth, her sister.

Grant that we, having set aside perverse errors, might consider the matters laid before us, not with sharp subtleties, but by weighing the certainty of the matters themselves, washing away the bitter stain of slander at the river of true reasoning.

Grant those who are wandering to be brought back to the right path. Give them to be not obstinate. Cause them to remember that ignorance, when recognized, is the highest wisdom; that the truth can be that which seems unbelievable to man, and the lie that which seems plausible; and that the greatest victory is to triumph over error exposed.

Since thou hast commanded us to pray for kings and princes, and for all who are placed in authority,[49] we pray, among others, for those governments whose theological professors are present in this solemn ecclesiastical assembly, as well as for those who are yet expected;[50] and for his royal majesty of Great Britain, James I, who is a courageous and conscientious protector of the true faith. We pray for his son-in-law, the illustrious Prince Elector of the Roman Empire and Palatinate on the Rhine,[51] and for the Chief Magistrate of the Empire. We pray for the illustrious Duke and Elector of Brandenburg,[52] for the illustrious Count of Hesse,[53] for the United Cantons in Switzerland, for the high-borne Counts of Nassau and

---

49 1 Tim. 2:2.
50 This list includes all the foreign countries that sent a delegation. It omits France, whose king prevented the delegates from making the trip. The modern reader will know where Great Britain, France, and Geneva (Switzerland) were. Bremen and Emden (also known as East Frisia) were in Germany, just across the border from the Netherlands. Brandenburg was in what is today eastern Germany. Nassau-Wetteravia and Hesse were in what is today western Germany.
51 Frederick V.
52 Johann Sigismund.
53 Maurice I.

Wetteravia,[54] and for the honorable and worthy council, the Republics of Geneva, Bremen, and Emden.

Especially we pray for those whom thou hast placed over us in the Reformed Netherlands: for the exalted lords the States General, and for their exalted deputies to this synod; for the illustrious and warlike hero, the Prince of Orange,[55] and for the entire house of Nassau; for the noble-minded lords states of Holland and West Friesland;[56] for the most wise noble-minded lords, the Presidents and Counselors of both of the Courts of Justice; and for the respectable council of this city, the Lord Sheriff, Mayor, Aldermen, and the eight judges.

Grant that each and every one of them might serve thee with reverence and rejoice with trembling. Confirm their scepter and secure their throne in ever-increasing measure, that they might remain faithful, nurturing fathers[57] of thy church in these regions.

Bless also the citizens of this city. Grant that they seek above all the kingdom of God and his righteousness.[58] According to thy

---

54 Nassau and Wetteravia were really one territory. Count John VI had ruled it until his death in 1606. After he died, his sons each ruled a part of the territory. That his sons ruled explains the use of the plural "counts." That their father had been a count explains in part, if not completely, the word "high-borne." Of the sons, Willem Lodewijk (William Louis) was prominent, having married the sister of Maurice, the Prince of Orange.

55 Prince Maurice, of Nassau.

56 In this paragraph Lydius prayed not for church officials, but for government officials. His mention of two provincial governments, Holland and West Friesland, is striking. For over a decade, the center of the Arminian controversy was in their political jurisdiction, and the provincial government for the most part favored the Arminians. Other provincial governments had to urge these two provincial governments to agree to a national synod. When finally they did agree, the States General set the date for the synod. Probably this is why Lydius referred particularly to these provincial governments. The interested reader can find more about this in the translated "Historical Foreword" in Hoeksema, *Voice of Our Fathers*, 567–624.

57 Isa. 49:23.

58 Matt. 6:33.

lovingkindness, provide them that of which they stand in need. Finally, grant that we all together in this assembly may be dedicated to produce what is pleasing to thee, to the honor of thy holy name, the preservation of the truth, and divine blessing for the church and the republic. Amen.

NOTES

NOTES

NOTES

NOTES

NOTES

NOTES

www.ingramcontent.com/pod-product-compliance
Lightning Source LLC
Chambersburg PA
CBHW050548160426
43199CB00015B/2577

Jane's book is not just written on paper—it lives through her speech and daily life. We met two years ago when we were both in an adventure season of finding a place to call home: our church. I had the chance to hear about her adventures first-hand and was encouraged again to fix my eyes on Jesus. And now you are getting that chance too. *Adventure Awaits* is full of honest thoughts, stories from the Bible and challenging questions. Be ready to listen, learn and grow, and to embrace the adventure that God calls you to.

Marie Bischoff, Pastor at MGE Peine, Germany

—

Adventure Awaits finds the perfect balance between simplicity and conviction. Jane combines real life stories from her own walk with biblical truths, and brings the reader along on a journey to uncover what God is truly calling us to as his children. She challenges comfort and complacency by sharing her own battle with the two, and is beautifully vulnerable in the honest sharing of her journals, prayers, and her wrestle towards surrender. *Adventure Awaits* acts as a preparation manual for all those who wonder "is there more?" After reading this book I can tell you, yes, there is more.

Liv deGroot, Social Worker and former Children's Ministry Director

—

Adventure Awaits portrays the walk of the Christian faith so well as a journey rather than a destination to reach, lived in a comfort zone. I love that Jane gives real life examples from her own life and uses this to capture our attention. It makes the book itself more relatable and interesting. The way that Jane tells how God guides and personally speaks to her gives us a glimpse of how her own relationship with Jesus is lived out daily through her faith.

Pamela Esslemont

Adventure Awaits is Jane opening up her heart and sharing her journey while leaving a trail of golden nuggets you can take away and apply to your own life. This book will help you take a fresh look at your adventure and the promises God has spoken over your life.

Jane, I'm humbled by your honesty, encouraged by your bravery and inspired to live a life that is surrendered to Jesus. Thank you for putting pen to paper and not giving up on your God-given dreams.

Lisa Ruth Lyall, Children's Pastor, AoG Central Church, UK

—

This book breaks the mould of religion and puts you in direct contact with the Holy Spirit. It has the depth to challenge and reshape the mindsets that guide us all. If you let her, Jane will take you on a journey to discover the word of God as a practical, faith-driven tool to shape your future.

Michelle Herrmann, Prophetic Voice to the Nations